The School Reform Landscape Reloaded

The School Reform Landscape Reloaded

More Fraud, Myths, and Lies
2nd Edition

Christopher H. Tienken

ROWMAN & LITTLEFIELD
Lanham • Boulder • New York • London

Published by Rowman & Littlefield
An imprint of The Rowman & Littlefield Publishing Group, Inc.
4501 Forbes Boulevard, Suite 200, Lanham, Maryland 20706
www.rowman.com

6 Tinworth Street, London SE11 5AL, United Kingdom

Copyright © 2021 by Christopher H. Tienken

All rights reserved. No part of this book may be reproduced in any form or by any electronic or mechanical means, including information storage and retrieval systems, without written permission from the publisher, except by a reviewer who may quote passages in a review.

British Library Cataloguing in Publication Information Available

Library of Congress Control Number: 2020946623

ISBN 978-1-4758-5028-4 (cloth : alk. paper)
ISBN 978-1-4758-5029-1 (pbk. : alk. paper)
ISBN 978-1-4758-5030-7 (electronic)

∞ ™ The paper used in this publication meets the minimum requirements of American National Standard for Information Sciences Permanence of Paper for Printed Library Materials, ANSI/NISO Z39.48-1992.

For Allison—unconditional love is the most power force in the world

Sempre—Francesca e Gabriella

Contents

Foreword		ix
C. M. Achilles		
Acknowledgments		xiii
Introduction		1
1	Education Equity and Democracy	5
2	Neoliberalism, Social Darwinism, and Consumerism Masquerading as School Reform	25
3	The Education Reform King with a Styrofoam Crown	43
4	A Catalogue of Reform Myths	61
5	The Path of High-Risk Implications in the Dual System	77
6	High Stakes, Low Quality	93
7	World-Class Standards That Are Too Big to Fail	115
8	Charter Schools: Separate but Legal	135
9	A Way Forward	155
Index		179
About the Author		185

Foreword

C. M. Achilles

According[1] to Gustav Schwab (1946), much of the early accounts of the progress of humankind can be attributed to the study of the myths and epics of western civilization, especially of the Greeks. Two major players in the early events were Prometheus (foresight) and his less well-known brother, Epimetheus (afterthought). One key point this story brings to us is that the future builds upon the past, or at least in the future those who advocate for progress should acknowledge its heritage.

One way to accomplish this feat in the education policy arena is for writers to to present their views on past and current social forces exerting much pressure on education in the United States. The author of this volume published by Rowman and Littlefield provides a highly accessible critical review of some threshold education reform issues. The author provides a look at some of the current and past myths that populate the reform landscape. Because education is cumulative throughout our lives, it should be framed as essentially a lifetime of discovery. As such, this volume assists current and future education leaders to discover the foresight and afterthought necessary to discern the truth from myth and the facts from lies that continue to drive education policy and practice.

The humorist/philosopher H. L. Mencken is reputed to have said, "For every complex question there is a simple answer—and it is wrong" (see Carson et al., 1991). In a similar vein, the philosopher George Santayana, citing the Roman philosopher Cicero, explained that those who cannot remember the past are condemned to repeat it. Consider Plato's allegory of the cave! Things are not always what they seem at first; each point, pro and con needs to be explored using the lenses of empirical facts, theoretical frameworks, and philosophical foundations. Such is the current landscape of education reform policies and practices.

Mencken's and Santayana's expressions taken together suggest that humans should study and know the past so they can improve the future. That is a large part of the purpose for education—to leave the world a better place by examining *what is* and encouraging people to influence *what may be* positive changes, while maintaining and advocating what research and practices have shown to contribute to social harmony and growth. One way to activate this challenge is for competent researchers to analyze education policies carefully and publish their conclusions for others to review or analyze deeply. Education must satisfactorily meet the norms of the diverse cultures within which it operates. Is the quality of US public education policy better, worse, or the same as in 2018, 2008, 2000, or 1992, for that matter?

Amid much disturbing national and world news these days, I'm pleased to see an effort by a scholar who reviews some major reports and policies in education and society in general and suggest alternative views about the continuing assault on American public education by big business, government, and advocacy groups. Christopher Tienken from Seton Hall University in New Jersey uses his talents to continue the important work of Gerald Bracey, PhD, and others who worked diligently to present a balanced picture of education in America, and explain the need for a carefully educated citizenry in a democracy, or, to paraphrase Thomas Jefferson, if a nation wishes to be ignorant and free, it wishes what never has been and never will be.

Professor Tienken traced some major education and cultural factors that educators should consider as they progress both in advancing knowledge and confronting social values such as freedom of choice and charter schools. For example, how do charter schools resonate with the *Brown v. Board of Education* Supreme Court decision? Is a legalized return to segregated schools disguised as charter schools imminent? For those interested in curriculum and assessment, the author critiques the Common Core State Standards and national testing to find that the emperor might not have clothes.

Although charter schools, standardized curriculum, and standardized testing have been generally accepted in some form by most professional organizations and educators, the profession as a whole seems woefully uninformed regarding the empirical facts on such subjects. Jack Culbertson, PhD, longtime director of the University Council for Education Administration, has warned educators to evaluate thoroughly what they advocate and do: perhaps to make haste slowly (festina lente).

> However, the last century has taught us pertinent lessons, two of which are noted. Borrowed concepts tend to enter textbooks before they are adequately tested in school systems. The result is that such concepts may be used indefinitely in training programs even though their actual relations to school management and leadership practices remain unknown. (1990, p. 109; emphasis added)

The Culbertson warning seems to have classical roots in the myth of Prometheus, the forward-looking brother, and his lesser-known brother, Epimetheus. Don't take the analogies too lightly. I believe that this book will fill a void in the education literature of today by challenging the status quo with evidence. The publishers, Rowman and Littlefield, have found a niche and a writer who will fill the void with challenging perspectives.

NOTE

1. This foreword is a slightly revised version of the original that was included in the first edition of this book. It represents one of Dr. Charles M. Achilles's last published works before his death on February 8, 2013. The foreword was lightly edited to reflect the change from two authors on the first edition of the book to one author for this edition. However, Achilles' message is timeless, as is much of the work he did in education on behalf of children.

REFERENCES

Carson, C. C., Hueleskamp, R. M., & Woodall, T. D. (1991, May 10). *Perspectives on education in America. Annotated briefing, third draft.* Albuquerque, NM: Sandia National Laboratories. See especially "A Call to Action," pp. 2–9.
Note: Education was such a hot topic at the time of this report from an esteemed federal laboratory that the Reagan administration tried to downplay this report's generally positive outlook about US education and the lab was told to recall the document. (You bury this report, or we'll bury you. Quite a threat to a government-funded entity.)
Culbertson, J. A. (1990, fall/winter). Tomorrow's challenges to today's professors of educational administration. *Record in Educational Administration and Supervision,* 100–107.
Schwab, G. (1946). *Gods on heroes: Myths and epics of ancient Greece.* New York: Pantheon. See especially pp. 31–36 about Prometheus.

Acknowledgments

Although you won't see them listed as authors, my wife Allison and daughters Gabriella and Francesca influenced large portions of this book. The joy of experiencing life through the eyes of a child is eclipsed only by the unconditional love of a wife. Love makes all things possible.

This book explores some of what I call the myths, frauds, and lies of the school reform landscape since the launch of Sputnik 1 in 1957. I would like to thank those who have the courage to use science, empathy, and love to serve the best interests of children and give a voice to the voiceless.

I acknowledge appreciatively the support from my Rowman & Littlefield editors, Carlie Wall and Dr. Thomas Koerner. Their encouragement and patience are much appreciated. Donald C. Orlich coauthored the first edition with me and I am forever grateful for his work on the book and I continue to be inspired by the legacy of scholarship he left on the field.

Thank you to Dr. Ted Creighton, NCPEA Living Legend, for his suggestions and careful review of the book. He is a great colleague. My graduate assistant Jessica Jones spent many hours reviewing chapters and provided a reader's perspective that was invaluable in helping to refine my ideas. Professor Carol Mullen continues to give selflessly of her expertise and encouragement—thank you!

I have been fortunate in my career to work with school administrators and teachers who stand out in their commitment to children. These educators take stances for children and fight for equity in the face of a policy apparatus hellbent on privileging only the wealthy. I benefit greatly and they inspire me. They are what my extraordinary dissertation mentor and friend Dr. Charles M. Achilles called the defenders of the defenseless. His work on the Tennessee STAR Study changed the face of education research and improved the lives of untold numbers of children. He was an inspiration and a role model. I miss you, Chuck.

Fortunately, I had Daniel Tanner to guide my work in curriculum and instruction research. His advice has been invaluable to my professional growth. Thanks to Pappy for keeping me grounded. God bless Lucille.

There are also those special places that inspire ideas, refresh the spirit, and bring clarity: *Tra il mare e la montagna c'e San Giovanni Montebello, the Campo, and i vicoli di Roma. Only in Sicily.*

Introduction

To better understand the current iteration of public education reform policies and practices it is important to know where education has been in terms of its evolution. In the first part of the book, I begin the process of unpacking modern school reform by providing an overview of the historical purposes and roles of public education in the United States. My purpose is not to create an exhaustive review of education reform or the history of public education in the United States; Tanner and Tanner (2007) already accomplished that task in their seminal text, *Curriculum Development: Theory into Practice*. My intent is to give readers the background knowledge necessary to engage in an analysis of the current education reform landscape in terms of its recent historical roots so they can better evaluate present and future school reform proposals and understand and propose ideas for change.

I use the terms "school reform" and "reformers" in two ways throughout this book. One way I use the terms is to describe processes and people that attempt to deride and degrade, without empirical evidence, the quality of public education in the United States. I provide evidence throughout the book of how the detractors of the unitary US public school system use misinformation, ideology, rhetoric, and/or less-than-accurate statistics to forward a thinly veiled agenda of creating a dual system of education. Some proponents of public education are actively building a two-tiered system that favors the wealthy elite over the rest of society.

The creation of a two-tiered, dual system is stripping the traditional unitary public school system of funding and support and it is creating a greater concentration of economically disadvantaged students and students with special needs in the public schools. The dual system is already evident in the nation's urban areas and it affecting other areas. The siphoning of less poor and less cognitive and linguistically needy students has created a system of educational "haves" and "have nots" under the umbrella of school *choice*. Students from poverty and students of color are most often negatively affected by such systems.

The other way I use the terms is to highlight positive efforts to improve schooling. The comingling of the "good" with the "bad" is purposeful because "school reformers" approach public education policy formation from at least two different camps. There are those who propose and have proposed changes to the system that I find undemocratic and harmful to the long-term health of education and democracy. Conversely, there are others whose proposals were or would be helpful to create a more participative and democratic country for children and adults.

One premise is that people concerned with safeguarding the democratic and unifying institution of public education must dig below the rhetoric and surface arguments of reform proposals to decipher the potential outcomes of the proposals. They must be able to determine whether the proposed reforms and the reformers advocate changes to benefit the greater good of society or if the changes are based on less ethical principles such as profit motives. I do some of that work in this book. The rest is up to reader.

LENSES OF REFORM

The unpacking process requires that I choose a framework from which to view and critique school reform initiatives, policies and practices. The choice of a framework is inherently biased based on those who do the choosing. My biases include a respect and preference for a participatory democracy led by people that develop policies, institutions, and cultural norms that promote the attainment of "liberty and justice for all" in an equitable society. I hold biases against state and corporate-sponsored education reform initiatives or policies that overtly or covertly structure public education in ways that favor one group over others or that have the potential to create long-term structural inequities in our societal systems. I believe public education reformers should not impede access to the opportunities needed to achieve "liberty and justice for all" as a nation of diverse peoples. My biases lead me to examine school reform through the lens of progressivise education philosophy with a reliance on the works of John Dewey.

Specifically, I use progressivist philosophy as the primary framework to critique and examine school reform and its influences on the ability of children, especially those who are members of groups not in the racial majority or wealthy minority, to overcome state sponsored policies, institutions, and norms that lead to intended or unintended consequences that foster inequality and inequity in education.

I also draw upon some aspects of Critical Theory as a secondary tool to analyze the current reform landscape. In its most basic form, Critical Theory requires one to examine the formal structures that exist in society and to be skeptical of those structures unless evidence demonstrates that the structures facilitate upward mobility and equity.

Freire (2000) coined the term "banking model" to describe education policies and practices that seek to deposit static information from the ruling class into the heads of children from the nonruling classes as a way to keep the current social structure, whatever that might be, in place for the foreseeable future. People with resources (money) usually do not subject their children to this type of model, as they can afford other "options" or have the state pay for those options through voucher programs or other types of schools that take public money, but do not serve all students.

I use the frameworks as lenses to examine past and present education reform policies and practices to determine whether those policies and practices can facilitate the attainment of "liberty and justice for all" or whether they lead to balkanizing students and communities along economic and racial/ethnic lines. I caution readers not to mistake my approach as one-sided. It is not. My approach at examining the current reform landscape requires I look through evidence-based lenses. For example, the empirical evidence, evidence derived via recognized scientific methods, suggests that current criticisms of the public school system as a "failing" institution that needs to be replaced with a system of choice and options is seriously flawed.

The evidence suggests there has been a manufactured crisis to make the public schools seem as if they are failing so neoliberal, market-based solutions can be introduced into the system (Berliner & Biddle, 1995). I examine critically some of the more common criticisms of public education that, although false, seem to permeate society as fact and lead to the development of policies and practices that jeopardize the unitary system.

Hopefully this book makes you question education reform policies before choosing to support or implement them. Perhaps the book will motivate you to take action to save the democratic, unitary system of public education so as to promote equity for all children. Overall, I hope this book makes you more skeptical of reform proposals and a more skilled reader of education literature.

ORGANIZATION OF THE BOOK

Chapter 1 presents a cursory historical overview of tensions that exist in public education between the unitary system and proposals for a dual system. It is a tension that has existed since the genesis of public schooling in America and continues today. Chapter 2 introduces the concept of neoliberalism, an economic policy model focused on market-oriented policies and programs. Neoliberalism pervades all of social policy making in the United States and has been a driving force in creating a dual system of education. Chapter 3 peels back the curtain on the genesis of public school bashing and misinformation, the launch of Sputnik 1. It presents evidence from declassified memos and shows how the rhetoric born from Sputnik has sustained the dual system movement since 1957. The chapter also presents an evidence-based critique of one of Sputnik's spawn, *A Nation at Risk*, published in 1983.

Chapter 4 debunks seven common myths about the perceived shortcomings of public education, such as "flat" test scores, and the ways in which principles from big business will save education. Chapter 5 presents risks associated with establishing a dual system of education and it provides an analysis of the root cause of under-achievement: poverty. Chapter 6 deconstructs high-stakes testing and lays bare the inherent weaknesses that should exclude the use of results from standardized tests as important indicators of student achievement or education quality.

Chapter 7 raises questions about the claims made by proponents of standardization. The chapter tests many of the claims made by the developers of the Common Core State Standards and shows how the latest version of revised state standards born from the Common Core suffer the same weaknesses as the Common Core itself. Chapter 8 takes charter schools, the primary tool of the dual system, to task and uncovers the neoliberal, profit-driven motives the charter industry now embraces. Chapter 9 presents practical and evidence-based solutions that focus on local control of curriculum, instruction, and student assessment.

REFERENCES

Berliner, D. C. & Biddle, B. J. (1995). *The manufactured crisis: Myths, frauds and the attack on America's public schools.* Reading, MA: Addison-Wesley.

Freire, P. (2000). *Pedagogy of the oppressed: 30th anniversary edition.* New York: Continuum.

Tanner, D. & Tanner, L. (2007). *Curriculum development: Theory into practice.* New York: Allyn & Bacon.

Chapter One

Education Equity and Democracy

Since the formation of the United States of America, there has been debate over the roles and purposes of education. Some envisioned a public education system that unified diverse people on a level playing field in the spirit of "all men are created equal." The unifiers envisioned a system built upon egalitarian principles in which one's social status, cultural background, socioeconomic position, skills, dispositions, or academic readiness did not matter. They wanted all students to have opportunities to reach or exceed their potential within a participative democracy.

The public education system is the only social system in America in which all members of society must theoretically pass through and it is the only public system that is capable of socializing diverse peoples to the customs, culture, and mores of a participative and representative democracy. Public education has unified diverse people around democratic principles, on a large scale, since Massachusetts enacted the country's first compulsory education law in 1852.

Others sought a dual system of education based on the European model of meritocracy in which the rich attended an education system separate and apart from the system attended by the rest of the population. The rich were perceived to be more worthy of better opportunities, simply because they were rich, and thus the rich wanted to preserve any advantages they had.

Children from the privileged ruling class received more exclusive education experience, usually private and segregated from the masses. Dual system supporters believed that children from the lower social classes should received more mechanized, impersonal education experiences based on a narrow curriculum, memorization, rote drill, and oral recitation. Some students of education history might list the Lancaster model, also known as monitorial instruction, as one example of a mechanized education for the masses, although there are many others.

Reflected Values

The theme of conflict between the vision of a unitary system of public schools for everyone versus a dual system of private schools, semiprivate schools, and special academies for the privileged and a stripped-down public system for the "rest" has been a reoccurring one and continues today in America. The conflict is played out in the "school reform" arguments with proponents lining up on either side of ideas like charter schools, school choice, vouchers, national curricula, standardized testing, selective public high schools, and virtual schools. Proponents of the unitary system fight for equality and equity, whereas proponents of the dual system fight to preserve privilege and elitism.

Thomas Jefferson's Unifying Views of Education

The Jeffersonian view of the role and responsibility of education was one of equity, progress, change, and evolution. Jefferson proposed a public education system that would act to level the playing field between those who came from a more privileged background and those who did not have such advantages.

He saw public education as a means to help society progress. Jefferson believed that if school were to prepare children to be participative citizens, it should reflect society. Jefferson emphasized that it was important not to segregate students based on economic status. Children needed to learn how to live, learn, and work with different types of people, and school was the place to do that. Jefferson saw the public school system as the melting pot of society where different perspectives, lifestyles, and ideas can be exchanged and democratic culture can be unified.

Formalizing Education

Jefferson's first formal call for a public education system came in 1776 when he attempted to push a bill through the Virginia legislature that would have established a free public education system (Jewett, 1997). Although the Virginia legislature did not pass the bill at that time, Jefferson continued to work to get the foundation for a public school system in the western territories included in the Ordinances of 1784, 1785 and 1787.

The Ordinance of 1784 created the footprint for what later became the states of the American Midwest. The Ordinance of 1785 defined subdivisions of land and resulted in the development of townships. It also mandated that one section of land within each township be set aside for the development of a public school (Williams, 1989).

By now most people know of (or have heard) Jefferson's statement, "If a nation expects to be ignorant and free in a state of civilization, it expects what never was and never will be" (Padover, 1939, p. 89). The Ordinance of 1785 operationalized Jefferson's aspiration to bring public education to the masses. The ordinance was struck just two years after the American Revolution ended on September 3, 1783. It led to the proliferation of public schools in the expanding territories west of Pennsylvania (Finkelman, 1993).

The Ordinance of 1787 cemented the importance of public education in the new states and territories. Education was stated as a necessary ingredient for good government. Jefferson drafted the ordinance, which outlawed slavery in the states that would later be formed in the American Midwest (Finkelman, 1993). The ordinance would work to proliferate public schools in the free states and territories.

James Carter

Thomas Jefferson's view of education was not lost after his presidency. James Carter continued the struggle for one system of public education in the New England states. Carter, a teacher and state legislator from Massachusetts, brought attention to the condition of public schools during the 1820s. Carter thought that if the public school was going to survive, its form and function needed to be reformed. Carter called for formal teacher-training institutions, supported by the state, to professionalize public school teaching (Tanner & Tanner, 2007).

Like Jefferson before him, Carter advocated for free public secondary schools and fought against the dual system of education that favored the rich and shunned children of lower social classes. At that time, there were secondary school academies for the wealthy, but nothing substantial existed in terms of a free public secondary school system.

Carter's persistence paid off in 1839 when the first public normal school opened in Massachusetts. Perhaps Carter's greatest contribution was his idea that the state should oversee and help direct the public school system to ensure a more equitable situation rather than relying solely on town control of education. He brought the idea of local control with state regulation to the policy discussion. This idea of state direction of a unitary system of public education laid a foundation for the later work of other proponents of the free public school system such as Horace Mann.

Mann and Barnard

Horace Mann and Henry Barnard worked to solidify the public school systems in Massachusetts and Connecticut, respectively. They built upon and extended Carter's proposals as they advocated for and eventually founded teacher education institutions to raise the quality of instruction taking place in classrooms. Mann advocated for the role of school principal as someone who could help improve the teaching that took place in classrooms and as someone who would be responsible for helping to develop a quality curriculum.

Mann understood the importance of heterogeneous grouping in public schools as a unifying practice to bring together students from diverse backgrounds. He was not naive in his understanding of how a public school system could improve and support democracy. Mann knew that a public school system, in and of itself, could not sustain a democracy without careful thought about what that system would provide in the way of curriculum. In his view, it was important to organize the system to help develop people who could question, think critically, and strategize in order to grow the democratic republic. Mann and Barnard stressed the importance of a curriculum that went beyond the basics of the time.

Mann realized that if the public school system was going to live up to its role as the equalizer of social classes and preparer of the next generation of democratic citizens, it needed a curriculum that fostered well-rounded individuals prepared for the future instead of being focused on the past or present. Mann fought for the inclusion of music, physical education, and the study of social issues (Mann, 1848), subjects that help to develop creative thinking and innovation. An expanded curriculum was revolutionary at that time, as most public schools taught only writing, reading, arithmetic, and oral recitations. Thanks in part to Jefferson, Carter, Barnard, Mann, and many others, a more "progressive" conception of education began to take shape during the first eighty years of the republic.

A Step Back

For every hard-won battle to take several steps forward, there seems always to be a step backward. That step back came in the form of Joseph Lancaster and monitorial instruction. The Lancaster method originated in London, England, in a school opened for children from poverty and was quickly brought to large cities in the United States, New York being one of the first.

Proponents of the method placed large numbers of students in a class, fifty not being uncommon (Rayman, 1981). The teacher followed a scripted drill lesson and then turned the monitoring of instruction over to several "bright" students in the room. Each bright student was responsible for monitoring a row of students. Then the teacher would move to another room to deliver instruction, and the process would continue.

The method was cost-efficient but highly mechanical. Fortunately, monitorial instruction faded from the scene, and by around 1850 it was no longer in vogue, but the idea of creating larger classes to maximize resources survives today, as was seen by Bill Gates's proposal to increase class sizes and pay teachers more. Gates stated that schooling would be more cost effective if the system were able to identify and eradicate less effective teachers while giving the more effective teachers more students and a raise in pay (Thompson, 2011).

Gates derided what he believed to an excessively low teacher-student ratio of 15.7:1, although the teacher-student ratio is not class size. Gates failed to mention that he and his children attended the prestigious Lakeside School, ranked seventh among all private schools in the country, with a teacher-student ratio of 9:1.

Both Lancaster's and Gates's proposals highlight a defining feature of the ongoing tension between a unitary system of public school and a dual system: educational inequity. The wealthy covertly advocate for and receive enhanced education treatment while the masses receive a mass produced version of education. Similar proposals and practices that foster a dual system of education include selective public magnet schools, selective public vocational schools, selective charter schools and charter schools that do not offer or provide a full range of special education services, private school vouchers, and tax credits for private schools.

Quincy

The battle against the dual system of education continued and the free public school system continued to grow. The town of Quincy, Massachusetts, was the site of the next great contribution to the unitary system and the systemic development of liberty and justice for all through a free and quality public education system. Francis Parker, who would later be referred to as the father of modern progressive education by John Dewey, became the superintendent of Quincy schools in 1875.

At Quincy, Parker found a school system with curricula and instructional practices based on memorization and recitation. The students could not answer questions or read passages not previously rehearsed and were unable to engage in real problem solving, strategizing, or socially conscious critical thinking (Campbell, 1967). Parker initiated a series of curricular reforms that would transform public education in Quincy and beyond.

Parker instituted curriculum and instruction methods such as open-ended conversations, divergent questioning, experiential learning through field trips and community-based education, integrated language arts, and a correlated curriculum that fostered connections and transfer of knowledge and skills between subjects. He worked to create a curriculum and instruction program that introduced content in more meaningful ways that were connected to the students through problem posing. The Quincy system, as some referred to it (Campbell, 1967), demonstrated that quality can be a hallmark of public schools and that a dual system of schools was unnecessary.

Dewey Speaks

John Dewey provided ongoing support for the important connection between a healthy public school system and a thriving representative democracy (Dewey, 1916). Dewey made many contributions to the developing public education system. I could not possibly do justice to all his accomplishments, nor will I try. My purpose in bringing him into the discussion is to give the reader an insight into Dewey's ideas of democracy and the role of public education to support and nurture a democratic society.

Dewey's conception of the connection between democracy and schooling and Paulo Freire's Critical Social Theory (Friere, 2000) along with the champions of public schooling mentioned earlier, form the foundation for my thinking about public school and school reform.

Although Dewey authored a pantheon of education publications, one can find poignant and important guidance for school reform in three of his works: "My Pedagogic Creed" (1897), *School and Society* (1899), and *Democracy and Education* (1916). Dewey (1897) stated, "I believe that education is the fundamental method of social progress and reform" (p. 80). In Dewey's mind, there could be no social progress, no national democratic progress, without quality democratic education for all children. But what was Dewey's conception of democracy and progress?

Education can be used as a tool to stoke ultranationalist fervor, as we saw after the launch of Sputnik during the Cold War, and now again with things like the continuing war on terrorism and issues related to immigration and America First policies. One's conception of democracy matters because it is the conception that drives action. Dewey saw democracy as a social process, something related to the greater good, but also as something deeply personal and connected to informed and thoughtful action.

Democracy Described

Democracy, as conceived by Dewey (1916), is "a way of personal life controlled not merely by faith in human nature but by faith in the capacity of human being for intelligent judgment and action if proper conditions are furnished" (p. 227). Public school is the only publicly funded and universally accessible social institution in the United States that provides a mechanism to socialize all future adults to a representative and equitable democracy.

Dewey (1929) explained the importance of the role of public education in nurturing a democracy:

> For the creation of a democratic society we need an educational system where the process of moral intellectual development is in practice as well as in theory a cooperative transaction of inquiry engaged in by free, independent human beings who treat ideas and the heritage of the past as means and methods for the further enrichment of life, quantitatively and qualitatively, who use the good attained for the discovery and establishment of something better. (p. 84)

Dewey and others viewed the unitary public system as a way to develop the individual to the best of his or her potential so that individual could study the problems of democracy in his or her community, state, and nation and take appropriate action to improve society.

Giles, McCutchen, and Zechiel (1942) warned of confusing individual development with individualism:

> The development of the individual as a goal is not to be confused with individualistic action as a method for its achievement. Unrestrained individualism is inconsistent with democratic values since it will not guarantee others the realization of their potentialities . . . a sharing of responsibilities are essential for the development of personalities to their maximum. (p. 10)

Dewey saw all members of the nation playing a part in the democracy, not just the privileged few making decisions for the rest of society. Like Jefferson before him, Dewey saw a thriving public school system in which the privileged and less privileged worked and learned side by side, just as they would have to do after leaving school.

Dewey demonstrated that students need to be engaged in socially conscious, problem-based, authentic learning as opposed to recitation and mindless acceptance of disjointed facts. If leaders of an education system wish to craft problem solvers, strategists, informed citizens, and a population that questions the status quo in order to improve it, then all students must be provided that type of education. Otherwise, a two-tiered society emerges, with one tier given the mental tools to excel and the other tier subservient to those who possess the tools. Dewey (1899) warned:

> Plato somewhere speaks of the slave as one who in his actions does not express his own ideas, but those of some other man. It is our social problem now, even more urgent than in the time of Plato, that method, purpose, understanding, shall exist in the consciousness of the one who does the work, that his activity shall have meaning to himself. (pp. 37–38)

Tiered systems of education produce tiered outcomes, and those outcomes are consistently better for those who already come to school with the most resources. Dewey and others saw the tiered system as a holdover from the European aristocracy and warned that it had no place in an equitable democracy.

REPORTS, COMMISSIONS AND LANDMARK STUDIES

Whereas some progressive educators viewed the roles and responsibilities of education an incubator of democracy and equity, the messages coming from various formal committees and commissions were sometimes mixed. Reports such as those from the Committee of Ten, Committee of Fifteen, and the *Cardinal Priniciples of Secondary Education* would come to shape policy and practice for decades to come.

Committee of Ten

The *Report of the Committee of Ten on Secondary School Studies* (1893) recommended reforms to the high school curriculum that were on one hand aimed at strengthening the democracy, yet were autocratic in nature because they were geared toward college entrance requirements at a time when less than 5 percent of the population graduated from high school. Driven by the concerns of Charles W. Eliot, the president of Harvard University, the Committee of Ten was formed. Eliot wanted to compress the time it took students to work their way through the traditional elementary and secondary programs in an effort to bring down the average age of freshmen entering the university.

The curriculum proposed by the Committee of Ten was highly programmed and based in part on the idea of mental discipline. There was a belief, which persists today, that some academic subjects are better than others and that some subjects actually exercise the brain. Some believed that there was one set of high school courses that better prepared students for college than other options.

Students were required to take four years of Latin and/or Greek, English literature and composition, math, and history because those subjects were better for brain development. The Committee of Ten report called for three years of laboratory science. Vocational coruses like woodshop were looked down upon and reserved for those students educators thought did not posses the intellect for higher education.

There was little room for electives, and the committee prescribed even those. Although the report was supposed to be aimed at reforming secondary education, it did more to promote the existing mechanistic system. The proposed high school curriculum included none of the creative subjects like the arts or physical education advocated years earlier by Mann.

The mechanistic view of high school curriculum became entrenched in the form of a new set of high school graduation requirements. Similar proposals exist today as some continue to market the idea of one best path through high school. The American Diploma Project (ADP) of the early 2000s was one such proposal.

Committee of Fifteen

Eliot was back to reform the elementary school curriculum two years later, in 1895, with the Committee of Fifteen. The major contribution of this committee was the reduction of elementary schooling from ten to eight years, thereby ultimately decreasing the entrance age of first-year college students, as desired by Eliot.

The recommendations from the members of the Committee of Fifteen prescribed, down to the minute, each subject at each grade level, along with the number of lessons per week for each subject in elementary school. Once again, a reform aimed at improving education for all students had the unintended consequence of creating a straitjacketed elementary school experience.

The *Cardinal Principles* Break the Mold

The National Education Association's (NEA) Commission on the Reorganization of Secondary Education released the *Cardinal Principles of Secondary Education* in 1918. The authors of the *Cardinal Principles* recognized that the reforms advocated by the members of the Committees of Ten and Fifteen were counterproductive to educating more children more effectively and more democratically. The *Cardinal Principles* included recommmendations for socially conscious, problem-based approaches to education formed from the tenets of the progressive/experimentalist philosophy.

The *Cardinal Principles* came down squarely on the side of democracy and equity through a unitary system of education that aimed to connect content to students through socially conscious and relevant learning experiences. The authors identified the crucial role of public education as the only public service capable of unifying the country around the ideals of democracy. The public school system was the only public entity in which all citizens, immigrants and native-born children alike, could be socialized and educated together on the tenets of democracy.

Another great wave of immigration occurred in 1918 with the end World War I. Women could not yet vote, many immigrant groups (e.g., Italians and other southern Europeans) were treated as less than human and discriminated against, less than 10 percent of children graduated from high school, and many did not attend school past grade 8. There were concerns that democracy might not be the best form of government as the first Red Scare occurred in 1917 based on the rise of Communism.

The members of the commission recognized the importance to democracy of having more students enter and stay in high school. They called for a massive reform of the secondary school curriculum. The *Cardinal Principles* presented a progressive vision of education. They embodied an inclusive and egalitarian vision of education, different from the existing mechanistic, one-size-fits-all approach in use around the country at the time.

The members of the commission provided a blueprint for an education program that connected school ocntent to the students through a curriculum based on social problem solving and the study of the problems related to democracy. The curricular plans included authentic learning of skills and knowledge students would need to become contributing members of their community, culture, and the larger society. The focus was to develop individuals to their maximum potential so that they would advance their culture, improve their community, and contribute to their country.

The *Cardinal Principles of Secondary Education* was education's Declaration of Independence from the ideas of an elitist dual system, and it sent shockwaves through the establishment. The authors of the *Cardinal Principles* called for educating all children through high school in the same system in an untracked, yet differentiated as needed, curricular program. All students would participate in a curriculum that included the fundamental processes (traditional subject matter).

The problems of democratic society formed the backbone of a core curriculum advocated in the *Cardinal Principles*. All students participated in the study of societal problems during all four years of high school and portions of middle school. Students learned about democracy through problem-based experiences, not just reading about it in a textbook.

Knowing that many students would not finish high school, the curriculum was sequenced so that those students who completed at least grade 10 would leave with basic academic content, an exploration of the problems of society, and a basic foundation in the role of a participative citizen. Students who stayed in school beyond grade 10 would have the chance to access various curricular programs aimed at college preparation or career specialization.

The *Cardinal Principles* called for a focus on three types of curricula to create a complete education program: (1) academic, (2) socio-civic, and (3) avocational. The complete program taught students how to work for the greater good through the fusion of what one might call white- and blue-collar career education with service learning and problem-based activities related to the problems of democracy. The authors envisioned a secondary school program where students take part in career education inside and outside the schoolhouse, with an emphasis on developing self, culture, community, and country.

A specialized set of electives in home economics were proposed for girls. The commission laid out ideas for a high school curriculum, known as Worthy Home Membership, that recognized women as the backbone of democracy because they had the responsibility to raise the next generation of citizens. The commission members believed that democracy started in the home and extended to the community and ultimately the country. Therefore, women deserved the opportunity to access a specialized curriculum.

The *Cardinal Principles* were truly futuristic in thinking about the role and importance of women in a democratic society. The *Cardinal Principles* placed women in a central role in the republic during a time when women could not even vote. The idea of the woman as the head of the household and matriarch of the community with primary responsibility for rearing the next generation of citizens continued another fifty years, until the advent of the modern women's liberation movement in the late 1960s. The commission identified the importance of women to the democracy.

The document was a democratic proposal and helped the suffrage movement succeed and it influenced the civil rights movement (D. Tanner, personal communication, May 2011). The country owes a debt of gratitude to the authors of *Cardinal Principles*. They illuminated an education program for secondary school students drawn from an equity perspective. The authors espoused that all citizens should possess the skills and information necessary to conduct their own business matters and be able to understand their role and responsibility as productive citizens to their family, community, and country.

The *Cardinal Principles* are responsible for some of the remaining progressive curricular and instructional practices in use in some schools today. The practices of differentiated instruction and problem-based learning were born out of the *Cardinal Principles*. Specialized course sequences, cocurricular activities, enrichment courses, exploratory elective courses, and comprehensive high school were other innovations that resulted from the application of the *Cardinal Principles* across the country.

The Principles Ignored

The *Cardinal Principles* were futuristic in their specific ideas about socializing all peoples to democratic life. The 1920s through the 1940s saw an explosion of egalitarian and equitable education experiments and the eventual operationalization of the *Cardinal Principles*. Edward Thorndike and Robert S. Woodworth's initial study in 1901 about the transfer of knowledge, or students' ability to use what they learn in school outside of school, and his 1924 landmark study of 8,564 children once and for all crushed the myth of mental discipline. Their results demonstrated that there was not a hierarchy of secondary school subjects and that no one subject was superior to the others when it came to overall growth in intelligence.

Thorndike's studies exposed the fundamental flaws in the Committee of Ten's recommendations for one set program of studies in high school. He found that the best subjects to promote transfer of knowledge were the vocational subjects, like woodshop. The vocational subjects were more complex in nature because students were required to use their content knowledge from various subjects to solve authentic life problems and create usable products or solutions.

Unfortunately, many of the state commissioners of education and various education bureaucrats in the United States either don't remember Thorndike or did not read the studies. This is evidenced by the majority of education bureaucrats who jumped on the bandwagon of the American Diploma Project vended by Achieve, Inc. (2008), the Common Core State Standards (CCSS) that arrived in 2010, national standardized testing, and other programs that attempt to standardize education and human outcomes

ADP and CCSS are simply reincarnations of an educationally bankrupt idea that was empirically destroyed more than eighty-five years ago. Due to a lack of understanding of their own history, some education leaders are willing to follow business interests over the cliff of botched reforms again and again.

Thorndike's studies added credence to the call of the *Cardinal Principles* for a large and varied curricular program, known as the macrocurriculum. As noted above, the *Cardinal Principles* focused on the three universal curricula first outlined by Lester Frank Ward in 1883 and later detailed by John Dewey in *Democracy and Education* (1916): (1) academic, (2) socio-civic, and (3) avocational.

A comprehensive macrocurriculum developed from the three universal curriclua allows students to take multiple paths through high school while (a) experiencing academic content to prepare them for a vocation, (b) participating in socially conscious problem-based activities to learn how to actively take part in a democracy, and (c) pursuing activities and hobbies based on personal interest. Regardless of the course paths individual students choose, all the paths embed authentic problem solving and socially conscious studies that connect the experiences of students to the larger society.

Demonstrated Successes

Wrightstone (1935) and Wrightstone, Rechetnick, McCall, and Loftus (1939) conducted a series of studies to determine the effects of activity-based curriculum on student achievement and social dispositions of students in the New York City public schools. Elementary school students in grades 4 through 6 in sixty-nine schools across the city were placed in experimental and control groups.

Activity-based curricula were piloted in large school districts as a way to increase educational equity. The idea was simple: All children—regardless of wealth, culture, race, or ethnicity—should receive the "good stuff" and be provided with the skills and dispositions necessary to lead a fulfilling life and participate in a vibrant democracy.

Students in the experimental groups were taught using socially conscious problem-based activities, whereas students in the control groups received the traditional instruction based on facts, figures, and reading comprehension. Problem-based activities were chosen based in part on topics that would interest students in the various grade levels. Students learned content by investigating interesting and socially conscious topics.

Wrightstone's first study included a sample of matched-pair students from thirty-two control classes and thirty-two experimental classes. The final sample of students matched for comparison purposes was approximately nine thousand. Students were tested before the experiment and found to be similar in academic achievement and social dispositions. The control group students had the advantage in intelligence by the equivalent of one month of schooling (Wrightstone, 1935).

The posttest results indicated that the students who engaged in the activity-based curriculum demonstrated more academic and affective growth than students in the traditional program. Students were assessed in the following areas: (a) comprehensive achievement in reading and mathematics, (b) cooperation activities, (c) experimental activities that require creation or construction of new ideas, and (d) critical activities such as critique, persuasion, or defending points of view.

The posttest results also showed superior gains in leadership activities, self-initiated activities, and work spirit activities. Students in the activity curriculum classrooms outscored their peers on all assessments except recitations. The effect size difference between the academic achievement on the comprehensive assessment was 0.21, favoring the activity group. The results demonstrated the efficacy of a nonstandardized curriculum.

Jersild, Thorndike, and Goldman (1939; 1941) reported on the results of what came to be known as the New York City experiment, which included seventy-five thousand elementary school students. Once again, the students involved in an activity-based curriculum outperformed their peers from traditional college preparatory programs on measures of academic and affective growth.

These studies demonstrated the power of the ideas communicated in the *Cardinal Principles of Secondary Education* and suggested that the ideas could be applied to elementary and secondary education. However, these studies paled in comparison to what is still considered *the* landmark study in education: The Eight-Year Study, discussed later in the chapter.

Educational Policies Commission

The Educational Policies Commission (EPC) emerged in 1938 with a report that set forth five "ideals" (EPC, 1938) that schools should seek to foster in students: (1) humanitarianism; (2) understanding and respect for the rights of other peoples; (3) civic participation in decision making; (4) methods of solving local, national, and international disputes that arrive at peaceful resolutions; and (5) the ability to evaluate the effectiveness of domestic and foreign policies in helping people progress in society (pp. 7–9).

Although the members of the EPC did not overtly recommend a unitary system in the 1938 report, one can infer that the ideals were not reserved only for a ruling class and that instead all children should experience the type of education that would help to achieve them. The connection between the EPC's ideals and the *Cardinal Principles* is clear. Another clue that the members of the EPC were not proposing a dual system was in the commission's admonition of standardized testing.

Standardized testing as a way of sorting students was gaining popularity at the time. Born out of the US Army's use of the Alpha Test to select officer candidates during World War I, the standardized test was quickly adopted into public schools to choose and sort students into programs and academic levels. The commission communicated clearly that standardized tests were limited in their ability and scope of measuring student achievement and their myopic focus on measuring isolated bits of information. It is interesting that over seventy years later, our education leaders and policymakers have yet to understand the commission's warnings and recommendations.

The EPC released several other reports in the years that followed (1944, 1952) that would add to their initial ideals. The report known as *Education for ALL America's Youth* proposed an eight-year curriculum beginning in grade 7 and extending into grade 14. This proposal, also known as the 2X2 model, created a bridge from high school to career or postsecondary schooling. Although the model never gained universal support, aspects of the idea remain today in some schools that offer work-study, apprenticeship, and dual-credit college enrollment programs.

The Eight-Year Study

If the *Cardinal Principles of Secondary Education* was education's Declaration of Independence from the dual system, then the Eight-Year Study (Aikin, 1942) provided a road map to achieving independence. The study grew out of the progressive/experimentalist philosophy and operationalized the

Cardinal Principles. The study included thirty high schools/districts from across the country.

The university professors and the educators from the thirty schools were troubled by the stranglehold that college admissions had on the high school curriculum. The college admissions requirements had a standardizing effect on high school curricula. The professors and educators sought a way to achieve excellence for all students, not just those who intended to go to college, by changing the college entrance requirements and broadening the curricula to reflect the three universal themes laid out by Ward and Dewey.

The participants set out to design and implement secondary school programs that brought the *Cardinal Principles* to life. They received approval from hundreds of colleges that waived the traditional admission requirements and standardized entrance exams. Students from the thirty schools could substitute portfolios of quantitative and qualitative evidence to demonstrate that they were prepared for college. The thirty schools were freed from standardized test prep curricula (Aikin, 1942).

The curricular programs of the thirty schools were not standardized. In fact, they were synthesized from the recommendations of the *Cardinal Principles*, and progressive education philosophy. They were based on research of the time about the nature of the learner, human development, the nature of knowledge, and the best ways to organize curriculum, as well as influence from social forces, including democratic ideals. The program at each school was unique, yet each was focused on a paradigm of curriculum and instruction and based on five overarching principles that are still vital to education quality today (Kridel & Bullough, 2007).

Guiding Principles

The first principle was that the learner is an active constructor of meaning who brings prior knowledge and experience to the classroom, and that school policies and practices should capitalize on those experiences. The second was that knowledge must be organized as a fusion of discipline-centered subject matter and personal/societal experiences, connecting the content to students through authentic socially conscious problem-solving situations that examined issues facing democracy. The third principle was that student social and cognitive development is ongoing and occurs in stages, not at finite points in time, like the end of grade 9.

Democracy was the fourth principle. Democracy is a strong cultural force that cannot be ignored. Any initiative that is authoritarian in nature or without involvement of important stakeholders is unlikely to achieve its stated goals. Authoritarian initiatives generally fail because they violate cultural norms of democratic participation and decision making.

Equity was the fifth and final principal. Equity is the idea that one gets what one needs (e.g., diversification of curriculum) and not the same as everyone else (e.g., standardization of curriculum and assessment). Equity should be a driving force in education planning and implementation.

Results

Students in the thirty schools pursued diverse interests within a large macro-curriculum. The curriculum provided a common core of study for all students on the challenges facing democracy. This was usually accomplished by a mandatory course for all students in middle and high school. The curriculum also provided for instruction in the basic academic subjects along with a large set of electives to allow for career specialization, personal exploration, and overall enrichment. The lack of standardization and the reduced emphasis on standardized testing produced superior results compared to students in high schools with traditional curricular sequences focused on mental discipline.

Ralph Tyler headed the evaluation of the project. The results suggested that when matched with similar students from traditional high schools, the students from the thirty schools outperformed their peers on all measures of academic achievement, including standardized tests. The students from the thirty schools achieved higher college grade point averages and demonstrated better problem-solving skills and civic-minded behaviors, among other things. The only academic area in which they did not statistically significantly outperform their peers was in a foreign language (Aikin, 1942).

The results from the Eight-Year Study demonstrated that public secondary schools can educate all students together through differentiated curriculum and instruction to meet their unique needs. Public secondary schools can diversify course offerings, operating in truly nonstandardized and democratic ways in which teachers, administrators, and university professors work together to increase educational equity and produce better results academically, socially, and civically.

The results demonstrated that ultimately public secondary schools could fill the equalizing role proposed by Thomas Jefferson and the other historic defenders of a democratic, classless education system. In the end it was diversification, guided by a progressive education paradigm informed by professional judgment and research, that trumped standardization and an exclusionary mentally of elitist education.

The Power of Politics

The Eight Year Study was published just as World War II was underway and the study of the problems that faced democracy was not a priority. Thus, its overall effect on education policy after World War II was rather diminished.

Keep in mind that the political climate at the time was not kind to school curriculum programs that taught students to question democracy or to study the problems of democracy. The rise of Russia and then China led to curricular retrenchment in the basics and away from problem-based learning.

Progressive/experimentalist education policy reforms as a whole, and their curricular programs, were falling out of favor. Curriculum materials and supporting resources such as the *Building America* series of problem-based units were under attack by the "conservative press and ultra right wing groups" (Tanner, 1991, p. 45) as being sympathetic to Communism. The *Building America* series was used by many schools that engaged in socially conscious problem-based work. In fact, in 1945—the year that regressive, antiexperimental/antiprogressive attacks began in earnest—the series sold 1 million copies per monthly issue (Tanner, 1991).

By 1948, publication of the *Building America* series and other progressive materials stopped due to the increasing false allegations that members of the *Building America* editorial board members were Communist sympathizers. Many schools boards across the country removed the books from school shelves and destroyed them. The questioning of democracy and study of its problems was not tolerated in the post–World War II era.

World War II, the rise of Communism and socialism, and an American inferiority complex dampened the large-scale progressive/experimentalist practices taking place across the country. A diminishing number of educators are familiar with the Eight-Year Study or the other landmark studies that create the foundation of quality education.

The lack of historical knowledge might be one reason the hamster wheel of education reform continues to turn unabated. Educators should reacquaint themselves with education's rich history and research in an attempt to once again reestablish the role and responsibility of public education as a unitary system devoted to leveling the playing field within a truly participative democracy.

EFFICIENCY: EDUCATION'S OTHER REFORM

Although education reform based on democratic ideals and a unitary conception of public education gained strength during the turn of the twentieth century up through World War II, there was another reform movement underway, perhaps even stronger in its intoxicating appeal. This reform was to become known as scientific management or the efficiency movement (Taylor, 1947). The efficiency movement in education was less concerned with equity, liberty and justice for all, and democratic ideals and more concerned with squeezing every ounce of perceived waste out of the system, at a cost to effectiveness.

The efficiency movement propelled the popularity of monitorial instruction and the Gary Plan, also known as platoon schools. The Gary Plan, named after a school structure used in Gary, Indiana, was developed by William Wirt in 1908 after he became superintendent (Callahan, 1962). Wirt proposed that classrooms should not be empty during the school day because that was an indication of waste.

There was controversy at the time that school buildings not were not used night and day, nor all year round. Wirt realized that if schools became departmentalized by academic subject, then all the students could move from room to room throughout the day and homerooms and specialty rooms could also be in use due to the rotating system. No longer would a room be used only for homeroom activities. With departmentalized instruction, the homeroom could become the math room for some additional periods during the day, followed by an English room, followed by a foreign language room.

The Gary Plan caught on, and by 1925 the plan was in use in 632 schools in 126 cities (Callahan, 1962, p. 129). Although the plan sounds commonsensical today, its focus was not on education as much as it was on economization. For example, the idea was brought to the elementary school level in New York City without the research to support its use at that level. The Gary Plan was also used to develop double and triple school sessions so that the school plant was in constant use, or as close to 100 percent utilization as possible.

Callahan (1962) noted that observers of the platoon school commented that students looked like machines marching in line and that the schools exhibited a hyperfocus on the number of students being educated within the shortest number of hours. Schooling was done "to" those students, not "with" or "for" them.

The use of the Gary Plan and platoon schools was adopted more frequently in the cities where more racially diverse and poorer students attended school. It seems that those in power prescribe a less democratic system for those who come to school with less. Efficiency is not the same as effectiveness, and effectiveness is not always efficient. Efficiency is more often concerned with maximizing profits at the expense of the best interests of human beings.

POINTS TO REMEMBER

Proponents of a democratic system of free public schools viewed public education as the great equalizer in terms of social mobility. The public schools are the only social institution that all children can pass through on their way to adulthood. The system has the ability, along with other policies and programs, to facilitate maximum vertical mobility within the social classes while developing a participative democracy with the representative republic model. Initial supporters of public education saw the system as a way to break out of the European class system and create an educated citizenry and a more equitable society.

A LOOK AHEAD

Chapter 2 transitions from education's distant past and introduces the genesis of modern school reform and the propaganda that continues to drive proposals related to the dual system. The chapter presents analyses of the Sputnik era and then *A Nation at Risk*. The analyses derive from empirical evidence and other facts. Facts should trump myths, frauds, and lies.

REFERENCES

Achieve, Inc. (2008). Closing the expectations gap. Retrieved from http://www.achieve.org/files/50-state-2008-final02-25-08.pdf
Aikin, W. M. (1942). *The story of the eight-year study*. New York: Harper.
Callahan, R. E. (1962). *The cult of efficiency*. Chicago: University of Chicago Press.
Campbell, J. K. (1967). *Colonel Parker: The children's crusader*. New York: Teachers College Press.
Commission on the Reorganization of Secondary Education. (1918). *Cardinal Principles of Secondary Education*. Bulletin No. 35. Washington, DC: US Bureau of Education.
Dewey, J. (1897). My pedagogic creed. *School Journal, 54*, 77–80.
Dewey, J. (1899). *School and society*. Chicago: University of Chicago.
Dewey, J. (1916). *Democracy and education*. New York: Macmillan.
Education Policies Commission. (1938). *The purposes of education in American Democracy*. Washington, DC: National Education Association of the United States and the American Association of School Administrators.
Education Policies Commission. (1944). *Education for ALL American youth*. Washington, DC: National Education Association.
Education Policies Commission. (1952). *Education for ALL American youth: A further look*. Washington, DC: National Education Association.
Finkelman, P. (1993). Jefferson and slavery: Treason against the hopes of the world. In Peter S. Onuf (Ed.), *Jeffersonian Legacies* (pp. 181–221). Charlottesville: University Press of Virginia
Freire, P. (2000). *Pedagogy of the oppressed: 30th anniversary edition*. New York: Continuum.
Jefferson, T. (1818). Report of the commissioners appointed to fix the site of the university of Virginia. In Roy J. Honeywell (1964). *The Educational Works of Thomas Jefferson*. New York: Russell and Russell, Appendix J.
Jersild, A. T., Thorndike, R. L., & Goldman, B. (1939). An evaluation of aspects of the activity program in New York City elementary schools. *Journal of Experimental Education, 8*, 166–207.
Jersild, A. T., Thorndike, R. L., & Goldman, B. (1941). A further comparison of pupils in "activity" and "non-activity" schools. *Journal of Experimental Education, 9*, 307–309.
Jewett, T. O. (1997). Thomas Jefferson and the purposes of education. *Educational Forum, 61*, 110–13.
Kridel, C., & Bullough, Jr., R. V. (2007). *Stories of the Eight-Year Study: Reexamining secondary education in America*. Albany: State University Press of New York.

Mann, H. (1848). *Twelfth annual report of the board of education together with the twelfth annual report of the secretary of the board*. Boston, MA: Dutton and Wentworth State Printers.

National Education Association of the United States, Committee of Ten on Secondary School Studies. (1893). *Report of the Committee of Ten on Secondary School Studies; With the Reports of the Conferences Arranged by the Committee*. New York: Published for the National Education Association by the American Book Co., 1984.

Padover, S. K. (1939). *Thomas Jefferson on democracy*. New York: Appleton-Century.

Rayman, R. (1981). Joseph Lancaster's monitorial system of education and American Indian education. *History of Education Quarterly, 21*(4), 395–409.

Tanner, D. (1991). *Crusade for democracy: Progressive education at the crossroads*. Albany: State University of New York Press.

Tanner, D., & Tanner, L. (2007). *Curriculum development: Theory into practice*. New York: Allyn & Bacon.

Taylor, F. W. (1947). *Scientific management*. New York: Harper and Brothers.

Thompson, D. (2011, Feb. 28). Bill Gates' idea to fix US education: Bigger classes. *Atlantic*.

Thorndike, E. L. (1924). Mental discipline in high school studies. *Journal of Educational Psychology, 15*, 1–22, 98.

Thorndike, E. L., & Woodworth, R. S. (1901). The influence of improvement in one mental function upon efficiency of other functions. *Psychological Review, 8*, 247–61, 384–95, 553–64.

Ward, L.F. (1883). *Dynamic sociology or applied social science*. Vol. 2. New York: D. Appleton.

Williams, F. D. (1989). *The Northwest Ordinance: Essays on its formulation, provisions, and legacy*. East Lansing: Michigan State University Press.

Wrightstone, J. W. (1935). *Appraisal of newer practices in selected public schools*. New York: Teachers College Press.

Wrightstone, J. W., Rechetnick, J., McCall, W. A., & Loftus, J. J. (1939). Measuring social performance factors in activity control schools of New York City. *Teachers College Record, 40*(5), 423–32.

Chapter Two

Neoliberalism, Social Darwinism, and Consumerism Masquerading as School Reform

Current national and state education policies and program initiatives in the United States are moving the public education system in a new direction. The country's locally controlled unitary system, based on egalitarian principles, is quickly being reshaped and cast toward a dual system based on economic principles foisted upon the system by for-profit business interests. Policies and programs in the United States born out of neoliberalism, commercialism, consumerism, and social Darwinian ideologies have penetrated almost all aspects of public education in some form.

Education legislation based on for-profit business principles overwhelm Thomas Jefferson's and John Dewey's views of a robust unitary system of public education. One-size-fits-all standardization programs and so-called public schools like charter schools and magnet academies, which use entrance requirements to exclude certain types of students, and the massive transfer of public education tax dollars to private education corporations casts a long shadow over the democratic public school system. Dewey (1916) warned of the dangers of a dual system in which the wealthy subjugate the less wealthy to an inferior education when he stated, "The more activity is restricted to a few definite lines—as it is when there are rigid class lines preventing adequate interplay of experiences—the more action tends to become routine on the part of the class at a disadvantage, and capricious, aimless, and explosive on the part of the class having the materially fortunate position" (p. 242).

The public education system now finds itself a victim of what Sandel (2012) called the "commercialization effect," in which government policy replaced a public social system of education with a market-based system of education (p. 120). The commercialization effect of the legally mandated market system of education entrenches what Freire (2000) termed a banking model of education.

The banking model describes a form of education in which students are viewed as passive receptacles, responsible for little more than unquestionably accepting knowledge and regurgitating it at a time and format decided upon by outside forces. The commercialization effect objectifies students by assigning labels such as college- and career-ready or partially proficient, based on the results from a standardized test. Then students are assigned to various commercial education products that correspond to their academic labels.

NEOLIBERALISM

Neoliberalism is born out of an economic ideology, or system of beliefs, that capitalistic free-market competition and privatization of social services is a more efficient way to increase economic growth (Steger & Roy, 2010). Mullen, Samier, Brindley, English, and Carr (2013) stated that neoliberalism is a "strategy of domination and subordination of the few over the many" (p. 189). Bourdieu (1999) called neoliberalism the "programme of methodical destruction of collectives" or any social services for the public, like education, libraries, and parks (p. 95). Neoliberal policies seek to destroy the public sphere and turn all public services into a private commodity to be purchased in the economic market (Bourdieu, 1998).

Underlying Theory

The theory of Pareto efficiency in part guides the ideology of neoliberalism (as cited in Adler, 2011, pp. 9–12). Pareto efficiency posits that there is a possibility that any form of economic redistribution hurts the wealthy more than it assists those in poverty or the middle class. The public is not worthy to receive services because those services will ultimately be paid for with higher taxes on the richest people and corporations, which is viewed as unfair in neoliberal ideology.

Neoliberals view services provided by the state as a form of wealth redistribution and an overall drag on economic development and the wealthy. Vilfredo Pareto postulated that rich people have more utility than poor people and that the elite wealthy class makes use of the resources provided in more effective ways (as cited in Adler, 2011, p. 10). The efficacy of Pareto efficiency has not been demonstrated empirically, yet it is an influential force in education reform policy and overall social policy in America.

Proponents of neoliberal policies opine that the ideology provides a more efficient framework to guide the management of society and sustain a growing economy (Steger & Roy, 2010) than policies that seek to lessen income inequality and provide quality social services for all. Policymakers and bureaucrats across the United States advocate limiting the role of the government in providing social services such as traditional public education. They and other bureaucrats who hold neoliberal worldviews advocate for education service delivery models derived from free-market structures, including charter schools, private schools, for-profit universities, and virtual or online for-profit schools.

Fraudulent Thinking

The market system does not run on ethics or morals; it runs on economics and selfishness. Neoliberal policies are disguised as efficiency and effectiveness, but the overriding objective is profit. Decisions are made based on money, not morals. Neoliberalism does not have a moral compass and is guided only by economic self-interest rather than the interest of the larger society and the greater good. Some wealthy elite want to separate themselves from the masses. Dewey (1916) explained that separation among groups in society serves only to make society selfish: "The essential point is that isolation makes for rigidity and formal institutionalizing of life, for static and selfish ideals within the group" (p. 245).

The neoliberal market system is ambiguous and amorphous, and that is one reason it is hard to stop. There is no one to call, no one to complain to, and no one place from which it is controlled. Neoliberal thinking is now embedded in the culture of American society.

Neoliberal Networks

A network of neoliberal think tanks and lobbying organizations financially support policymakers to ensure market-friendly legislation permeates the halls of federal and state governments. Organizations like the Business Roundtable, the US Chamber of Commerce, National Alliance for Public Charter Schools, Americans for Prosperity, the American Bankers Association (ABA), and the American Legislative Exchange Council (ALEC) contributed more than $90 million to senators and members of Congress in 2011. By 2018, contributions exceeded $113 million to forward the big business agenda of liberalizing the economy (Open Secrets, 2012, 2019).

ALEC is particularly dangerous in terms of influencing neoliberal education policy at the state and national levels. ALEC has a team of people who write neoliberal education legislation for policymakers. Many of the education bills submitted in state legislatures are written by ALEC authors; they most commonly attack teacher tenure and pensions and advocate for high-stakes testing, privatization, vouchers, charter schools, weakening of student data protections, gutting special education law, and the general degradation of public school in favor of private options.

International organizations such as the International Monetary Fund (IMF), the World Bank, the European Commission, and the World Trade Organization (WTO) advance neoliberal agendas around the world. They work with governments to deregulate and denationalize industries, destabilize unions, and globalize trade and labor to lower wage costs. The IMF, World Bank, and WTO support poilcies that undermine workers' rights and benefits.

Neoliberal Welfare for the Rich

The US banking industry presents an overt example of welfare for the rich. The industry profited immensely from the 1999 repeal of the Banking Act of 1933, known as the Glass-Steagall Act. President Bill Clinton signed the Gramm-Leach-Bliley Act of 1999 and set in motion the liberalizing of the American banking industry. Provisions within the legislation allowed large banks to create subsidiary companies to engage in high-risk securities trading. Before 1999, traditional banking operations and securities trading were separated and that separation helped to insulate the taxpayer from irresponsible investing strategies of the largest US banks.

Five years after the passage of the Gramm-Leach-Bliley Act, the US Securities and Exchange Commission changed another set of banking rules and allowed banks to increase their leverage for securities trading operations. The change in regulations increased the amount banks could "bet" on financial positions without requiring the banks to have the money on hand to cover their bets (McLean & Nocera, 2010).

The confluence of weak federal and state regulations, liberalizing legislation, and increased risk-taking behaviors on the part of big bank leadership helped lead to the financial crisis of 2008 and the taxpayer-funded multitrillion-dollar financial bailouts of those financial institutions (McLean & Nocera, 2010). Neither the networks that lobbied for the legislative changes on behalf of the banks and financial institutions nor the bankers who took risks—and taxpayer money—have been held accountable (Carney, 2011).

Shaping the Narrative

Neoliberal policymakers and bureaucrats around the globe narrate a consistent message that social services are a form of wealth redistribution. They espouse the view that the state should not be involved in redistributing wealth to the poor or middle class, although they do advocate for redistribution of wealth upward to the rich (Stiglitz, 2012). Some examples of upward wealth redistribution in the United States include tax cuts to the wealthiest citizens, corporate welfare via bank bailouts, low dividend and capital gains taxes for the wealthiest people, low estate taxes on the wealthiest citizens, and tax loopholes that allow the richest Americans and corporations to hide their money in offshore accounts and pay lower tax rates than most middle-class citizens (Adler, 2011; Friedman & Kakoyiannis, 2019).

EGALITARIANISM

In the most basic sense, egalitarianism is the concept that everyone should be afforded equal treatment to a society's social mobility apparatus in order to lead a productive and sustaining life (Roemer, 1998). Egalitarianism is a necessary component of equity, and a comprehensive public education system is part of the apparatus to operationalize an egalitarian and equitable society. Egalitarian ethos is exemplified in the phrase from the US Declaration of Independence (1776) "that all men [sic] are created equal, that they are endowed by their Creator with certain unalienable Rights, that among these are Life, Liberty, and the pursuit of Happiness" (para. 2).

The aims of equitable education policies can be fully realized only if supported by wider egalitarian and equitable social policies, due to the close link between socioeconomic status and student achievement in the United States (Sirin, 2005). Just as the flower needs the rain, education policy needs broader participation by other societal supports, tax policy included, to facilitate upward economic growth for those students most displaced in an economy (Atkinson & Leigh, 2008; Hungerford, 2012).

MERITOCRACY

In a meritocracy, those with the most ability are viewed as having the most value, and they are selected to receive access to the quality services and experiences. In other words, the good stuff is reserved for the chosen few. Meritocracy can be seen playing out in many aspects of neoliberal school policy within the dual system of education. Some states allow publicly funded specialty academic high schools, including magnet schools, charter schools, and vocational-technical academies, to use entrance criteria to select students for enrollment or retention in the schools.

Wealthier students most often meet the criteria for enrollment, while the poorest students and students with special needs are more often excluded from such schools. Even in cases in which bureaucrats use lotteries for random selection, many charter schools and magnet schools have more homogenous student populations than their neighborhood schools, based on socioeconomics, race, prior academic achievement, or special needs categories (Frankenberg, 2011; Miron, Urschel, Mathis, & Tornquist, 2010; Weber and Rubin, 2018). The neoliberal market system allows for discrimination, segregation, and the commercialization of the public schools because decisions are made based only on economic impact, not moral or ethical considerations.

Entrance and/or retention criteria are hallmarks of meritocracy. The students who are better off socioeconomically generally do better academically on standardized tests. Those students go on to receive better education opportunities. Students who do not perform well on traditional measures of academic achievement receive limited access to quality education opportunities and are usually remanded to mechanistic test preparation curricula and programs. The segregation of education opportunity and quality is the Matthew effect in action: The academically and socially rich get richer (Stanovich, 1986).

CONSUMERISM

Veblen (1994) described consumerism as a social-economic orientation that values the purchase of goods and services as part of an overall accumulation of possessions. Consumerism links to materialism and commercialism in that they all emphasize amassing goods and personal effects (Foster, 2000), but consumerism also values unrestrained choice. Advocates of a consumerist ideology suggest that consumption of goods and services relates positively to the overall well-being of a society. The more goods and services that people in society consume, the more developed that society must be. Former president George W. Bush (2001) went so far as to say that consumption was patriotic.

MARKETING THE MYTH

Overall, the average US citizen has more choices for material possessions and services than was available fifty years ago. Cars, televisions, cell phones, larger homes, and other consumer items can be obtained on credit to satisfy the need for immediate gratification brought on by unrestrained choice. However, US society is not more developed according to indicators like the percentage of children living in poverty, child suicide rates, and the percentage of children living in single-parent households (National Center for Education Statistics, 2010, 2018). The percentage of children living in poverty shrank minimally under the Obama administration, from 21.1 percent in 2010 to 19.1 percent in 2017, but is still one of the highest rates in the industrialized world.

Much of the school reform marketing revolves around the idea of treating parents and students as consumers: "Students and parents are our clients" is a rallying cry heard throughout the education reform market. Two tenets underlying the treatment of students and parents like clients are consumerism and the free market. Should we relegate students and parents to the passive position of consumers? Is a free market the best idea for public education? The market is about competition. So someone must lose in order for another to win.

Choice without Voice

Consumption of education based on choice equates to quality in the market-based education reform world when viewing the choice through the consumerist and neoliberal lenses. Parents and students are sold the idea that the consumption of education via nonpublic, nontraditional, corporatized delivery systems demonstrates modernization of the public school system. Bush (1999) used charter schools as an example of how choice equates to quality:

> Charter schools encourage educational entrepreneurs to try innovative methods. They break up the monopoly of one-size-fits-all education. These diverse, creative schools are proof that parents from all walks of life are willing to challenge the status quo if it means a better education for their children. More competition and more choices for parents and students will raise the bar for everyone. (pp. 233–34)

Freire (2000) delineated between modernization via choice and societal development, stating that "the basic, elementary criterion is whether or not the society is a being for itself. If not, the other criteria indicate modernization rather than development" (p. 162). Choice does not automatically beget quality of life improvements or better education.

Partners versus Consumers

The act of choosing or consuming a commodity does not equate to involving oneself in decision making about the design, development, leadership, or management of that commodity. In the consumerist marketplace, education is a commodity and students and parents are reduced to purchasers or users, not decision makers, contributors to the quality of the product, or partners.

Many nonpublic schools, including charter schools, do not have democratically elected boards of education. They commonly have appointed boards of directors, with many of those directors having a monetary interest in the school. Parent and student involvement is relegated to superficial activities such as fundraising, signing student homework folders, or attending school events. There is no involvement in the decision making about programs, policies, or procedures because there is no democratic mechanism for involvement—there is only forced choice without an authentic voice. Parents and students have the "choice" to either comply with the policies or leave the school.

Public school educators and supporters can elevate students and parents out of the bowels of neoliberal consumerism by treating them more like partners in education and less like clients.

SOCIAL DARWINISM

Social Darwinism is a concept that suggests only the strongest and best-adapted humans should excel in society (Bannister, 1989). It is the human equivalent of survival of the fittest. It is the opposite of "liberty and justice for all" as recited by millions of public school children daily in the Pledge of Allegiance.

Social Darwinism is visible through the use of one-size-fits-all curriculum standards and the use of results from mandated standardized testing to make important decisions about children and teachers. For children, poor performance on a single state test can result in being (a) denied entrance into quality academic program tracks, (b) retained in grade, (c) placed in low academic tracks, or (d) denied the opportunity to graduate high school. Students who do not perform as expected on one state-mandated test do not merit higher quality opportunities. Based on their test results, they are not the academically strongest and therefore do not deserve to be in the top classes or programs.

Teachers can be penalized with salary reduction, loss of tenure, or denial of merit pay if their students do not score well enough on the mandated tests. The logic holds that the teacher of a student who struggles academically must be weak and therefore does not deserve to have the same rights or provisions to salary and tenure provisions as teachers whose students score higher on the tests.

Meritocracy Meets Darwin

Social Darwinism and meritocracy collide when students who perform poorly on state-mandated testing receive impoverished education opportunities narrowly focused on only those topics most likely to be tested. Their chances of receiving an enriched education or performing better in the future on such tests decrease the longer they are in the system because they continue to receive educationally austere opportunities (Booher-Jennings, 2005). The cycle of education austerity destines many struggling students to failure. However, that is what the free market has decided is appropriate.

In effect, a dual system of education is being constructed that could ensure unequal access to education opportunities and inequitable access to quality education for students from poverty because the mandated tests favor students who come from less impoverished backgrounds. The academically successful fittest students receive the benefits of access to more educational opportunities. These students are commonly those who come from wealthier backgrounds and environments, and who more frequently score proficient on state-mandated tests.

Standardized tests are heavily influenced by socioeconomic status, and the results can be predicted by community census data (Tienken, Colella, Angelillo, Fox, McCahill, & Wolfe, 2017). The standardized test is one tool used frequently by neoliberal policymakers to sort children under the guise of equity. They claim the test results identify the students who are being left behind by educators, but the results do nothing more than provide insights into the zip code in which a student lives (Badger & Bui, 2018). The longer students are kept in the system, the greater the education achievement differences between students of wealth and those from poverty become, and they further entrench two classes of educated persons—the educated and the undereducated.

The more educated students move to higher levels of education, wider ranges of job opportunities, and access to better healthcare. The undereducated are relegated to a high school diploma or less, and a life destined to labor for the educated. Education level correlates to personal wealth and life expectancy (Denney, McNown, Rogers, & Doubilet, 2012). The Darwinian theory of natural selection will play out in the end, as the life expectancy of the wealthy educated citizenry will continue to rise and that of the poor and those dispossessed by the new education system will stagnate.

The difference in life expectancy in America between rich and poor men now favors the rich by almost fifteen years (Karma, 2019). The life expectancy gap has almost doubled in the last thirty years, and the difference correlates to the increasing wealth gap in the United States (Karma, 2019; National Academies of Sciences, Engineering, and Medicine, 2015). It seems as if the free market decided that some people do not merit longer lives.

Testing the System

The standardized testing provisions in federal and state legislation have the effect of stripping control of assessment away from the local education agencies and placing it in the boardrooms of large corporations such as McGraw-Hill and Pearson. Karier (1972) predicted such a situation almost thirty years before the signing of the No Child Left Behind Act (NCLB) in 2002. The outsourcing of assessment and other aspects of schooling to big business align to the neoliberal model of shifting public funds and decision making to private entities and out of the public sphere (Hursh, 2007).

The outsourcing of assessment from school personnel to corporate personnel acts to deskill educators, lessen the in-house capacity of school personnel, and further weaken local control. The entire process of assessment, aside from the actual proctoring, is outsourced. Educators do not need to know or understand the assessment design. Educators become mere assessment implementers and imitators, not decision makers or creators.

Over time, educators come to rely on prepackaged corporate education programs, many of which are never fully vetted or demonstrated effective on the populations for which they are marketed (Tanner & Tanner, 2007). In many cases, the same corporations that make the standardized assessments also make programs to address deficiencies identified by the assessments, thereby creating a neoliberal system of education that some students never can escape.

CEMENTING THE NEW CASTE SYSTEM

The sixth reauthorization of the 1965 Elementary and Secondary Education Act, signed by Barack Obama on December 10, 2015, and now known as the Every Student Succeeds Act (ESSA), preserved many of the structural features of its predecessor, NCLB. ESSA maintained the testing mandates in grades 3–8 and high school as well as the mandate that at least 95 percent of students participate in testing. ESSA continued to require states to set school and district accountability targets and identify subgroup performance. All states must report results to the public via school and district report cards and use curricula that have been deemed college and career aligned. However, ESSA includes a neoliberal nail in the coffin of the publically funded, unitary system of education that did not exist in NCLB: the social impact bond (SIB), known as pay-for-success initiative.

The ESSA (2015) defined the pay-for-success initiative as

> a performance-based grant, contract, or cooperative agreement awarded by a public entity in which a commitment is made to pay for improved outcomes that result in social benefit and direct cost savings or cost avoidance to the public sector. Such an initiative shall include—(A) a feasibility study on the initiative describing how the proposed intervention is based on evidence of effectiveness; (B) a rigorous, third-party evaluation that uses experimental or quasi-experimental design or other research methodologies that allow for the strongest possible causal inferences to determine whether the initiative has met its proposed outcomes; (C) an annual, publicly available report on the progress of the initiative; and (D) a requirement that payments are made to the recipient of a grant, contract, or cooperative agreement only when agreed upon out-

comes are achieved, except that the entity may make payments to the third party conducting the evaluation described in subparagraph (B). (STAT. 2096)

Social impact bonds are a way to funnel public money to private companies to perform services traditionally provided by public entities, like public schools, with the private companies and investors getting paid based on results reported by the private company.

Social Impact Bonds

Social impact bonds change the rules of the game. They further commercialize education by treating it as an investable commodity. Roy, McNeil, and Sinclair (2018) discussed a fundamental flaw in SIBs that subjugates the interests of the students to those of economics:

> The introduction of a profit incentive fundamentally alters the relationship between the service provider and user. The principal client and dominant stakeholder of any given SIB is its financier, not those who receive the services it finances and whose voice rarely figures into any discussion. The motivation propelling private investment in SIBs is profit or return on investment, rather than assisting or changing the circumstances of citizens in need. SIBs reduce this latter feature—which we might regard as the central purpose of social and public policy—to a by-product of investment. (p. 3)

Pay for success is just a slogan to camouflage SIBs. Leith (2017) explained:

> In the case of the ESSA, social impact bonds are a way for investors to speculate on education outcomes; essentially making bets on programs and then measuring if kids meet these benchmarks—which trigger a payout to investors by the state or local government agency that signed onto the contract.

Leith provides an in-depth example of a SIB program in Utah in which Goldman Sacks gets paid 5 percent interest on the loan plus reward money every year for every student in the private preschool program who is deemed not in need of special education services up through grade 6. She explained:

> In Utah, [Senator Orrin] Hatch's home state, Goldman Sachs and the investor J.B. Pritzker agreed to invest millions of dollars in an expansion of a preschool program in the Granite School District and later the state as a whole. The payoff for investors would occur if the expansion of preschool to underserved populations cut down on the number of students requiring special education services later in their academic careers. The bet was preschool would reduce the number of kids in special education based on scores determined by the Peabody Picture Vocabulary Test.
> The sell to the school district was the potential savings of $2,600 dollars [sic] for every child who didn't need special education or other remedial services.

The payout plan to Goldman Sacks and J.B. Pritzker is tricky, and makes me wonder if any of the politicians who supported the statewide preschool plan took the time to crunch the numbers and imagine worst case scenarios. Here's the terms for The Utah High Quality Preschool Program America's First "Results-based Financing" for Early Childhood Education.

Determining Pay-for-Success Payments

- Children participating in the high impact preschool program are given the Peabody Picture Vocabulary Test which is a predictive evaluation that will serve as an indicator of their likely usage of special education and remedial services. Students that test below average and are therefore likely to use special education services will be tracked as they progress through 6th grade
- Every year that they do not use special education or remedial services will generate a Pay-forSuccess payment
- School districts receive a fixed per annum payment of approximately $2,600 per student to provide special education and remedial services for students in general education classrooms from the State of Utah. The amount of the Pay-for-Success payment is based on the actual avoided costs realized by the State of Utah
- Pay-for-Success payments will be made equal to 95% of the avoided costs or $2,470 per child for every year, Kindergarten through Sixth Grade, to repay the senior and subordinate debt plus a base interest rate of 5.0%
- Thereafter, Success Payments will equal 40% of the savings, or $1,040 per child per year of special education services avoided, to be paid as Success Fees to Goldman Sachs and Pritzker

And this disclaimer, which in my mind seems to contradict the point made above. I'm thinking interpretation will hinge on whether Goldman Sachs and Pritzker are making money on their investment at the 7 year mark:

- Pay-for-Success payments are only made through 6th grade for each student; but all savings that are generated after that point will be captured by the school district, state and other government entities.

The New York Times took a look at the first year results of the Utah program and found some troubling issues. First off, Goldman Sachs reported a payout of $260,000 dollars [*sic*] by claiming their program helped 99% of the students enrolled avoid special education, even though the highest rate of prevention in well funded preschool programs is a 50% success rate. Oh, and the Goldman Sachs program isn't considered to be well funded.
"Goldman said its investment had helped almost 99 percent of the Utah children it was tracking avoid special education in kindergarten. The bank received a payment for each of those children.
"The big problem, researchers say, is that even well-funded preschool programs—and the Utah program was not well funded—have been found to re-

duce the number of students needing special education by, at most, 50 percent. Most programs yield a reduction of closer to 10 or 20 percent.

"The program's unusual success—and the payments to Goldman that were in direct proportion to that success—were based on what researchers say was a faulty assumption that many of the children in the program would have needed special education without the preschool, despite there being little evidence or previous research to indicate that this was the case."

Another problem was the Peabody Picture Vocabulary Test or P.P.V.T. overestimated the kids at risk for special education services, even though this test isn't really used as a screener for special education in the first place.

"Before Goldman executives made the investment, they could see that the Utah school district's methodology was leading large numbers of children to be identified as at-risk, thus elevating the number of children whom the school district could later say were avoiding special education. From 2006 to 2009, 30 to 40 percent of the children in the preschool program scored below 70 on the P.P.V.T., even though typically just 3 percent of 4-year-olds score this low. Almost none of the children ended up needing special education.

"When Goldman negotiated its investment, it adopted the school district's methodology as the basis for its payments. It also gave itself a generous leeway to be paid pack. As long as 50 percent of the children in the program avoid special education, Goldman will earn back its money and 5 percent interest—more than Utah would have paid if it had borrowed the money through the bond market. If the current rate of success continues, it will easily make more than that."

As of August 2020, the yield on a ten-year government Treasury bond was less than 0.75 percent and the amount of interest investors receive in their savings accounts is about .09 percent. Goldman Sachs is guaranteed 5 percent interest on their education scheme, and they seem to have been able to set the metrics for success and the measures used to judge success.

REFUSING TO PLAY IN THE CORPORATE BOARDROOM

Standardized products from the education marketplace, like CCSS or rebranded/renamed versions of the CCSS, and standardized testing products extend the education reform ideas put forth by Dwight D. Eisenhower, the authors of *A Nation at Risk*, and legislation like NCLB and ESSA. Dewey (1938) warned that standardization impedes society's movement toward more equity and progress: "It is to large extent the cultural product of societies that assumed the future would be much like the past, and yet it is used as educational food in a society where change is the rule, not the exception" (p. 19).

One can see the intersection of neoliberalism, social Darwinism, consumerism, and meritocracy in cases in which education bureaucrats, school administrators, or other policymakers use results from mandated standardized tests of the standardized curriculum as triggers to make life-influencing decisions about public school students, teachers, or the structure of public schooling.

Because historically the lower academic tracks do not adequately prepare students for their federally mandated state tests in high school, the prophecy becomes self-fulfilling. It is the Golem effect when students who are consistently told they perform poorly lower their expectations and continue to perform poorly. Neoliberal education practices encrust the Golem effect in policy (Babad et al., 1982; Rowe & O'Brien, 2002).

The policy shifts perpetrated by neoliberal ideology already produced changes in the system that affected children negatively. For example, more than one hundred thousand high school students are denied high school graduation or made to jump through additional hoops to find a path to graduate every year because they did not pass state-mandated exit exams in either language arts or mathematics (Tienken, 2011). Many of these students are poor and nonwhite. Enough information about the dangers to equity of creating a dual system is already known about the policy initiatives currently used in the US conceived from neoliberalism, social Darwinism, consumerism, and meritocracy have no place in a democratic system of public education.

TAKING ACTION

The dismantling of the public space and its services is one consequence of neoliberalism; dehumanizing children is another. Educators are simultaneously the first and last line of defense. They see firsthand and early on how neoliberal education policy treats children as a commodity and how that commodification dehumanizes them. Neoliberalism represents legalized economic violence against democracy and the common good. Egalitarianism and dignity are ideas, like democracy; and like democracy, egalitarianism and dignity must be defended and nurtured by educators at the local level in order to cultivate and preserve them.

Educators can lead by example and not label students or educators in ways that dehumanize them. They can overtly correct those who label students as inanimate objects, like "basic skills" or "advanced" or some other term. School is the primary venue in which students become socialized to egalitarian and democratic community life. It is a place where they learn how their actions impact others and the greater good.

If educators label students or allow the practice of labeling to occur, then some human beings will be deemed as more worthy of dignity than others based on a test score or some other measure outside of their control. Those individuals will then learn to devalue egalitarian principles in favor of principles aligned with meritocracy, and the cycle of commercialization and commodification will continue.

A LOOK AHEAD

The next chapter examines the genesis of the modern school reform rhetoric that public schools are failing with a deep dive into the launch of Sputnik. The chapter uses declassified memos from the Eisenhower presidency and declassified reports from the US Army to tell the true story about the space race and education's role. The chapter concludes with an evidence-based debunking of the claims made by the report *A Nation at Risk*, the blueprint for the modern standardization movement.

REFERENCES

Adler, M. (2011). *Economics for the rest of us: Debunking the science that makes life dismal.* New York: New Press.
Atkinson, A. B., & Leigh, A. (2008). Top income in New Zealand 1921–2005: Understanding the effects of marginal tax rates, migration threat, and the macro-economy. *Review of Income and Wealth, 54*(2), 149–65.
Babad, E. Y., Inbar, J., & Rosenthal, R. (1982). Pygmalion, Galatea, and the Golem: Investigations of biased and unbiased teachers. *Journal of Educational Psychology, 74,* 459–74.
Badger, E., & Bui, Q. (2018, October 1). Detailed maps show how neighborhoods shape children for life. *New York Times.*
Bannister, R. (1989). *Social Darwinism: Science and myth in Anglo-American social thought.* Philadelphia: Temple University Press.
Booher-Jennings, J. (2005). Below the bubble: "Educational triage" and the Texas accountability system. *American Educational Research Journal, 42*(2), 231–68.
Bourdieu, P. (1999). The abdication of the state. In P. Bourdieu (Ed.), *The weight of the world: Social suffering in the contemporary society* (pp. 181–88). Stanford, CA: Stanford University Press.
Bourdieu, P. (1998). *Acts of resistance: Against the tyranny of the market.* New York: New Press.
Bush, G. W. (1999). *A charge to keep.* New York: William Morrow.
Bush, G. W. (2001, September 27). At O'Hare, president says get on board: Remarks by the president to airline employees [Transcript]. Speech at O'Hare International Airport, Chicago, IL. Retrieved from http://georgewbush-whitehouse.archives.gov/news/releases/2001/09/20010927-1.html
Carney, J. (2011, December 14). The size of the bank bailout: $29 trillion. CNBC. Retrieved from http://www.cnbc.com/id/45674390
Denney, J. T., McNown, R., Rogers, R. G., & Doubilet, S. (2012). Stagnating life expectancies and future prospects in an age of uncertainty. *Social Science Quarterly, 94*(2). https://doi.org/10.1111/j.1540-6237.2012.00930.x
Dewey, J. (1916). *Democracy and education.* New York: MacMillan.
Dewey, J. (1938). *Experience and education.* New York: Kappa Delta Pi.
Every Student Succeeds Act (ESSA). (2015). Pub. L. No. 114-95, § 129, Stat. 2096. Retrieved from https://www.congress.gov/114/plaws/publ95/PLAW-114publ95.pdf
Frankenberg, E. (2011). Educational charter schools: A civil rights mirage? *Kappa Delta Pi Record, 47*(3), 100–105.
Friedman, N., & Kakoyiannis, A. (2019, September 17). How the super-wealthy hide billions using tax havens and shell companies. *Business Insider.* Retrieved from https://www.

businessinsider.com/jake-bernstein-panama-papers-offshore-banking-shell-companies-2018-2

Foster, J. B. (2000). *Marx's ecology: Materialism and nature*. New York: Monthly Review Press.

Freire, P. (2000). *Pedagogy of the oppressed: 30th anniversary edition*. New York: Continuum.

Hungerford, T. L. (2012, September 14). *Taxes and the economy: An economic analysis of the top tax rates since 1945*. Congressional Research Service. Retrieved from http://graphics8.nytimes.com/news/business/0915taxesandeconomy.pdf

Hursh, D. (2007). Assessing "No Child Left Behind" and the rise of neoliberal education policies. *American Educational Research Journal, 44*(3), 493–518.

Karier, C. J. (1972). Testing for order and control in the corporate state. *Educational Theory, 22*(2), 154–80.

Karma, R. (2019, May, 10). The gross inequality of death in America. *New Republic*. Retrieved from https://newrepublic.com/article/153870/inequality-death-america-life-expectancy-gap

Leith, C. (2017, July 11). Pay for success—also known as social impact bonds, Senator Orrin Hatch & the Every Student Succeeds Act (ESSA). *Seattle Education*. Retrieved from https://seattleducation.com/2017/07/11/pay-for-success-also-known-as-social-impact-bonds-senator-orrin-hatch-the-every-student-succeeds-act-essa/

McLean, B., & Nocera, J. (2010). *All the devils are here: The hidden history of the financial crisis*. New York: Portfolio Hardcover–Penguin.

Miron, G., Urschel, J. L., Mathis, W, J., & Tornquist, E. (2010). *Schools without diversity: Education management organizations, charter schools and the demographic stratification of the American school system*. Tempe, AZ: Education and the Public Interest Center & Education Policy Research Unit. Retrieved from http://epicpolicy.org/publication/schools-without-diversity

Mullen, C. A., Samier, E. A., Brindley, S., English, F. W., & Carr, N. K. (2013). An epistemic frame analysis of neo-liberal culture and politics in the US, UK, and the UAE. *Interchange, 43*, 187–228.

National Academies of Sciences, Engineering, and Medicine. (2015). *The growing gap in life expectancy by income: Implications for federal programs and policy responses*. Washington, DC: National Academies Press. https://doi.org/10.17226/19015

National Center for Education Statistics. (2018). Number and percentage of related children under age 18 living in poverty, by family structure, race/ethnicity, and selected racial/ethnic subgroups: 2010 and 2016. Table 102.60. Retrieved from https://nces.ed.gov/programs/digest/d18/tables/dt18_102.60.asp

National Center for Education Statistics. (2010). The condition of education: Participation in education. Retrieved from http://nces.ed.gov/programs/coe/tables/table-cse-2.asp

No Child Left Behind Act of 2001 (NCLB). (2002). Pub. L. No. 107-110, § 115, Stat. 1425 Retrieved from http://www2.ed.gov/nclb/landing.jhtml

Open Secrets. (2012). Influence and lobbying. Retrieved from http://www.opensecrets.org/index.php

Open Secrets. (2018). Influence and lobbying: Business associations. Retrieved from https://www.opensecrets.org/lobby/indusclient.php?id=N00&year=2018

Roemer, J. (1998). *Equality of opportunity*. Cambridge, MA: Harvard University Press.

Rowe, W. G., & O'Brien, J. (2002). The role of Golem, Pygmalion, and Galatea effects on opportunistic behavior in the classroom. *Journal of Management Education, 26*, 612–28.

Roy, M. J., McNeil, M., & Sinclair, S. (2018, May 1). A critical reflection on social impact bonds. *Stanford Social Innovation Review*. Retrieved from https://ssir.org/articles/entry/a_critical_reflection_on_social_impact_bonds

Sandel, M. (2012). *What money can't buy: The moral limits of markets*. New York: Farrar, Straus and Giroux.

Sirin, S. R. (2005). Socioeconomic status and academic achievement: A meta-analytic review of research. *Review of Educational Research, 75*(3), 417–53.

Stanovich, K. E. (1986). Matthew effects in reading: Some consequences of individual differences in the acquisition of literacy. *Reading Research Quarterly, 21*(4), 360–407.

Steger, M. B., & Roy, R. R. (2010). *Neoliberalism: A very short introduction.* New York: Oxford University Press.

Stiglitz, J. (2012). *The price of inequality: How today's divided society endangers our future.* New York: W.W. Norton.

Tanner, D., & Tanner, L. (2007). *Curriculum development: Theory into practice.* New York: Allyn & Bacon.

Tienken, C. H. (2011). Structured inequity: The intersection of socio-economic status and the standard error of measurement of state mandated high school test results. In B. Alford (Ed.), *Blazing new trails: Preparing leaders to improve access and equity in today's schools* (pp. 257–71). [The 2011 yearbook of the National Council of Professors of Educational Administration]. Lancaster, PA: DES *tech* Publications/Pro>Active Publications.

Tienken, C. H., Colella, A. J., Angelillo, C., Fox, M., McCahill, K., & Wolfe, A. (2017). Predicting middle school state standardized test results using family and community demographic data. *Research on Middle Level Education, 40*(1), 1–13.

United States Declaration of Independence. (1776). Paragraph 2. Retrieved from http://www.archives.gov/exhibits/charters/declaration_transcript.html

Veblen, T. (1994/1899). *The theory of the leisure class: an economic study of institutions.* Mineola, NY: Dover Publications.

Weber, M., & Rubin, J. S. New Jersey charter schools: A data-driven view—2018 update, part I. Retrieved from https://doi.org/doi:10.7282/T39Z983M

Chapter Three

The Education Reform King with a Styrofoam Crown

In the category of Events That Make History, October 4, 1957, was marked by the shocking announcement from Moscow that the Soviets had successfully launched their Sputnik 1 space satellite. The Soviets beat the Americans into space! The shockwaves rocked democracies around the world. But the Soviets launched more than a satellite on that October day; they helped launch the rhetoric that has powered a wave of modern school reforms aimed at creating a dual system of education.

MAKING HISTORY

The Myth and The Fraud

The Soviet launch of Sputnik 1 was hailed as proof that the Soviet Union had eclipsed American scientific prowess. Although it was initially the scientific community that came under scrutiny, the focus and blame quickly turned to public education, especially in the areas of math and science. It was claimed that the perceived lag in education caused America to lose the space race and that the space race was an indicator of the larger Cold War battle being fought over political, educational, and economic ideologies. The Soviets and the Chinese lauded Communism as the superior political, educational, and economic system compared to democracy and capitalism, and the blame was laid at the feet of the American public schools.

The Rebuttal

The fact that America *could* have launched a satellite many months earlier than the Soviets was never made public. Political leaders in Washington, DC, chose not to share that information for geopolitical reasons. Many Americans still accept that the launch of Sputnik was an indicator that the American public education system was inadequate. Anecdotally, many education professionals and preservice educators also believe this. They, like many other citizens, fail to look below the surface and critique the conventional wisdom. They accept the headline.

The fact that the Soviets launched Sputnik 1 before America launched its first satellite was not related to the quality of America's public education system at that time. Dwight D. Eisenhower's administration made a political choice to allow the Soviets to launch a satellite first. Eisenhower and his team went on to use Sputnik as a vehicle to inject more funding into public schools and research universities.

American presidents since Eisenhower—and their secretaries of education—have used Sputnik, the original king of the modern school reform movement, as an instrument of fear to advance their education reform initiatives. These reforms have typically been based on standardization and privatization of the public school system. Bureaucrats since Eisenhower have used Sputnik to legitimize education reform policy actions aimed at entrenching the dual system in some way, even though the truth about Sputnik is easily accessible.

Obama Doubles Down

Barack Obama used Sputnik to build support for policies aimed at helping to stave off the economic crisis that began in September 2008 by investing in programs aimed at increasing innovations in technology and programs for energy independence. Obama stated in his 2009 remarks at the National Academy of Sciences:

> When the Soviet Union launched Sputnik a little more than a half-century ago, Americans were stunned. The Russians had beaten us to space. Furthermore, we had to make a choice: We could accept defeat or we could accept the challenge. Moreover, as always, we chose to accept the challenge. (p. 2)

Obama's secretary of education, Arne Duncan (2009), used the Sputnik myth and lie to push the Race to the Top (RTTT) initiative:

> In 1957, the Soviet Union launched Sputnik. They showed the world that they were leading the space race. President Eisenhower and Congress responded by establishing NASA. But they also funded efforts to create new curriculum and

programs to advance mathematics and science in our schools. They understood that education would help us win the Space Race—and any other race. (p. 1)

Unfortunately, Obama and his education secretary continued to perpetuate the myth, at that point a lie, with their frequent calls for a "Sputnik moment" in education. Education had nothing to do with the financial crisis of 2008, yet it was being used to deflect the blame and the attention from Wall Street firms and the mortgage industry that took advantage of lax financial regulations instituted during the 1990s to fuel a housing and mortgage lending bubble that later exploded (Baker, 2008). Obama and Duncan were not the first to invoke Sputnik to push a political policy. They were following a tradition of myth spinning. It seems that whenever high-ranking bureaucrats want to push an initiative to standardize or further privatize education, they wheel out Sputnik.

Reagan, Clinton, and Bush Launch Sputniks of Their Own

Rod Paige, secretary of education under George W. Bush, used Sputnik to support the 2003 Mathematics and Science Initiative:

> When the federal government last launched a major initiative promoting mathematics and science education after *Sputnik*, within 12 years, America had upgraded mathematics and science education, launched satellites, and seen its astronauts orbit the Earth and land on the Moon.

Bill Clinton's secretary of education, Richard Riley (1995), used Sputnik to justify further federal involvement in education as part of the America2000 legislation:

> If you look at our nation's history—going all the way back to Morrill Act in 1862 during the middle of the Civil War—the American people have always turned to the Federal government for support in education during times of great economic transition—just like the one we are going through now—or times of national emergency when our national security was at risk. . . . When the Russians woke us up by flying Sputnik over our heads late at night—a few of you may remember that experience—Congress passed the 1958 National Defense Education Act, which sent millions of Americans to college and educated a generation of scientists who helped us to win the Cold War.

Ronald Reagan used Sputnik as a tool in 1982 to support his plan to give tax credits for parents to send their students to private schools. He painted a picture of failing public schools to stump for tax credits for the rich, who could already afford private schools. Is this crowning of Sputnik as the king of modern school reform justified? Did American public education let down the country and compromise national security?

America Chose to Be Second

A review of some declassified memos and communications made during the Eisenhower administration tell another story of Sputnik and provide factual evidence that the United States was not lagging in scientific or education prowess. Sputnik became a manufactured crisis, to borrow a term by Berliner and Biddle (1995). In reality, it is just a vagabond king wearing a Styrofoam crown (Bon Jovi & Sambora, 1995). What follows is a review of presidential memos and speeches that expose the use of Sputnik as an example of the need for reform as misguided and intellectually weak.

Eisenhower held a meeting with his top staff on October 8, 1957, to discuss the launch of Sputnik. Declassified records indicate that Eisenhower was not overly upset or worried about the situation. The quality of the US education system was not a concern. According to Deputy Secretary of Defense Donald A. Quarles, who was present at the meeting, "The Redstone [military rocket] had it been used could have orbited a satellite a year or more ago" (Goodpaster, 1957a, p. 1).

Eisenhower did not want to be the first into space because he feared igniting a third world war with the Soviets. The president was pleased when Sputnik launched first because, to him, the Soviets opened up space for the United States. He stated during the October 8 meeting that the Russians "have done us a good turn unintentionally in establishing the concept of internationalizing space" (Goodpaster, 1957a, p. 2).

At the 339th meeting of the National Security Council on October 10, 1957, six days after the launch, Quarles stated, "Our Government had never regarded this program as including as a major objective that the United States should launch an Earth satellite first, though, of course, we have always been aware of the cold war implications of the launching of the first Earth satellite" (Gleason, 1957, p. 3).

As best as can be determined through access to declassified documents found in the National Archives and the Eisenhower Library, the idea that US public schooling was inferior first came from propaganda put out by Nikita Khrushchev and the Communist Chinese government immediately following the launch.

The Education Scapegoat

The Soviets and the Chinese seized upon the launch to initiate their propaganda offensive in an attempt to show the world that Communism was a superior form of government. Keep in mind that at the time, the Soviets were expanding their Communist bloc and looking for any positive press to help them overcome the unsavory picture being painted of the iron curtain. Likewise, the Chinese Communists were under constant pressure to control the population and needed positive propaganda to support their fledgling government.

Not until an October 15, 1957, meeting between Eisenhower and several scientific advisors did education begin to enter into the conversation, and then only casually, as a way to persuade Congress and the American public to support more funding for basic and specialized scientific research, not K–12 science education. Dr. I. I. Rabi told the president, "We can now see some [scientific] advantages on our part. However, the Soviets picked up tremendous momentum" (Goodpaster, 1957b, p. 2). Dr E. H. Land then stated that the scientific community needed the president's support to bring more of a focus to science: "At this time, scientists feel isolated and alone, but all of this could change" (Goodpaster, 1957b, p. 2).

Although worldwide public opinion saw the launch as a Soviet victory and indication of a scientific lead in the Cold War, US officials were not concerned that Sputnik represented a concrete indication of US inferiority in terms of scientific capacity or education. A memo dated October 16, 1957, "Reaction to the Soviet Satellite: A Preliminary Evaluation," acknowledged the propaganda value of the launch but clearly stated that informed opinion was less definite: "The satellite, is of course, most widely and readily accepted as proof of scientific and technological leadership by those with the least scientific and political sophistication. . . . Sophisticated opinion is, of course, far less likely to be impressed by the drama of the satellite or its being a first" (White House Office of the Staff Research Group, 1957).

The scientists helped create the lore of Russian superiority in science education. That lore would fan the flames of attacks on public schools for years to come. Land told the president, "They [the Soviets] regard science both as an essential tool and a way of life. They are teaching their young people to enjoy science" (Goodpaster, 1957b, p. 2). Land went on to accurately portray the tenor of the times and the rising role of consumption in the United States as it influenced science and discovery during those years leading up to Sputnik: "Curiously, in the United States, we are not now great builders for the future, but are rather stressing production in great quantities of things we already achieved" (p. 2).

To his credit, Eisenhower pushed back against the idea that the Soviets were superior in science education. Eisenhower said it was his understanding that the Soviets did not have a superior education system; they simply "followed the practice of picking out the best minds and ruthlessly spurning the rest" (Goodpaster, 1957b, p. 2). Nevertheless, Eisenhower did see the need for a "coordinated effort" on the issue and stated that he was in favor of trying to "create a spirit, an attitude toward science similar to that held toward various kinds of athletics in his youth" (p. 2).

The group of scientists saw the potential of attaching basic education to this issue as a way to mobilize support for more funding in the research labs and universities. Eisenhower agreed and stated that "now is a good time to try such a thing. People are alarmed and thinking about science, and perhaps this alarm could be turned to a constructive result" (Goodpaster, 1957b, p. 2). The federal government had very little influence on the K–12 curriculum at the time of the Sputnik launch, and the idea of federal incursions into the classroom was not welcomed. The researchers, Congress, and to some extent the president saw Sputnik not as an education crisis but as an opportunity to inject federal money into education on a large scale.

Eisenhower Takes the Bait and Runs

A little more than one month later, on November 7, 1957, the president made a speech on science and national security to announce a series of actions he was prepared to take. Education was not mentioned in that speech. It was not until November, 13, approximately six weeks after the launch of Sputnik, that Eisenhower brought education to the forefront. This is perhaps the speech that created the myth of US education inferiority that haunts education to this day. In this speech, Eisenhower painted the picture of a superior Soviet education system and of the US falling behind educationally.

The Lie Heard around the World

Several statements made by Eisenhower are quite poignant and illustrate how the Sputnik myth fueled a lie that would alter the trajectory of public education in the United States. Eisenhower (1957) stated, "We know of their rigorous educational system and their technological achievements." (Even though one month earlier, he had rebuked one of the researchers who made that comment in his office.) Eisenhower then made a direct connection between the support for research desired by the scientists, weaving in their idea to link this to the general public through a connection with basic education: "Time is a big factor in two longer-term problems: strengthening our scientific education and our basic research."

Eisenhower went on to make an amazing claim: "As you do this, my friends, remember that when a Russian graduates from high school he has had five years of physics, four years of chemistry, one year of astronomy, five years of biology, ten years of mathematics through trigonometry, and five years of a foreign language."

We were the country that invented the atomic bomb before anyone else. Had our scientific education and basic research degenerated to a place so low that in just twelve years, Russia could be superior in science education and technological development?

No nation on the planet graduates even a majority—let alone "all"—of its students having taken all of those courses, and in fact the statement was not true. Eisenhower asked that the public "scrutinize your school's curriculum and standards. Then decide for yourselves whether they meet the stern demands of the era we are entering." He helped to start the disinformation and distrust of America's public schools. This was the creation of the failing schools myth, the modern dual-system reformer's book of Genesis.

Project Horizon

Not only did the US never intend to be first into space, but it was known that the United States had the technological capacity to land a man on the moon as early as 1966. According to the 1959 declassified US Army feasibility study, the United States determined it could begin landing humans on the moon for the eventual construction of a military outpost. Lieutenant General Arthur G. Trudeau headed the ambitious plan, called Project Horizon (Department of the Army, 1959a).

Volume 1 of the two-volume report, released on June 9, 1959, stated that the United States was on track to deliver supplies to the moon by 1964:

> Advances in propulsion, electronics, space medicine, and other astronautical sciences are taking place at an explosive rate. The first penetration of space was accomplished in 1959, when a two-stage V -2 rocket reached the then unbelievable altitude of 250 miles. . . . In 1960, and after that. there will be other deep space probes by the US and the USSR, with the US planning to place the first man into space with a REDSTONE missile, followed in 1961 with the first man in orbit. . . . As will be indicated in the technical discussions of this report, the first US manned lunar landing could be accomplished by 1965. Thus, it appears that the establishment of an outpost on the moon is a capability which can be accomplished. (p. 2)

The report explained that the required technology to achieve the goals of the project was already in place or would be in place within a few years and a base consisting of 12 men could be ready in less than a decade:

> By the end of 1964, a total of 72 SATURN vehicles should have been launched in US programs, of which 40 are expected to contribute to the accomplishment of HORIZON. Cargo delivery to the moon begins in January 1965. The first manned landing by two men will be made in April 1965. The buildup and construction phase will be continued without interruption until the outpost is ready for beneficial occupancy and is manned by a task force of 12 men in November 1966. (p. 7)

The US Army (1959a) concluded not only that a manned military outpost on the moon was feasible but that no barriers, other than financial and political, would stand in the way. The authors wrote, "There are no known technical barriers to the establishment of a manned installation on the moon" (p. 2).

Furthermore, in volume 2: *Technical Considerations and Plans* (Department of the Army, 1959b), the authors stated, "The establishment of a lunar outpost is considered to be technically and economically feasible" (p. 6).

Education was never mentioned as a problem in the report. The space race was viewed only as a psychological, military, and political issue (Department of the Army, 1959a):

> From the viewpoint of national security, the primary implication of the feasibility of establishment of a lunar outpost is the importance of being first. Clearly. we cannot exercise an option between peaceful and military applications unless we are first. For political and psychological reasons, anything short of being first on the lunar surface would be catastrophic. Being first will have so much political significance that no one can say at this time what the absolute effects will be. However, it is apparent from past space accomplishments that being second again cannot be tolerated. (p. 59)

As best can be determined through access to declassified documents found in the National Archives and the Eisenhower Library, the United States never had an education problem. The idea that US schooling was inferior first came from propaganda put out by Nikita Khrushchev and the Communist Chinese government immediately following the launch. Almost every presidential administration since Eisenhower then has used the myth and propaganda of Sputnik to create a crisis mentality to advance school reform proposals.

Education's Role

None of the astronauts who first orbited Earth as part of NASA's Mercury space exploration missions or those who landed on the moon during the Apollo missions were in K–12 public school at the time of the reforms instituted immediately following Sputnik. They and the thousands of people involved in the space race were products of the education system that Eisenhower claimed was lacking. Sputnik was an exercise in propaganda, not an example of education failure. Its use to support a proposed reform is nothing more than political theater and nothing short of educational malpractice.

The Modern Reform Roadmap

Eisenhower laid out what now appears to be the road map for modern-day "reform" efforts in terms of creating a dual system through standardization, educational meritocracy, and diversion of public funds to private and semi-private education options: "We should, among other things, have a system of nation-wide testing of high school students; a system of incentives for high aptitude students to pursue scientific or professional studies; a program to stimulate good-quality teaching of mathematics and science; provision of more laboratory facilities; and measures, including fellowships, to increase the output of qualified teachers."

One can see Sputnik's mutated spawns—the *A Nation at Risk* report, the No Child Left Behind Act, Race to the Top, Common Core State Standards, and the Every Student Succeeds Act—waiting in the wings of that speech. Eisenhower legitimized Sputnik as the symbol of American education's inferiority when, in fact, the United States had technological and educational superiority over the Soviets at that time and never lost it. Yet the king was crowned, and so it began.

A New King Comes Calling

In April 1983, the Reagan administration controlled the US Department of Education and assembled the National Commission on Excellence in Education (NCEE, 1983), a "blue-ribbon panel" with the unannounced yet clear purpose of debasing the public schools. The Reagan administration used the report as one piece of a total strategy to lay the groundwork for an unsuccessful attempt to legislate school vouchers and tax credits for parents who sent their children to private and religious schools. The idea of vilifying public schools as a way to introduce vouchers, choice, privatization, and other neoliberal free-market concepts would continue, but *Risk* reinvigorated the Sputnik-era strategy of manufacturing an education crisis based on misleading and false data.

Risky Claims and Evidence-based Rebuttals

In *A Nation at Risk: The Imperative for Educational Reform*, the NCEE claimed to illustrate the gravity of the situation with the following assertion: "If an unfriendly foreign power had attempted to impose on America the mediocre instructional performance that exists today, we might well have viewed it as an act of war." Education researchers David Berliner and Bruce Biddle observed that using a war metaphor intentionally created a manufactured crisis, which is the title of their 1995 book. The report sent a new set of shockwaves through the education establishment and gave the would-be school reformers the shot in the arm they had been lacking since King Sputnik arrived on the scene.

The war metaphor was nonsensical rhetoric, but it worked. Once again, national security was used to drive an ideological public school reform agenda. Perhaps it was the sense of national inferiority compared with the Soviets that drove many to accept and endorse the report uncritically. Virtually every state board of education and local school board, whose members knew little about the history of American education, put their support behind the report or mentioned the report when they attempted to drive local reforms.

The report's writers also referred to Sputnik and used it as the springboard for more federal intervention into schooling. The report was loaded with antischool agendas, spurious references to pseudoscientific claims, and cause-and-effect fallacies that would make any university doctoral dissertation committee member reject a candidate's proposal on the spot. A few sample quotes capture the tenor of rhetoric used in *A Nation at Risk*.

Claim 1: "Our once unchallenged preeminence in commerce, industry, science, and technological innovation is being overtaken by competitors throughout the world" (p. 6).

What does this claim have to do with public schools? It has more to do with monetary, labor, trade, fiscal, and tax policy than with how students score on a standardized test (Cremin, 1989).

The claim is false. For example, every year from 1965 to 1983, the year *Risk* was released, the United States produced and was awarded more utility/invention patents than the entire rest of the world combined. Utility patents are one indicator of economic competitiveness In 1980, 1981, and 1982, the United States was awarded 37,350, 39,218, and 33,889 utility/invention patents, respectively, compared to 24,469, 26,553, and 23,999 for the rest of the world (US Patent and Trademark Office, 2018).

The US rankings of per capita gross domestic product (GDP) for 1981, 1982, and 1983 were seventh, fourth, and fourth, respectively, out of more than 165 countries (International Monetary Fund, 2018). Per capita GDP is the total amount of economic output of a country in current market prices divided by the total population and is one indicator of the standard of living in a county.

Claim 2: "The educational foundations of our society are presently being eroded by a rising tide of mediocrity that threatens our very future as a Nation and people" (p. 6). This assertion was plugged into the report with virtually no supporting evidence or detailed documentation. For example, before the release of *Risk*, the percentage of males and females attaining college degrees had increased unabated since 1940 (Statista, 2017).

Claim 3: "23 million adults are functionally illiterate by the simplest tests of reading, writing, and comprehension" (p. 8). The writers never stated which tests they were referencing. Large-scale national or international tests of adult literacy did not exist before the publication of *Risk*. The first National Adult Literacy Survey (NALS) was not administered until 1992. The young adult portion of the National Assessment of Education Progress (NAEP) for ages 21–25 was not released until 1985 and it only tested thirty-six hundred young adults.

Claim 4: "The average achievement of high school students on most standardized tests is lower than it was 26 years ago when Sputnik was launched" (p. 8). This is an interesting statement given that in 1983, there was only one test that could have been used to make this claim about high school students: the Iowa Test of Educational Development (ITED). Not every student in the country took that test, and the test questions and student populations had changed immensely over almost thirty years, making valid comparisons difficult. Achievement on the ITED indeed did decline between the late 1960s and the mid-1970s; then achievement rose unabated for ten years, and in 1985 student achievement on the ITED was at an all-time high (Bracey, 2003).

Claim 5: "Average tested achievement of students graduating college is also lower" (p. 9). The authors never cited which test or tests were used to gather these data. Perhaps that is because it was impossible to gather the data to make this claim as a mandated college exit exam does not exist.

Claim 6: "The College Board's Scholastic Aptitude Tests (SAT) demonstrate a virtually unbroken decline from 1963 to 1980. Average verbal scores fell over 50 points, and average mathematics scores dropped nearly 40 points" (pp. 8–9). This claim is misleading. There is no doubt that the average score declined over the period, but why and so what? The decline of SAT scores was due to a confluence of several factors. First, the statistical phenomenon known as Simpson's paradox could contribute to part of the decline. The general idea behind Simpson's paradox is that the results and conclusions from a large aggregate group data set are sometimes different than the results and conclusions from the underlying subgroup data sets.

There were more nontraditional (not college-bound) students taking the test due to policies aimed at increasing educational equity for poor and minority students. States had to demonstrate they were affording more educational experiences to traditionally low-achieving students. More students who had no interest in college and who did not take college-level course work in high school were encouraged or made to take the SAT to show that the opportunity to attend college was being offered to more students from historically underrepresented populations.

Additionally, the period between mid-1960s and the early 1970s was a time of great cultural upheaval in the United States. To think that social forces did not influence education outcomes is a bit naive. One should also ask, so what if the scores dropped? What do they tell us anyway? The SAT was never designed to measure education quality. At best, SAT scores predict between 10–16 percent of a first-year college student's grade point average (Korbin et al., 2008); and parental income is the best predictor of student SAT scores (College Board, 2012; Geiser & Santelices, 2007; Tienken, 2014).

Chapter 3

THE EMPIRICAL REBUTTAL YOU NEVER READ: THE SANDIA REPORT

Two definitions of *fraud* provided by the Merriam-Webster Online Dictionary are deceit and trickery. The unscientific and empirically absent claims made by the authors of *A Nation At Risk* seem at least deceitful. The authors provided no empirical evidence to support their rhetoric. The publication of *Perspectives on Education in America* (Carson, Huelskamp, & Woodall, 1993)—known as the Sandia Report because it was conducted by the Sandia National Laboratory at the request of Admiral James Watkins, who was then secretary of energy—demonstrated that *A Nation at Risk* was a fraud. The study challenged the assertions made in *Risk* and did so on an empirical level, with data.

The Sandia Report was completed in 1990 but was suppressed by the deputy secretary of the US Department of Education, former Xerox CEO Dave Kearns. Kearns was reported to say at a meeting with the Sandia researchers that either the researchers would suppress the report and not release it or they would be suppressed (Miller, 1991).

Suppression makes sense when one considers the political climate of the time and the positive results of the report. George H. W. Bush was presiding over a tanking economy and recession. The Republican White House needed a scapegoat, and once again the public education system was there for the chiding. Bush needed to pin the recession on something other than faulty economic policy. The fraud perpetrated in *A Nation at Risk* had worked once before, and members of the administration saw a way to recycle the argument, claiming the weak economy was caused by a supposedly poor education system.

Some of the major findings from the Sandia Report that contradicted the fraudulent claims and lies in *Risk* were:

- The high school graduation rate increased between 1960 and 1990.
- Between 1960 and 1990, the percentage of the population aged 25–29 who completed high school rose more than 30 percentage points to seven out of every eight persons in that age category.
- The dropout rates for both Black and White students declined steadily between 1968 and 1990, whereas the rate remained somewhat stable for Latino students, due mostly to first-generation immigrants failing to complete high school.
- Among the class of 1982, 83 percent completed high school on time (four years) and 91 percent earned a diploma or GED.
- Average SAT scores declined 5 percent between 1965 and 1990. This was attributed to changing demographics of test takers to include more minorities and lower socioeconomic students, more students who were not col-

lege bound, and more students from lower high school class ranks. When controlling for the demographic makeup of the test takers in the class of 1975, SAT scores rose without a hitch between 1975 and 1990. Again, this was Simpson's paradox at work. More students from the bottom half of their high school class took the SAT, whereas proportionately fewer students at the top 20 percent of their class took the test.

The authors of the Sandia Report further noted that:

- the number of students enrolling in higher education increased from less than 5 million in 1965 to more than 13 million in 1990;
- the number of bachelor's and master's degrees awarded increased by 20 percent and 25 percent, respectively, between 1971 to 1987;
- Graduate Record Exam (GRE) math scores rose 32 points between 1973 and 1988, while verbal scores remained stable; and
- the United States led the world in 1987 in the percentage of twenty-two-year-olds obtaining a bachelor's degree in science and engineering with more than 5 percent, compared to approximately 3.75 percent in 1965.

The results of the Sandia Report demonstrated that the education system was not at risk; in fact, it was performing quite well given the massive demographic, social, and political changes faced by the nation between 1963 and 1982. The Sandia Report exposed the factors listed in *A Nation at Risk* as indicators of risk as empirically lacking.

Read *A Nation at Risk*, found easily online, and look with a critical eye at the indicators of risk. Attempt to discern for yourself which data are being referenced by the authors and where the data were found. It is difficult, but also amusing. For a brief, easy-to-read, nonstatistical debunking of the report, see Bracey (2003).

The Lingering Hangover of Risky Frauds, Myths, and Lies

Although *A Nation at Risk* was an intellectually vapid and data-challenged piece of propaganda easily debunked by facts, the frauds, myths, and lies continue to haunt democratic public school policy. Many states plunged headlong into reform movements based on the advice of the presidential commission that wrote the report. *A Nation at Risk* recommended tougher coursework requirements for high school graduation, more standardized testing of students, higher admissions standards for universities, a longer school day and school year, and merit pay for teachers.

As a blueprint, *Risk* offered nothing that had not been urged and discarded one hundred years earlier. Edson (1983) critiqued *Risk* shortly after its publication and concluded that it very closely resembled the 1893 report issued by the Committee of Ten. Membership on the Committee of Ten and the NCEE, which wrote *Risk*, were dominated by people who were not public school personnel. The reports of both groups included intuitive recommendations. Both groups recommended longer school terms and endorsed a brand of social Darwinism: the survival of the academically fittest. *A Nation At Risk* continues to provide false legitimacy to those who covertly—under the banners of school choice, charter schools, lower standards to enter the teaching profession, or school vouchers—attempt to energize the movement toward a dual system of education.

The Three-Punch Combination of Reform Fraud

Although dual system school reformers generally throw Sputnik and *Risk* as their opening one-two punch in their attacks against the public school system, they always sneak in the body shot with National Assessment of Education Progress. Sometimes referred to as the Nation's Report Card, the NAEP is administered to a representative sample of public and private school students ages nine, thirteen, and seventeen through the US Department of Education. Subject area tests are given on a rotating basis every two to four years.

The NAEP Claim

Reformers make the consistent claim that NAEP scores in reading and mathematics have remained stagnant or have not risen fast and far enough over the last several decades. They claim that what they view as the stagnant nature of the average scale scores proves that public schools are failing. They use comparisons of the average scale scores across multiple years to demonstrate their point.

Evidence-based Rebuttal

The scale score results from the NAEP seem particularly susceptible to misinterpretation due to Simpson's paradox. For example, from 1971 to 2017 the NAEP reading scores for nine-year-olds improved 12 scale score points, from 210 to 222, yet the scale scores of the underlying subgroups (White, Black, and Hispanic) all improved by more than 12 scale score points individually (United States Department of Education, 2018a, 2018c).

Black students made 36 scale score points of progress, from 170 to 206, triple the progress made by the average score over that time. Hispanic students made 26 scale score points of progress, from 183 to 209, more than double the average progress. White students also outpaced the average progress, with 18 scale score points of progress from 214 to 232. Black students demonstrated twice the growth of whites during the time period between 1971 and 2017 (see table 3.1).

Simpson's Paradox

Simpson's paradox comes into play because the Black and Hispanic students, whose average scores were lower, make up a greater proportion of the population compared to higher-scoring White students. This is due in part to ongoing demographic shifts in the United States and the increasing percentage of students living in poverty. Thus, the average gain looks depressed, when in reality the minority subgroups' growth is more than double that of the White students in some cases. Are our schools really failing our minority students, or is it something else?

The same phenomenon occurs with NAEP mathematics scores. For example, the NAEP mathematics average scale scores for students in grade 8 rose 20 points between 1990 and 2017, from 263 to 283. But the scores for Black and Hispanic students started out much lower compared to that of White students. The 1990 average scale score for Black students was 237 and 246 for Hispanic students, whereas White students started at 270 in 1992 (United States Department of Education, 2018b, 2018c).

Table 3.1. Subgroup Age 9 NAEP Reading Scale Scores

Year	Average	White	Black	Hispanic
2017	222	232	206	209
2015	223	232	206	208
2012	221	229	206	208
2008	220	228	204	207
2004[1]	216	224	197	199
1999	212	221	186	193
1996	212	221	186	195
1992[2]	211	218	185	192
1988	212	218	189	194
1984	211	218	186	187
1980	215	221	189	190
1975	210	217	181	183
1971	208	214	170	N/A

[1] NAEP began a revised testing format.
[2] Data from 1971 to 2012 derived from the *Digest of Education Statistics*. Data after 2012 derived from the NEAP Data tool.

All of the subgroups made larger average gains (23 points) than the gains made by the total population (20 points) between 1990 and 2017. By 2017, average scores for White students rose 23 points, to 293. The average score for Black and Hispanic students rose 23 points, to 260 and to 269, respectively (United States Department of Education, 2018b, 2018c).

The influence of Simpson's paradox can be seen throughout the NAEP data at all age levels. Although it might be true that numbers do not lie, the dual system reformers who use NAEP numbers to claim that public education achievement is stagnant certainly do.

TAKING ACTION

The school reform landscape is littered with the bones of great reform ideas. It is as if any idea that standardizes, centralizes, and mechanizes education for the majority and provides more opportunities for the wealthy elite has no downside. Yet, like so many reformers before them, the bulk of all national or state reformers fail to heed James Conant's advice that US high schools should be improved at the local level, "school by school" to provide a high quality, egalitarian, democratic system of education. Those who understand the importance of public education as a vehicle to support a participative democracy must play an active role in evaluating reform proposals and developing proposals to ensure a vibrant future for the unitary system of public schools.

Bracey (2006) created a set of thirty-two practical principles for diving under the surface of quantitative claims. Five of those are particularly useful when evaluating the statistical claims about failing public schools:

- When making quantitative comparisons of two things (schools, countries, groups of students) make sure the things are comparable on all the factors that can influence the results.
- Beware of selectivity/cherry-picking of the data used to support the claims being made.
- Be on the lookout for Simpson's paradox any time average scores or aggregate data are used to make claims.
- Do not except simple explanations or ready-made solutions for complex problems.
- Review the actual data.

Educators and those who care about public education do not have to sit idle and accept the statistical claims made by reformers and pundits at face value. Question everything. Dig below the surface of the headlines and the initial statistics.

A LOOK AHEAD

In the next chapter I dissect some of the most common school reform fallacies. Examples include the seemingly unending chorus from corporate privateers and wannabe business tycoons that education needs to be run more like a business. We discuss eight such fallacies in an attempt to demonstrate that most reform claims rest more on a bed of sand than of concrete.

REFERENCES

Baker, D. (2016). *Rigged: How globalization and the rules of the modern economy were structured to make the rich richer.* Washington, DC: Center for Economic and Policy Research.

Berliner, D. C., & Biddle, B. J. (1995). *The manufactured crisis: Myths, frauds and the attack on America's public schools.* Reading, MA: Addison-Wesley.

Bon Jovi, J., & Sambora, R. (1995). These days. On *These Days* [CD]. Nashville: Mercury Records.

Bracey, G. (2006). *Reading educational research: How to avoid getting statistically snookered.* New York: Heinemann

Bracey, G. (2003). April foolishness: The 20th anniversary of *A Nation at Risk*. *Phi Delta Kappan, 84*(8), 616–21.

Bracey, G. (1999). The propaganda of A "Nation At Risk." Retrieved from http://www.america-tomorrow.com/bracey/EDDRA/EDDRA8.htm

Carson, C. C., Huelskamp, R. M., Woodall, T. D. (1993). Perspectives on education in America. *Journal of Educational Research, 86*(5), 259–309.

Cremin, L. J. (1989). *Popular education and its discontents.* New York: Harper and Row.

College Board. (2012). *2012 college bound seniors: Total group profile report.* Author. Retrieved from https://secure-media.collegeboard.org/digitalServices/pdf/research/TotalGroup-2012.pdf

Connant, J. B. (1959). *The American high school today: A first report to interested citizens.* New York: McGraw-Hill.

Duncan, A. (2009, October 16). Partners for success: Secretary Arne Duncan's remarks to the National Association of State Boards of Education Oct 16, 2009. Retrieved from http://www.ed.gov/news/speeches/2009/10/10162009.html

Edson, C. H. (1983). Risking the nation: Historical dimensions of survival and educational reform. *Issues in Education*, Vol. 1, pp. 171–84.

Eisenhower, D. D. (1957, November 13). Text of address on "Our Future Security" delivered by the president in Oklahoma City. Subjects include military programs and satellite projects. Retrieved from http://www.presidency.ucsb.edu/ws/index.php?pid=10950

Gleason, E. S. (1957, October 10). National Security Council Discussion at the 339th Meeting of the National Security Council. NSC Series, Box 9, Eisenhower Papers, 1953–1961 (Ann Whitman File), Dwight D. Eisenhower Library, Abilene, Kansas. Retrieved from http://www.eisenhower.archives.gov/research/Digital_Documents/Sputnik/10-11-57.pdf

Goodpaster, A. J. (1957a, October 9). Memorandum of conference with the president, October 8, 1957. National Archives. ARC Identifier 186623. Retrieved from http://www.archives.gov/education/lessons/sputnik-memo/#documents

Goodpaster, A. J. (1957b, October 15). Memorandum of conference with the president on American science education and Sputnik DDE's Papers as President, DDE Diary Series, Box 27, October '57 Staff Notes (2). Retrieved from http://www.eisenhower.archives.gov/research/Digital_Documents/Sputnik/10-16-57.pdf

International Monetary Fund. (2018). World economic outlook database: Gross domestic product (nominal) per capita, current prices, (millions of) US dollars. Author. Retrieved from https://www.imf.org/external/pubs/ft/weo/2018/02/weodata/index.aspx

Korbin, J. L., Patterson, B. F., Shaw, E. J., Mattern, K. D., & Barbuti, S. M. (2008). *Validity of the SAT for predicting first-year college grade point average.* New York: College Board.

Miller, J. (1991, 9 October). Report questioning "crisis" in education triggers an uproar. *Education Week.* Retrieved from http://www.edweek.org/ew/articles/1991/10/09/06crisis.h11.html

National Commission on Excellence in Education. (1983). *A nation at risk: The imperative for educational reform.* Washington, DC: US Department of Education.

Obama, B. H. (2009, April 27). Remarks by the president at the National Academy of Science Annual Meeting. Retrieved from http://www.whitehouse.gov/the_press_office/Remarks-by-the-President-at-the-National-Academy-of-Sciences-Annual-Meeting/

Paige, R. (2003, February 5). The secretary's Mathematics and Science Initiative. Retrieved from http://www.ed.gov/rschstat/research/progs/mathscience/describe.html

Rich, A. (2005, spring). War of ideas: Why mainstream and liberal foundations and the think tanks they support are losing the war of ideas in American politics. *Stanford Social Innovation Review, 18*–25.

Riley, R. (1995, March 13). US secretary of education before the Subcommittee on Human Resources and Intergovernmental Affairs of the House Committee on Government Reform and Oversight. Retrieved from http://www.ed.gov/Speeches/03-1995/shays.html

Geiser, S., & Santelices, M. V. (2007). *Validity of high-school grades in predicting student success beyond the freshman year: High-school record vs standardized tests as indicators of four-year college outcomes.* Berkeley: Center for Studies in Higher Education, University of California, Berkeley.

Statista. (2017). Percentage of US population who have completed four years of college or more from 1040 to 2017 by gender. Retrieved from https://www.statista.com/statistics/184272/educational-attainment-of-college-diploma-or-higher-by-gender/

Tienken, C. H. (2014). SAT as a poor predictor of school or teacher quality. Retrieved from https://christienken.com/2014/12/12/sat-as-poor-indicator-of-school-teacher-quality/

Time. (1982, April 26). A boost for private schools: Reagan offers tax credits. Retrieved from http://www.cnn.com/ALLPOLITICS/1997/04/28/back.time/

United States Department of Education, National Center for Education Statistics. (2018a). *Digest of Education Statistics. Table 221.85: Average National Assessment of Education Progress (NAEP) reading score by age and selected student characteristics: Selected years, 1971 through 2012.* Retrieved from https://nces.ed.gov/programs/digest/d17/tables/dt17_221.85.asp?current=yes

United States Department of Education, National Center for Education Statistics. (2018b). *Digest of Education Statistics. Table 222.10: Average National Assessment of Education Progress (NAEP) mathematics score by sex, race/ethnicity, and grade: Selected years, 1990 through 2017.* Retrieved from https://nces.ed.gov/programs/digest/d17/tables/dt17_222.10.asp?current=yes

United States Department of Education, National Center for Education Statistics. (2018c). NAEP data explorer. Retrieved from https://www.nationsreportcard.gov/ndecore/landing

United States Patent and Trademark Office (USPTO). (2018). Extended year set: Patent counts by country, state, and year utility patents. Retrieved from https://www.uspto.gov/web/offices/ac/ido/oeip/taf/cst_utlh.htm

White House Office of the Staff Research Group. (1957, October 16). Reaction to the Soviet satellite: A preliminary evaluation. Box 35, Special Projects: Sputnik, Missiles and Related Matters; NAID #12082706. Retrieved from https://www.eisenhowerlibrary.gov/sites/default/files/research/online-documents/sputnik/reaction.pdf

Chapter Four

A Catalogue of Reform Myths

In this chapter, I present seven common myths associated with the modern education reform movement. Each of the myths is what those who live in the western US call a box canyon, a three-sided ravine used to trap the minds of the complacent. I am confident that most people who believe the following myths will be able to see through them if they simply apply a skeptical eye and are willing to question their assumptions about the current reform agenda.

MYTH 1: FEDERAL LEGISLATION IS MEANT TO STRENGTHEN PUBLIC EDUCATION

A review of the No Child Left Behind Act of 2001 (No Child Left Behind, 2002) provides an opportunity to see the creation, via national education legislation, of the dual system. Hindsight allows readers to see that NCLB was nothing more than a thinly veiled neoliberal attempt to cripple the public school system and allow corporate interests to hijack public funds.

Assessment-driven education policies have been in place in all fifty states the since the 2003–2004 school year. Two examples of assessment-driven legislation in the 2000s are the test-based accountability of NCLB and the Every Student Succeeds Act. But the modern-day groundwork for recent federal education reform initiatives was laid in 1978 with the release of the report *Improving Educational Achievement* (Committee on Testing and Basic Skills, 1978). That report seemed to be the foundation for NCLB.

The authors of the 1978 report called for changes in schooling and recommended a return to "Basic Skills," increased achievement test scores as a goal of government, greater teacher quality, and test-score driven accountability of teachers and administrators as ways to "improve" education. Several statements seem prophetic now: "American education should be paying much more attention to doing a thorough job in the fundamentals of reading, writing, and arithmetic" (p. iii). The authors went on to state, "Tests can play several different roles. One is as a means of public accountability" (p. 7). It seems as though the underlying concepts of NCLB and ESSA have been around for quite some time.

Don't Be Fooled

Do not be fooled into thinking the intent of NCLB was noble based on the opportunistic name given to it by its creators. Leaving no child behind was a myth spun by neoliberal reformers to justify the regressive and draconian standardization requirements put into place to cement a dual system. Reading the act with a critical eye helps illuminate overt and covert attempts to separate the public from public education through the increased use of sanctions that ultimately led to private, semiprivate, and corporate intrusion into public education on a national scale. The corporate intrusion did not have a positive impact on academic achievement (Heinrich & Nisar, 2013; Lee & Reeves, 2012).

NCLB was a classic bait-and-switch routine. Beyond the catchphrase "No Child Left Behind," seemingly plagiarized from the Children's Defense Fund's motto "Leave No Child Behind," the act had very little redeemable value in terms of improving the social welfare of children. It seems as though most supporters of the law never read the entire legislation and just latched on to the title. It is now known from former officials inside the George W. Bush administration that the law was not created to strengthen and grow the public education system; it was meant to destroy it.

The myopic focus on a narrow interpretation of English language arts and mathematics, as defined by the small number of questions on state-mandated standardized tests, has had a dehumanizing effect on students and teachers (Slouka, 2009). NCLB, and now its younger cousin ESSA, relegate human beings to a test score and strip them of their dignity and worth.

Assistant Education Secretary Speaks the Truth

Former Assistant Secretary for Elementary and Secondary Education Susan Neuman stated in a June 8, 2008, *Time* magazine interview that there were some in the Bush administration and US Department of Education (USDOE) who viewed NCLB as a way to destroy public education so that the populace would support school choice, vouchers, privatization, and marketization; in effect, the law was being used as a Trojan horse to drive the wedge between the public and public education (Wallis, 2008).

Neuman's statement might sound counterintuitive or even outlandish to those who view the USDOE as a pro–public school institution, but it stands up under scrutiny. For those readers who have tracked USDOE policy making over the years it is clear that since the Reagan administration, the USDOE has become more antagonistic toward public education and increasingly focused on finding ways to funnel money to private schools and faux public schools like charter schools.

MYTH 2: TEST SCORES ARE FLAT

Student achievement has been monitored over most of the past hundred years by a battery of standardized tests. In general, the claim that test scores are have remained flat is fatally flawed. The results show an upward trend in student achievement when data are disaggregated into subgroups. The subgroup scores for the mathematics, science, and language arts portions of the National Assessment of Education Progress demonstrated remarkable growth for more than thirty years, as presented in the last chapter.

The aggregate scores of tests like NAEP, SAT, and ACT appear flat because of Simpson's paradox. There is a more socioeconomically diverse sample of students taking the ACT and SAT examinations than in past decades. More students from lower socioeconomic backgrounds are included in the testing pool than ever before. Poverty has a negative impact on standardized test results. Although the national test indicators have risen very slowly, the SAT shows that the students in all subgroups, especially non-White students, are achieving at rather modestly higher levels.

For example, in 2012 the average SAT score for reading was 496 and the average math score was 514. These average scores dropped by the 2016 testing year, just one high school cohort later: Reading was down to 494 and the average math score was 508. It appears as if SAT scores are getting worse, not better! Are the pundits right?

A closer look reveals Simpson's paradox at work. The average scores in reading and math for students living in poverty—those whose family income was $40,000 or less—were slightly higher in 2016 than in 2012. The average 2016 reading score was 435, compared to 433 in 2012, and the average math score was 465, compared to 463 in 2012.

This seems counterintuitive at first glance, but there were more students from poverty in the testing pool in 2016 (283,199) compared to 2012 (231,662)—and SAT scores, like most other standardized tests results, are influenced by out-of-school factors like family wealth. Not only were there more students from poverty in the 2016 SAT sample, but the overall number of students taking the test was also lower (1.637 million versus 1.664 million), making for a higher overall percentage of students from poverty in the

2016 sample compared to 2012 (17 percent versus 14 percent). The larger concentration of low scores in 2016 dragged down the overall scores. (See table 4.1.)

Overall, the testing pool of students in 2016 was smaller and poorer than the testing pool in 2012. Although the average scores on all parts of the 2016 SAT were higher for students from families with an income of $60,000 or more than on the 2012 SAT, the overall average SAT score for all students in 2016 decreased due to the larger pool of lower-scoring students from families with incomes of $40,000 or less. Simpson's paradox is one tool used by dual system reformers to make the case that public schools are failing.

The focus on "flat" test scores on the SAT and other large-scale tests takes attention away from the real problem: The SAT and other standardized tests do not measure learning; they measure money. The scores correlate almost perfectly with family income. In no instance does a group of students from a lower family income bracket outscore a group of students from a higher income bracket. Average SAT scores rise as average family income rises. (See table 4.2.)

That is not to imply that some individuals do not "beat the odds" and score above their family income range. But that is the exception and not the rule. An education system in a democratic country cannot be based on exceptions. In order for education to fulfill its democratizing function, equity must be at the core of the system. Dual systems favor the wealthy exceptions at the expense of everyone else. Dual systems increase inequity.

MYTH 3: COERCION WILL IMPROVE FLAT TEST SCORES

The common narrative of modern-day state and national educational reformers is that student achievement is at an all-time low, the entire public school is failing, and educators and students must be coerced by a government-imposed free market system to improve the situation. Education reform policies based on coercion lack theoretical and empirical support; they are not

Table 4.1. Characteristics of SAT Testing Populations for 2012 and 2016

Factor	2012	2016
Total Students Tested	1.664 million	1.637 million
# of Students in Poverty	231,662	283,199
% of Students in Poverty	14	17
Average SAT Reading	496	494
Average SAT Math	514	508

Table 4.2. 2016 Family Income and Average SAT Scores

Family Income	Reading	Math	Writing
Less than $20,000	435	453	426
About $20,000 to $40,000	465	477	452
About $40,001 to $60,000	488	495	471
About $60,001 to $80,000	503	509	485
About $80,001 to $100,000	517	527	501
About $100,001 to $140,000	530	539	513
About $140,001 to $200,000	542	553	528
More than $200,000	569	586	562

Source: The College Board. (2016). *2016 college-bound seniors: Total group profile report*. Author. Retrieved from https://research.collegeboard.org/programs/sat/data/archived/cb-seniors-2016

scientifically demonstrated. Coercion is an utterly anti-intellectual approach toward education improvement.

Advocates of coercion-based school reform policies such as school takeovers, school closures, outsourcing schools to big-box charter corporations, private school vouchers, and sanctioning schools generally harvest policy frameworks from rational choice theory and behaviorist theories. The frameworks are operationalized via state education policies that use positive reinforcement and negative reinforcement, also known as carrots and sticks. Bryk and Hermanson (1993) termed reforms based on this type of theory "instrumental use models."

The theory of action is that a policy body develops a set of expected education outcome measures (e.g., state standards) that monitors the relationship between the measures and school processes, usually through high-stakes testing, and then implements rewards or sanctions to change behavior through external force to maximize performance. The measures rest upon arbitrary academic proficiency levels and external control.

Of course, there is an underlying assumption in the theoretical framework for instrumental use models: Teachers and students do not work hard, and therefore need external motivators to improve. One example of an instrumental use model is the use of threats from state education agencies to withhold funding for poor performance on high-stakes tests to compel school personnel to work harder because they do not want to lose funding. An offshoot of the threat to withhold funding is the use of public castigation via the press and ratings and/or rankings of districts by state education personnel to spur educators to work harder to achieve outcomes.

One major weakness of instrumental use policies is that they do not have a demonstrated record of success. That is because such policies are harvested from behaviorist and rational choice theories. Behaviorism rests upon the idea of control. Stimulus-response psychology is at the heart of behaviorism—and is known as the—"science for controlling others" (Bredo, 2002, p. 25). Policies created from theories and science-based on controlling others have no part in an education system that serves a free, participative democracy.

The rational choice theory assumes that people will make logical choices when presented with various options. For example, when someone is presented with the choice to raise test scores or be publicly humiliated, the person will often choose to raise test scores at any cost. However, people do not always make rational choices. Sometimes they resist, especially when they are made to implement practices that are harmful to others.

Collective Punishment

An interesting characteristic of current education policies at the state and national levels related to sanctioning schools and educators for perceived low test scores is that those policies mirror closely something known as collective punishment. Collective punishment is a policy of punishing a large group for the actions of a small group.

It should be known that the Soviet Union utilized collective punishment, and totalitarian governments like the one in China use collective punishment on a regular basis to control populations. The British used the strategy during the years leading up to the American Revolution through the implementation of the Intolerable Acts. There are countless other examples throughout history of authoritarian nations using collective punishment to force their political wills on the population. History is also replete with examples of how collective punishment ultimately backfires and liberty and justice for all prevail (e.g., the American Revolution, the fall of the Soviet Union).

Undemocratic

An education system that models policies based in part on collective punishment seems unconstitutional, or at least undemocratic. Collective punishment policies appear to violate due process rights, and they do not provide a model of democratic behavior to future bearers of democratic ideals. Are not those who are punished supposed to receive a due process hearing? As a taxpayer, I request mine regarding the billions of dollars that have been diverted from public schools since 2002 on the creation of a dual system and education welfare for the rich.

In essence, the carrots and sticks used in instrumental use policies have little effect and might have negative effects, if the people believe that they are in a no-win situation. Coercion, intimidation, collective punishment, and policies based on broken theories and anti-intellectualism are unnecessary, unproductive, and bordering on institutional abuse.

MYTH 4: BIG BUSINESS VALUES WILL IMPROVE PUBLIC EDUCATION

Close to the center of all education reform policies and proposals is the not-so-quietly kept assumption that the values of big business should be incorporated into the culture of the schools. Nationally Achieve, Inc. is a business advocacy group aimed at "reforming" the nation's schools. In 2001 this corporate group was cochaired by Louis V. Gerstner Jr., chairman and CEO of IBM Corporation. Achieve, Inc. is now chaired by Mark B. Grier, vice chairman of Prudential Financial. The board of directors of Achieve Inc. has several other CEOs or former CEOs and governors. The "Inc." portion of the name intriguing, as it suggests an overt focus on the business model as the model for education reform.

Business Core Values

What are the core values of American big business? Unarguably, the hallmark of American business is maximizing shareholder value, known as profit. The focus on profit appears explicitly in every business-oriented educational "partnership" or "educational roundtable." The obsession with profit is exemplified by big business support of competitive testing for students, support for publicly funding the privatization of schools through vouchers and "big box" charter school chains, and the intense focus on the economic output of schools.

The following list of very apparent business values seems to be included in most education reform proposals:

- competition, takeover of public schools, and monopolies in the form of large charter school chains in urban areas across the country;
- the "bottom line" of test scores as all-important regardless of the means;
- communities and workers are expendable, management is not as exemplified in most charter schools not allowing unions;
- loyalty is not a mutual trait;

- workers obey management without questioning and dissent is not permitted;
- products are sought at the cheapest price; and
- the importance of individuals is related to their net dollar worth.

Granted, the examples above might show some of my bias against a corporate education system and toward a democratic system oriented toward equity. But I prefer policies and practices based on evidence that increase equity, help children become participating members of a democratic society, and help them to question the status quo in order to pursue liberty and justice for all. I prefer policies and practices that facilitate all children attaining life, liberty, and the pursuit of happiness, not just those whose parents can afford to purchase those things.

Read any issue of the *Wall Street Journal* or *Forbes* magazine and you will have to agree with the overall basic premise of business: Business leaders care about the business, and business is about profit. Chomsky (2011) eloquently explained that business leaders, in most cases, will put profit above people. In fact, in most publicly traded companies, it is the primary job of the CEO to maximize shareholder value (higher profits = higher share price). This is not a secret.

Broken Promises and Questionable Values

I suggest that business values are not appropriate to drive American education. True, we all want the most efficient use of the taxpayer dollar in the public schools. But that is not an educational core value. Certainly, parents want their children to receive that elusive "best education," but businesslike competitive practices are unlikely to provide it. Democracy is not efficient, and thus, democratic education is not efficient. In fact, it is the inefficiency in the system that perhaps produces some of its greatest qualities among American students: Creativity and innovation.

Zhao (2012) masterfully explained how the historically decentralized US public school system created the most dynamic, innovative, and entrepreneurial workforces on the planet, whereas nations with more centralized and standardized systems, like China, Singapore, and South Korea, strive to catch up. Similar arguments about the high quality of the US education system were dramatically illustrated in *The Manufactured Crisis: Myth, Fraud, and the Attack on America's Public Schools* (Berliner & Biddle, 1995). Another "cult of efficiency" (Callahan, 1962), accomplished through mass standardization and cost cutting, is being forced upon the public schools from a business community all too eager to earn profits off of the backs of children and educators.

One conclusion is that big business interests are now in the process of conditioning the American public (recall Pavlov's dog) to the lie about education failure so that a profit-driven dual system of education based on myth and fraud can replace the unitary system. Business leaders have been spinning myths and lies about public education and implementing fraudulent practices for a long time.

Chubb and Moe (1990) are examples of business apologists for school vouchers. They argued that private school vouchers, paid for by taxpayers, are needed because the public schools are incapable of reforming themselves due to bureaucratic and political restraints. They then praise private schools as exhibiting superior academic performance.

As of 2020, twenty-seven states had laws supporting the transfer of public tax dollars away from public schools and into private coffers. There are three main products used to divert the funds: (1) school vouchers, (2) scholarship tax credits, and (3) education savings grants. School vouchers are taxpayer money given to families to offset the cost of private schools. Scholarship tax credits allow individuals and corporations (usually corporations and the superrich) to divert part of their state taxes to private scholarship organizations that then use that public tax money to give scholarships to students to attend private schools.

As Molnar (1999) observed, the research on the topic has revealed no clear evidence showing private schools to be better than public schools. The rhetoric in favor of the dual system based on a free market of choice does not hold up under empirical scrutiny. Lubienski and Lubienski (2013) conducted a thorough review of the data on private school and public school achievement. They examined the mathematics portion of the NAEP and found that when one looks at socioeconomically comparable groups of students, the claims that private school students do better academically than public school students were wrong. Public school students, as a group, posted higher scores on standardized tests, and the public schools achieve those gains more cheaply than the private schools.

Lubienski and Lubienski (2013) wrote:

> These results indicate that, despite reformers' adulation of the autonomy enjoyed by private and charter schools, this factor may in fact be the reason these schools are underperforming. That is, contrary to the dominant thinking on this issue, the data show that the more regulated public school sector embraces more innovative and effective professional practices, while independent schools often use their greater autonomy to avoid such reforms, leading to curricular stagnation. (p. xvii)

Results from international tests of academic achievement confirm Lubienski and Lubienski's findings. Average mathematics scale scores for fifteen-year olds on the Programme for International Student Assessment (PISA) consistently show an advantage to public school students when comparing students from the same socioeconomic strata (Tienken, 2017). The 2015 PISA average mathematics scale scores for students in schools with 10 percent or less of students eligible for free lunch (the wealthiest private and public schools) favored public schools by a wide margin: 530 versus 493.

Utility Model

If one really must impose a business model on the public schools, the model should be that of a regulated utility. The schools are a giant public utility, established to promote the public welfare in a democracy. I acknowledge that there are bad schools, poor teachers, inept administrators, and parsimonious legislators, just as there are inept doctors, lawyers, and corporate executives.

Yet a public utility delivers its services to all who sign up—or, in the case of the traditional public schools, all who show up at the schoolhouse door, no matter what social baggage they bring. Achieve, Inc. and its edu-business clones ignore that feature.

They totally ignore corporate corruption cases like Enron, Tyco, Global Crossing, JPMorgan Chase, Barclays, WorldCom, Arthur Andersen, ImClone, Piper Jaffray, Goldman Sachs, Bear Stearns, Washington Mutual, Lehman Brothers, and all the other manipulative corporations and investment banking houses, their senior analysts, and traders on the stock exchanges who have been repeatedly been found in violation of state and national laws. The business path to reform is a very muddy detour at best. Its players may praise ethics, but practicing them seems to be a problem, and the results do not justify the costs.

MYTH 5: CORPORATELY INFLUENCED CURRICULA LEAD TO BETTER EDUCATION

An observation of the many sets of standards shows the misapplication of technical specifications to human nature. Each published standard resembles a product specification. For example, most begin with a statement that the student will (fill in the blank). Replace the student with battery, and the specifications are that the battery will light a three-watt bulb for two hours.

Such technically oriented pronouncements of student achievement lack mention of the conditions under which the learning is to take place and completely ignore the needed educational prerequisites and materials required to learn. This dimension of the standards movement is plainly dehumanizing the educational process. Education policy treats students like inanimate objects to be manipulated.

I suggest reading Buber (1970), who vividly illustrates how your actions toward fellow human beings are shown in how you perceive them. If you view children, adolescents, or early adults only as objects rather than as humans to be nurtured, then schooling takes on a mechanistic dimension. Kozol (2005) illustrated how standards and high-stakes tests become more important than the cultivation of a child's potential.

An unintentional result of the hyperfocus on standardization is that schools are, now more than ever, considered assembly lines of knowledge. Students are simultaneously repositories for static knowledge and standardized products. Such industrial metaphors are completely inappropriate for delicate human endeavors. Yet these same technical specifications are praised as the means for reaching those questionable world-class standards.

Children are not machines with specified tolerance values, voltage regulators, or assembled packages. Editorial writers and industrialists who heap praise and advocate adoption of standards show a bias to industrial values. Pervasive caring is a quality found in the best schools in this country and the best schools around the world. Caring, empathy, and love are not listed in any educational or business standard, but they are found in the best of schools.

The notions of caring, empathy, and love that the school is a safe haven: a place you can make friends, and be accepted, regardless of your demographic characteristics. Caring, empathy, and love mean that even if you arrive with heavy social baggage, someone in the school will lend a hand—the janitor, a secretary, the principal, your peers, your teachers. These three notions profoundly affect how children are respected and how they enjoy the challenge to learn. In some cases, the school is the only setting where students feel they are valued, loved, and cared about.

MYTH 6: RESULTS FROM STANDARDIZED TESTS ARE ACCURATE

The unintended consequences of the state and national standards movement have been rather well documented and for a long time. For example, in most states, if a student throws up on the state-mandated high stakes standardized test, the school personnel are instructed to place all the contents into a sealed plastic bag and return it to the Superintendent of Public Instruction. No directions are given on what to do with the child. Oh, and in some states, if your kid is in the hospital, a school-appointed monitor must administer the state test and nurses will be observed for any cheating.

One linchpin in the marketing of the tests themselves is the perceived accuracy of the results. In reality, large-scale errors occur regularly with scoring. A short and incomplete list of some high-profile instances of scoring mistakes reveals a systemic problem with corporate testing.

New York City provides a stark example of how the scoring of standardized tests can go wrong. Almost 9,000 students were required to attend a summer school program in 1999 based on the results of their standardized tests, developed and scored by CTB/McGraw-Hill. The testing corporation used the wrong norming table to calculate the number of students who scored below the national average on their reading tests (Archibold, 1999). The testing company initially denied the error but later had to admit it scored the tests incorrectly.

Then, in Nevada, the same company employed in the New York scandal used the wrong scoring table, causing third and fifth graders in 220 elementary schools to receive wrong test results. In Clark County (Las Vegas), 21,000 third- and fifth-grade students had incorrectly reported scores, noted the *Las Vegas Sun* (Ryan, 2003). In 2002 Harcourt was fined $425,000 because it had informed 736 high school sophomores and juniors in Las Vegas that they had failed the proficiency test. Similar errors were found in Tennessee, Wisconsin, and South Carolina during that testing year (Rhodes & Madaus, 2003).

The scoring company NCS Pearson made thousands of errors in 2000 on Minnesota's high-stakes tests, including its graduation exit exam. The errors prohibited hundreds of seniors from graduating from high school. The courts held for the students during the ensuing court case based on psychological duress and awarded approximately $12 million in damages to these individuals and their parents, plus attorney's fees and court costs (Court Order No. 00-11010, 2003).

The *Star Tribune* reported that NCS Pearson was sued in a class action suit by 7,900 of the 8,000 students on whom testing errors were made. The exact settlements ranged from $362.50 to $3,250 per student, depending on selected criteria. Students who were denied high school graduation received $16,000 each (Draper, 2000).

Almost 27,000 SAT tests taken in October 2005 had scoring errors. The errors accounted for almost 20 percent of the individuals' total exam score (Romano, 2006). A series of class action lawsuits followed this little "technical glitch." For sure, there are parental and student concerns about test abuses, but they are muffled by the sound of cash registers with more than $3 million paid out to aggrieved students and their families.

Wyoming experienced a large scale scoring error in 2009–2010 on its Proficiency Assessment for Wyoming Students (PAWS) test, developed and scored by NCS Pearson. As a result of the error, the company paid $5 million in fines to the state (Fair Test, 2014).

More than 4,000 students in Virginia received inaccurate test scores in 2013 due to an error in converting student scores to proficiency levels. Students were categorized as not proficient when in fact they had scored in the proficient range. Then, in 2014, scores from 500 students in Virginia had to be changed due to scoring errors; it was found that 224 students had been labeled as failures when in reality they passed their state's civics exam (Fair Test, 2019).

More than 1,000 students in Mississippi were labeled as failures on the state's graduation exam in 2017 because of a scoring error. Many of those students had to scramble to take an alternative graduation test in order to graduate high school (Fair Test, 2019). The stress, confusion, and time wasted by those students and their parents, through no fault of their own, cannot be remedied.

The previous examples are just a drop in the large bucket of scoring errors that have taken place. Scoring errors occur every year in multiple states, and they call into question the claim that standardized test results are an objective measure of student achievement.

MYTH 7: CENTRALIZATION OF EDUCATIONAL DECISION MAKING BENEFITS OUR NATION

If there is one truism, it is that NCLB and ESSA were clear and bold attempts to centralize America's three centuries of decentralized schools. Elmore (2002) put the concept of mass centralization in context when he wrote for the very conservative Hoover Institution:

> The federal government is requiring annual testing at every grade level, and requiring states to disaggregate their test scores by racial and socioeconomic backgrounds—a system currently operating in only a handful of states and one that is fraught with technical difficulties. The federal government is mandating a single definition of adequate yearly progress, the amount by which schools must increase their test scores in order to avoid some sort of sanction—an issue that in the past has been decided jointly by states and the federal government. And the federal government has set a single target date by which all students must exceed a state-defined proficiency level—an issue that in the past has been left almost entirely to states and localities.
>
> Thus, the federal government is now accelerating the worst trend of the current accountability movement: that performance-based accountability has come to mean testing, and testing alone. It doesn't have to. In fact, in the early stages of the current accountability movement, reformers had an expansive view of performance that included, in addition to tests, portfolios of students' work, teachers' evaluations of their students, student-initiated projects, and formal exhibitions of students' work. The comparative appeal of standardized tests is easy to see: they are relatively inexpensive to administer; can be mandated relatively easily; can be rapidly implemented; and deliver clear, visible results. However, relying only on standardized tests simply dodges the complicated questions of what tests actually measure and of how schools and students react when tests are the sole yardstick of performance. (pp. 1–2)

NCLB stated that the federal government controls the nation's public schools, and ESSA continued that control. Considering that the federal government contributes about only 7 percent of the total funding necessary to sustain K–12 public education, this is a classic case of the tail wagging the dog.

POINTS TO REMEMBER

Most of what is marketed to the general public regarding the core principles of school reform seem to weaken under close examination. The more one digs, the more one comes to the conclusion that the former Soviet Union concept of centralized command and control mixed with unrestrained neoliberalism was the initial blueprint for the education reforms driven by NCLB.

Originally authorized for five years, NCLB lasted almost thirteen. The federal government dictated the terms of education reform with NCLB beginning in 2002 under the George W. Bush presidency. ESSA was the follow-up five-year plan to NCLB, authorized on December 15, 2015.

ESSA maintained federal control over testing requirements but provided state education officials the opportunity to set their performance targets; standardized test performance targets were still part of the overall program—no choice. Although states were no longer bound to 100 percent proficiency, ESSA required that states test at least 95 percent of students. This mandate was a direct response to the opt-out movement and pressure from the corporate testing complex to keep the money flowing in the over $2-billion-a-year testing business (Strauss, 2015).

According to the Center for Media and Democracy, Educational Testing Service (ETS), Houghton Mifflin Harcourt, McGraw-Hill, and Pearson Education collectively spent more than $20 million over a six-year period starting in 2009 through 2015 to keep the testing provisions embedded in ESSA (Strauss, 2015). Regardless of how long ESSA remains in place, another reauthorization of the Elementary and Secondary Education Act must take place by law.

If the trend toward centralized planning continues, public school policy making will be eerily reminiscent of the five-year plans begun under Joseph Stalin in the Soviet Union. In 1928, Stalin announced the first of what would be thirteen five-year plans. The thirteenth plan was dumped when the "Evil Empire" dissolved in the early 1990s.

Every Soviet five-year plan ended in failure; they never achieved their stated goals. So too did NCLB. It never achieved its legislated goals and it seriously undermined the democratic unitary public school system. ESSA appears to be further eroding the public school system with centralized bureaucracy and neoliberal exploitation of children and educators.

A LOOK AHEAD

Chapter 5 presents high-risk implications of the dual system. The chapter explains the risks to children associated with poverty, stress, and learned helplessness. Ecological systems theory is introduced to illustrate that the root cause of underachievement cannot be solved by education reforms that rely on standardization and constant measurement of academic achievement.

REFERENCES

Achieve, Inc. (2000). *Achieve Policy Brief, 1*(1), 1–8.

Archibold, R. C. (1999, September 16). 8,600 in summer school by error, board says. *New York Times*. Retrieved from https://archive.nytimes.com/www.nytimes.com/library/national/regional/091699school-tests-edu.html

Berliner, D. C., & Biddle, B. J. (1995). *The manufactured crisis: Myths, frauds and the attack on America's public schools*. Reading, MA: Addison-Wesley.

Bracey, G. (2003). April Foolishness: The 20th Anniversary of a Nation at Risk. *Phi Delta Kappan, 84*(8), 616–21.

Bredo, E. (2002). The Darwinian center to the vision of William James. In J. Garrison, P. Poedeschi, & E. Bredo (Eds.), *William James and education* (pp. 1–26) New York: Teachers College Press.

Bryk, A., & Hermanson, K. (1993). Educational indicator systems: Observations on their structure, interpretation and use. In L. Darling-Hammond (Ed.), *Review of research in education*, vol. 19 (pp. 451–84). Washington, DC: American Educational Research Association.

Buber, M. (1971). *I and thou*. New York: Free Press.

Callahan, R. E. (1962). *Education and the cult of efficiency: A study of the social forces that have shaped the administration of public schools*. Chicago: University of Chicago Press.

Chomsky, N. (2011). *Profit over people: Neoliberalism and global order*. New York: Seven Stories Press.

Chubb, J. E., & Moe, T. M. (1990). *Politics, markets and America's schools*. Washington, DC: Brookings Institute.

Court Order No. 00-11010. (2003, January 24). Order Granting Plaintiffs' Motion for Final Approval of Class Action Settlement and for Final Judgment. Fourth Judicial District Court, State of Minnesota, Hennepin County. Allen Oliskey, Judge.

Draper, N. (2000, August 16). Test denied diplomas for 54 at most: Scoring mess affected fewer seniors than first thought.*Star Tribune*.

Elmore, R. F. (2002, spring). Unwarranted intrusion. *Education Next*. Retrieved from http://www.educationtext.org/20021/30.html

Fair Test. (2018). Pearson's history of testing problems. Retrieved from https://www.fairtest.org/pearsons-history-testing-problems

Heinrich, C. J., & Nisar, H. (2013). The efficacy of private sector providers in improving public educational outcomes. *American Educational Research Journal, 50*(5), 856–94. Retrieved from https://doi.org/10.3102/0002831213486334

Kozol, J. (2005). *The shame of the nation: The restoration of apartheid schooling in America*. New York: Crown.

Lee, J., & Reeves, T. (2012). Revisiting the impact of NCLB high-stakes school accountability, capacity, and resources: State NAEP 1990–2009 reading and math achievement gaps and trends. *Educational Evaluation and Policy Analysis, 34*(2): 209–31. Retrieved from https://doi.org/10.3102/0162373711431604

Lubienski, C., & Lubienski, S. (2013). *The public school advantage: Why public schools outperform private schools*. Chicago: University of Chicago Press.

Molnar, A. (1999, October). *Educational vouchers: A review of the research.* Milwaukee: Center for Education Research, Analysis and Innovation, University of Wisconsin–Milwaukee.

No Child Left Behind Act of 2001 (NCLB). (2002). Pub. L. No. 107-110, § 115, Stat. 1425. Retrieved from http://www2.ed.gov/nclb/landing.jhtml

Rhoades, K., & Madaus, G. (2003). *Errors in standardized tests: A systemic problem.* Chestnut Hill, MA: National Board on Educational Testing and Public Policy.

Romano, L. (2006, March 24). College Board acknowledges more SAT scoring errors. *Washington Post.*

Ryan, C. (2003, August 22). School testing company flunks again. *Las Vegas Sun.*

Slouka, M. (2009, September). Dehumanized: When math and science rule the school. *Harpers.* Retrieved from https://harpers.org/archive/2009/09/dehumanized/.

Strauss, V. (2015, March 30). Report: Big education firms spend millions lobbying for pro-testing policies. *Washington Post.* Retrieved from https://www.washingtonpost.com/news/answer-sheet/wp/2015/03/30/report-big-education-firms-spend-millions-lobbying-for-pro-testing-policies/

Wallis, C. (2008, June 8). No Child Left Behind: Doomed to fail? *Time Magazine.* Retrieved from http://content.time/com/time/nation/article/0,8599,1812758,00.html

Zhao, Y. (2012). *World class learners: Educating creative and entrepreneurial students.* Thousand Oaks, CA: Corwin Press.

Chapter Five

The Path of High-Risk Implications in the Dual System

A case can be made that the nation's education policy has been guided into reform by fraud, myth, and lies. The new "reforms" are a result of business interests and anti–public school political forces that prescribe arbitrary levels of academic achievement of a narrow set of curriculum standards. In some cases, education bureaucrats impose developmentally inappropriate standardized testing schemes to force compliance with educationally dubious content standards.

To borrow from one popular political slogan: "Students and teachers, are you better off today than you were before federal and state coerced standards were mandated?" Or: "Administrators, have you been able to provide your teachers with the tools, support services, instructional materials and training to reach more students as a result of state and federal mandated reform?"

Momentum for contemporary American school reform can be traced to the 1983 publication of *A Nation at Risk* (NCEE, 1983). The anti–public school report manufactured another education crisis and used a time-tested tool to drive more dual system reforms: fear. Global economic competition is the new hobgoblin, and the public schools are now erroneously considered the exclusive engines for worker productivity. One must ask a rhetorical question: "Have the schools ever been assigned this role?"

In his 1861 book *Education: Intellectual, Moral and Physical,* Herbert Spencer asked a parallel question, "What knowledge is of most worth?" Spencer answered with five educational purposes: (1) self-preservation, (2) meaningful work, (3) familial support, (4) social and political responsibilities, and (5) worthy use of leisure time. Spencer's landmark question about the purposes of education predated Lester Frank Ward's and John Dewey's three fundamental purposes of public education: (1) academic/economic, (2) socio-civic, and (3) avocational.

HIJACKED LEGISLATION

Some of the people you elect to write bills and policies outsource their job to corporate legislation writers. The dual system reform movement gains energy from political and unrestrained profit-seeking legislation and regulations that stress only economic output and neglect all the other purposes of education. Socio-civic responsibilities and the personal development found in avocational education pursuits become bludgeoned in a dual system driven by profit margins.

In the years 2002 and 2003, more than 1,000 different bills were introduced in the fifty state legislatures to "fix the schools." That figure almost doubled to 1,976 in 2018 (National Conference of State Legislatures, 2019). Almost 1,000 of those bills were written by the American Legislative Exchange Council, the neoliberal group made up of politically conservative state and corporate representatives.

One goal of ALEC is to advance legislation that supports neoliberal policies. About two hundred ALEC bills are adopted each year. Rob O'Dell (2019) from *USA Today* and the *Republic* conducted a study to determine the influence of ALEC on legislation around the country. O'Dell reported that at least ten thousand bills introduced in state legislatures around the country were essentially copied from model legislation written by ALEC in the years between 2010 and 2018. Approximately 21 percent of them—more than twenty-one hundred—were signed into law.

The bills supported things like charter schools, school vouchers and tax credits for people that send their children to private schools, increased standardized testing, and more ways to punish public schools. Somewhere along the way to *fixing* the schools, somebody—maybe everybody—forgot to ask, "What needs fixing?" People think they elect officials to create policies based on the needs of the public, but the evidence shows that conservative lawmakers are getting their policies written for them from corporate representatives.

Rather than examining the underlying social factors that impact learning and achievement, the education reform movement degenerated into a legislated hijacking of the public system for private interests. None of the ALEC-sponsored bills strengthened the social system in evidence-based ways that reduce poverty. Like all school systems around the world, the United States has educational problems, but it is still one of the most productive systems in the world (Tienken, 2017). No social institution is perfect. And if you get a small enough sample or finagle numbers in certain ways you can make any situation look "at risk."

Academic Achievement and Socioeconomics

School reform legislation ignores the root cause of academic underachievement: socioeconomic status (SES). Some researchers use eligibility for free and reduced lunch as the proxy for SES of individual students or a proxy for the overall SES of a school or school district. Sirin (2005) conducted one of the largest meta-analyses of the influence of SES on student outcomes and found that approximately 20 percent of the studies conducted between 1990 and 2000 used free and reduced lunch as the only variable to describe SES at the individual student, school, or school district level.

Although student eligibility for free and reduced lunch is one variable that can help provide a general description of student SES or overall family human capital, Harwell and LaBeau (2010) presented an argument against using the variable of free and reduced lunch status as the sole indicator of student family capital, school SES, or school district SES.

Harwell and LaBeau suggested that student eligibility for free and reduced lunch is not as precise an an indicator of overall student or community SES as some researchers might think. To overcome the potential limitation posed by using free and reduced lunch eligibility as a predictor variable, some researchers use multiple variables from the US Census data to create a multidimensional view of the family and community characteristics that influence student achievement on standardized tests.

The Layers of Learning

Some researchers use the term "human capital" to refer to the broad collection of people's skills, experiences, and abilities that allow them to potentially become more economically successful and act with greater skill (Becker, 1993; Coleman, 1988). In the context of research, the family is the closest level of human capital to the student. Family human capital directly influences the student's academic outcomes.

Results from the existing literature suggest that students who live in families with more human capital have greater access to academically oriented life experiences, collateral learning experiences that extend school learning, and more supports to help them connect to and capitalize on academic content embedded in formal education (Scherrer, 2014). As a group, students with more family human capital often perform better on standardized tests of traditional academic achievement (Tienken, 2020).

Family demographic factors such as income and living in a single-parent versus a two-parent household, or the percentage of female-headed households in poverty are factors that help describe the level of human capital in a family. Those demographic factors can be used as some proxies for the human capital experienced by the student.

The community in which a student lives also plays an important complimentary function, and in some ways has a reciprocal relationship with the human capital of a family. Coleman (1988) explained the connection between community demographics and social capital:

> Social capital is defined by its functions. It is not a single entity but a variety of different entities, with two elements in common: they all consist of some aspect of social structures, and they facilitate certain actions of actors—whether persons or corporate actors—within the structure. Like other forms of capital, social capital is productive, making possible the achievement of certain ends that in its absence would not be possible. . . . A given form of social capital that is valuable in facilitating certain actions may be useless or even harmful for others. (p. 98)

Formal and informal interactions and relationships within a community create community social capital (World Bank, 2011). The types of professionals that live in a community and the community resources and services intersect to contribute to the overall social capital of the community (Tienken, 2017). Resources and services such as the community groups, structured recreation programs for children, religious groups, libraries, services for senior citizens and disabled residents, art commissions, local social advocacy groups, quality and affordable daycare, quality preschool opportunities, influence the fabric of a community (Putnam, 2000).

When children grow up in communities with access to high levels of social capital, the chances are greater than those children and their families will interact with and develop formal and informal relationships with people who have high levels of human capital. Children have the potential to be exposed to and influenced by more academic ideas and life experiences that influence their learning in school directly and indirectly through the people that they interact with on a regular basis.

Children living in communities with higher levels of human and social capital are more likely to have access to varied life experiences that build academic background knowledge. They are more likely to come to school with existing academic knowledge that they can use to connect their life experiences to new content and better transfer ideas from school to other situations (Tanner & Tanner, 2007).

Access to varied types and quality of social and human capital influences student learning in traditional classroom situations where children need to connect the content of the classroom to their life experiences. Community social capital and family human capital plays a role in ultimate achievement on standardized tests. Children who are surrounded by higher levels of human and social capital can make greater use of educational resources at their disposal (Scherrer, 2014).

Ecological Systems Theory

The various layers of learning are situated within the broader theoretical framework of ecological systems theory, as described by Bronfenbrenner (1979). He posited that children exist in an ecological system and various layers of the system exert influences upon them. Family, school, peer groups, and community characteristics and resources intersect, and they directly and indirectly influence academic, social, and emotional behaviors and outcomes of children. (See figure 5.1.)

Ecological systems theory provides support for the concept that key layers of family human capital and community social capital surround children. Ecological systems theory helps explain how those layers of environmental influence can hinder or encourage academic achievement and general development and influence results on standardized tests and overall academic achievement. Researchers use a combination of indicators related to family human capital and community social capital to accurately predict student standardized test results at the school and district levels. The school and districts are within the ecological systems of children and influenced by the other factors within the system.

Ecological systems theory comports with research-based perspectives of poverty that suggest children need quality formal education resources but also appropriate family and community supports so that children can make full use of the resources they encounter in formal learning environments. Known as the capabilities perspective, the line of research suggests students have varying capabilities to "convert resources into their intended benefits" (Scherrer, 2014, p. 203). The realized output from the resources provided is influenced by the capability of the student to fully utilize the resources as intended.

Factors such as health and access to quality healthcare, stable living situations in which basic needs are met, and access to academically oriented life experiences are necessary to support students being able to connect their experiences to the formal curricular content of school. Children are inspired to learn more when they see the lessons learned in school used in real-world situations by themselves and others to whom they aspire.

Children learn more when they are able to transfer their formal learning to their everyday lives and participate in life experiences that extend and enhance their capability to make the most of formal schooling (Kelly, 2010). Learning becomes a recursive process and cumulative over time, evolving to a more sophisticated understandings of subject matter content and how to use the content.

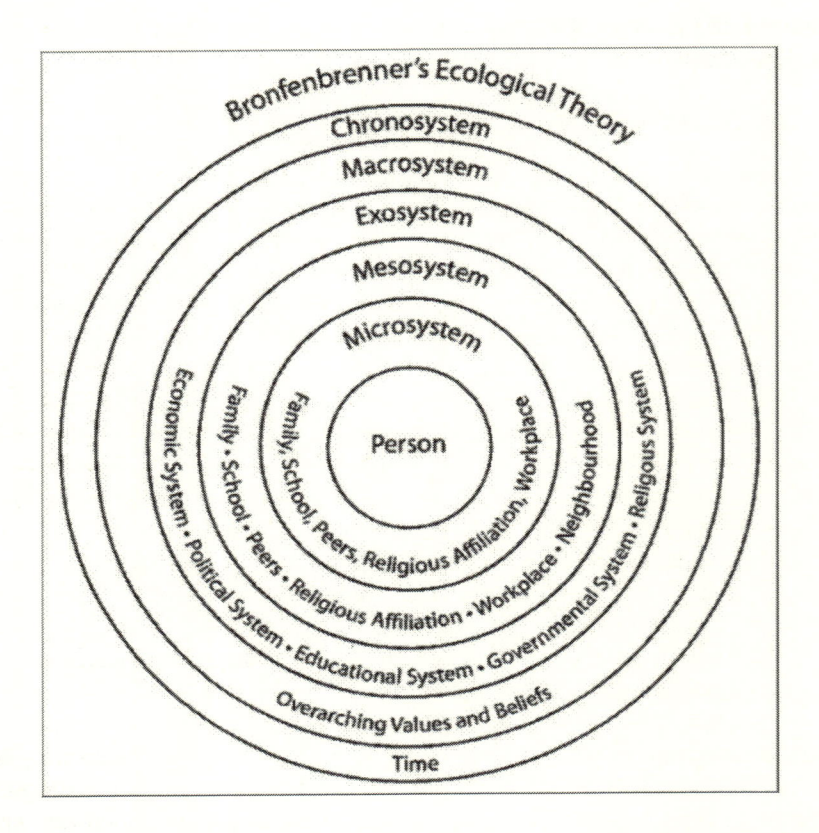

Figure 5.1. Illustrated model of a Bronfenbrenner's Ecological Theory adapted from Berger, K. S. (2007). *The developing person through the life span.* New York: Worth Publishers and published in Stanger, N. (2011). "Moving 'Eco' Back Into Socio-Ecological Models: A Proposal to Reorient Ecological Literacy Into Human Developmental Models and School Systems." *Human Ecology Review*, 18(2), on page 169.

A description of the evolution of learning that occurs for children who grow up in ecological systems with higher levels of human and community capital aligns with the definition of curriculum put forth by Tanner and Tanner (2007). They defined curriculum as "that reconstruction of knowledge and experience that enables the learner to grow in exercising intelligent control of subsequent knowledge and experience" (p. 99). Active construction of meaning on the part of the learner is implied in the definition, as is active learning through collateral and direct experiences of the child in highly enriched ecological systems. The formal curricular content and the students connect via reciprocal learning relationships. How can educational equity be achieved if the opportunity to live in a vibrant ecological system is not distributed equally?

THE PATH OF POVERTY

According to the US Department of Commerce, almost 13 million children, 17.5 percent of all children in the United States, lived in abject poverty during the 2018 school year. The Department of Commerce defined poverty as a family of four with an annual income below $25,283, which is equivalent to $486 a week or about $12.15 an hour based on a forty-hour week.

Internationally, the United States ranks near the top of industrialized countries for the highest levels of child poverty according to the Organisation for Economic Co-operation and Development (OECD, 2018). The OECD calculated that about 20 percent of children in the United States lived in relative poverty in 2018, ranked with Lithuania, Russia, Mexico, and Chile.

The OECD defined relative poverty as:

> The child relative income poverty rate, defined as the percentage of children (0–17 year-olds) with an equivalised household disposable income (i.e. an income after taxes and transfers adjusted for household size) below the poverty threshold. The poverty threshold is set here at 50% of the median disposable income in each country. (p. 1)

The level of child poverty in the United States leaves many children, by no fault of their own, at a social and educational disadvantage. The ecological systems of children in poverty do not support the realization of their academic, social, and emotional potential. Poverty is a powerful force in educational underachievement and underachievement in life. One rarely hears proponents of dual system solutions willing to tackle poverty head-on with substantial changes to the social welfare system to support families and children.

One simply has to ask, "Why the silence?" One could speculate that Americans have been subtly conditioned and misled by neoliberal lies and myths into believing that childhood poverty is really not a social problem. Neoliberal rhetoric blames the victim and claims things like culture, laziness, and a lack of grit are the cause, not the system that is rigged in favor of the wealthy.

Dual system reformers claim that poverty is an individual problem created by slackers who refuse to pull themselves up by their own bootstraps to achieve the American Dream. Let us not forget the antipoverty messages carried by the nation's media from the 1970s to the 1990s about all those "welfare queens."

Problems of Poverty

There are several attributes of childhood poverty that negatively impact school outcomes. Inadequate nutrition is a key contributor. There is a definite relationship between malnutrition and cognitive dysfunction. Chronic vitamin B1 and B12 deficiencies have a demonstrated relationship to cognitive impairment that has been known for a long time (Venkatramanan, Armata, Strupp, & Finkelstein, 2016). Other actors include single-parent family structures and less access to life experiences that build sight vocabulary necessary for reading (Shim, Felner & Shim, 2001).

Poverty itself—the lack of money—is a key factor. The resource allocation for schools is directly related to community property tax bases. Poverty in the United States is often concentrated due to housing patterns and decades of housing segregation and racial discrimination. The concentration of community-based poverty creates a vicious cycle of impoverished ecological systems.

People in poverty do not have the fiscal resources to provide optimal learning environments for their children. State and federal bureaucrats have become increasingly unwilling to equitably distribute wealth. The ecological systems students living in poverty experience are more educationally depressed compared to students in middle- and upper-class ecological systems. State education bureaucrats provide funding to schools in impoverished communities, but that funding is for the act of schooling. It does little to ameliorate the environmental effects of living in an impoverished ecological system.

Effects of Poverty

A national review of test score data revealed that students labeled as economically disadvantaged, as a group, always have lower scale scores on all statewide tests of academic achievement, including high school exit exams, than their non–economically disadvantaged peers. The average effect size difference is greater than 0.50.

Pogrow (2018) defined effect size as the size of the difference between two outcomes. He explained that it is a helpful statistic when one wants to compare differences between two outcomes. Effect size relates to standard deviation, which is a calculation that explains the variation in a set of values or how much something deviates from the mean. A set of values with a low standard deviation do not differ much, whereas a large standard deviation signifies greater differences. Generally standard deviations range from 0.00 to 3.00.

Cohen (1988) provided some general guidelines to determine relative size. Cohen described effect sizes of 0.20 as difficult to detect, 0.50 as "visible to the naked eye" (p. 26), and effect sizes of 1.00 or more as "grossly perceptible" (p. 27). Another way to interpret the meaningfulness of a standard deviation is to look at through the lens of percentile ranks. A student who scores one standard deviation above the mean score of his reference group scored higher than 84 percent of that group. A two-standard-deviation difference puts the student at about the 95th percentile and a three-standard-deviation difference places the student at the around the 98th percentile.

Table 5.1 includes examples of effect size differences from several states' high school exit exams between students labeled economically disadvantaged or eligible for free or reduced lunch and more advantaged students. The range of effect sizes in table 5.1 is 0.59 to 1.05. In other words, the achievement differences between students and poverty and those students not in poverty are *big*. Reduce poverty and the so-called achievement gap evaporates: no other reforms necessary.

The effect size differences between students in poverty and students not in poverty remain relatively consistent for all statewide tests given in grades 3–11 (Tienken, 2011). If the United States continues to pursue policies that disregard poverty as the root cause of underachievement, the country will continue to obtain the same results, regardless of how many standardized tests children are made to take and regardless of the school-based interventions used.

Noted educator Stephen Krashen (2011) summed up the influence of poverty on education in two sentences when he wrote, "Poverty is clearly the most serious problem. In fact, it may be the only serious problem in American education" (p. 17). That sobering idea was also suggested by Benjamin S. Bloom in 1964 in his seminal work *Stability and Change in Human Characteristics*. Bloom indicated that early learning deficits would require greater and more powerful instructional interventions later in schooling. To date, the only interventions provided by dual system school reformers have been more testing and standardization of curriculum and teaching. Standardized testing is not teaching and has no impact on learning. In fact, continued testing of students who historically do not perform well on standardized tests creates another debilitation effect of poverty: learned helplessness.

Table 5.1. Percentages of Students Performing Proficient or Above Proficient on NAEP Mathematics, Ages 9, 13, and 17, for 1990, 2003 and 2017.

	Grade 4—Age 9	*Grade 8—Age 13*	*Grade 12—Age 17*
2017	40	34	25*
2003	34	28	23*
1990	13	15	N/A

*12th grade comparison scores were only for years starting at 2005 and ending at 2015.

Learned Helplessness?

Poverty appears to be at least one condition that exacerbates the creation of adverse educational consequences due to taking high-stakes tests. Failing students are apparently exhibiting characteristics of learned helplessness. Cosgrove (2000) noted that "learned helplessness is a specific consequence of one particular form of psychological stress: being given an impossible task" (pp. 45–46).

Sapolsky (1994) cited the research of Donald Hiroto and Martin E. P. Seligman showing how learned helplessness is a function of environmental conditions that are adverse. If children in grades 3, 4, or 5 have negative experiences with high-stakes tests and receive predictable negative consequences, they are more likely to perceive passing that test as another impossible task when they reach the middle school grades.

The theoretical construct of Maslow's (1954) hierarchy of needs provides a lens to better understand learned helplessness and the connection to poverty. Maslow constructed eight ascending psychological needs, of which five are germane to my argument. Level 1 relates to basic physiological necessities such as food and water. Level 2 relates to safety needs, including shelter and security, while level 3 describes the belongingness needs.

Level 4 is esteem—the need to achieve, be competent, gain approval and recognition. Children who are informed that their test scores are not meeting standard are being denied an element of esteem. Being involuntarily subjected to standardized tests that include questions outside of the cognitive or life experience purview of some children helps produce the condition of learned helplessness.

Level 5 of Maslow's hierarchy is cognitive—the need to know, understand, and explore. It is claimed by the reformers that hundreds of thousands of children nationally have not reached that level—again, based on test scores. With the cognitive need being contingent on the four basic physiological and psychological needs below it in the hierarchy, it becomes apparent that poverty in general and learned helplessness specifically may be playing a more tragic role in student achievement than previously believed.

Children who live in impoverished ecological systems with little chance to feel secure may be severely limited in their attempt to ascend beyond levels 1 and 2 in Maslow's hierarchy. This is because they must attend to their basic living necessities. Additionally, youth in these circumstances tend to be exposed to violence, remaining at level 2 since their safety needs are unmet.

Stress develops as a consequence of a combination of learned helplessness and lack of meeting the first four needs in the Maslow hierarchy (1954). Depression can set in when a stressful situation is perceived to be hopeless.

This being the case, then no amount of testing will help children perform any better; they will probably perform worse.

The Path of Psychological Stress

One can look to the international scene to see where we are headed in terms of student stress and psychological issues. Thousands of students worldwide are believed to commit suicide over exams each year, but figures are sketchy, as some cases are not reported as exam related. China, India, and South Korea are three examples of test-based cultures, and all three countries have issues with teen suicides.

Almost four hundred teen suicides in China related to exam pressures were uncovered by a private think tank, the 21st Century Education Research Institute, in just eleven months during 2016 and 2017 (Yan, 2018). Like many statistics reported in China, the suicide statistic is almost certainly artificially low, with hundreds, if not thousands, more student suicides going unreported each year. The Chinese government claims not to even collect data on the actual number of student suicides.

Almost nine thousand student suicides were reported in India in 2015. Many people blamed the intense pressure to succeed on college exams as the culprit (Gupta, 2019). South Korea has the highest suicide rate for all of the OECD member countries for children and young adults ages 9–24 (Singh, 2017). The OECD is a group of the top thirty industrialized countries in the world.

India, China, and Korea are not the United States. But teenagers in the United States are now being subjected to the same inhumane stress as their Indian, Chinese, and Korean counterparts with state-mandated tests, college entrance exams, local benchmark and formative testing, and other types of testing. Teenage suicides are not a pleasant thought, but current pressures brought on by high-stakes testing predict that these tragic acts of self-destruction will occur. Policymakers have subverted our long-standing social contract with youth in terms of providing them with quality educational experiences, and the corporate contract will undoubtedly precipitate the suicides of the more fragile youth as a result of that breach.

The Path to Educational Corruption

In the business sector, financial statements often carry the category of goodwill costs that refer to the excess of a purchase price over the fair market value. Nichols and Berliner (2005) identified another insidious factor of high stakes testing, the social cost related to hyper quantification of academic achievement. Students, educators, and the public school system become dehumanized in the eyes of policy makers and in the media by being associated with numbers that supposedly reflect their worth. Campbell's (1976) law predicted such dehumanization.

Campbell explained that "the more any quantitative social indicator is used for social decision-making, the more subject it will be to corruption pressures and the more likely it will be to distort and corrupt the social processes it is intended to monitor" (p. 49). During the period of 2004–2005, Nichols and Berliner systematically monitored hundreds of news stories and research papers in America related to high-stakes testing as a hallmark of school reform. They found ten categories of corrupting effects on high-stakes testing.

High-stakes tests corrupt and distort the educational processes and decision making. These ten categories of corruption illustrate the exorbitant social costs being extracted from students, educators, and society in general that can never be repaid: (1) administrator and teacher cheating, (2) student cheating, (3) exclusion of low-performaning students from testing, (4) misrepresentation of student dropouts, (5) teaching to the test, (6) narrowing the curriculum, (7) conflicting accountability ratings, (8) questions about the meaning of proficiency, (9) declining teacher morale, and (10) score reporting errors.

Speaking of social costs, this is an opportune moment to add a postscript and reflect on Michael Harrington's (1962) *The Other America: Poverty in the United States*. Harrington's examination of the nation's conscience appeared at a time when the United States was celebrating the achievements of post–World War II America. Harrington argued and provided substantive data that several millions of Americans were trapped in a culture of poverty. President John F. Kennedy was profoundly influenced by this work, which led to his own "war on poverty." Of course, mainline politicians viewed Harrington's work as simply a socialist's view and not really germane to mainstream Americans.

Dionne (2000) observed that Harrington had great impatience with capitalism's tendency to privatize success while socializing failure. Private enterprise produces what sells in the marketplace. The government is stuck with dealing with tough social issues and problems not addressed in the private sector. Politicians realize that if the public schools' success stories continue, people may well begin to think at a higher level and see through the rhetorical nonsense that is amply expressed in education accountability plans.

The Path to Bureaucratic Overload

Any public school educator who entered the system prior to the passage of the No Child Left Behind Act in 2002 can describe how much bureaucracy has been placed upon schools since the beginning of the NCLB era. Pekow (2006) provided an example of how Title I inspectors checked for almost 600 compliance measures on all agencies that are affected by NCLB. The Office of Inspector General (OIG) at the Department of Education identified 588 requirements needed for Title I, Part A of NCLB.

None of the state guides include all 588 indicators and even the Department of Education's guides include only 360 of them. Any school leader who has gone through a Title 1 audit since the passage of NCLB knows how it feels to be buried by bureaucracy. Sleep well tonight knowing that your school district will be spending much-needed tax resources on submitting reports and certifications galore.

What began as a test makers relief bill, NCLB has truly evolved into an accountants employment act. The bureaucracy did not improve with the passage of the Every Student Succeeds Act in 2015. The gravity and sheer madness of the political nonsense that is being perpetrated on public schools as a measure to improve education has reached a fever pitch.

All Paths Lead to the Opportunity Gap

The difference in achievement between various groups of students on standardized tests is termed the achievement gap. The term is pejorative in nature, and I believe it to be offensive. It describes a symptom of a root cause. It connotes a deficiency or something that is lacking. The term is most often used to describe differences in achievement between White and non-White students, specifically Black and Latino students.

The term "achievement gap" is misleading because the difference in test results between various groups of students is not an achievement gap, it is an opportunity gap (Carter & Welner, 2013). Certain groups of students are not afforded the same opportunities as other groups in American society to grow in develop in enriched ecological systems. Welner (2013) stated that the "opportunity gap that exists across racial and associated class lines is expansive, and it widens as income and wealth inequality continue to rise" (p. 2).

TAKING ACTION

Inequality and inequity are choices societies make based on policies they pursue. Those policies in most cases become laws voted on by elected officials. This country's citizens choose to have one of the highest levels of child poverty in the industrialized world and they choose to have the levels of income inequality. The levels of income inequality in 2020 were similar to those in Thailand, Ecuador, and Peru. According to the Central Intelligence Agency (CIA, 2020), the United States ranked 118 out of 157 countries for income equality, whereas counties like Norway and Sweden ranked in the top ten of all nations. Citizens can make different choices through changes to voting patterns and advocating for change.

A LOOK AHEAD

Chapter 6 dives further into the belly of the testing beast to uncover the flawed technical characteristics and less-than-stellar results of high-stakes testing policies. Statistical evidence of the strong link between money and test scores is presented via studies that have used ecological systems theory and US Census data to predict the percentages of students who will score proficient or above on state mandated tests.

REFERENCES

Becker, G. S. (1993). *Human capital: A theoretical and empirical analysis, with special reference to education*, 3rd ed. Chicago: University of Chicago Press.
Bloom, B. S. (1964). *Stability and change in human characteristics.* New York: John Wiley & Sons.
Bronfenbrenner, U. (1979). *The ecology of human development: Experiments by nature and design.* Cambridge, MA: Harvard University Press.
Campbell, D. T. (1976, December). *Assessing the impact of planned social change.* Hanover, NH: Public Affairs Center, Dartmouth College.
Carter, P. L., & Welner, K. G. (2013). *Closing the opportunity gap: What America must do to give every child an even chance.* New York: Oxford University Press.
Central Intelligence Agency. (2020). *The world factbook: Distribution of family income—Gini index.* Retrieved from https://www.cia.gov/library/publications/the-world-factbook/fields/223rank.html.
Cohen, J. (1988). *Statistical power analysis for the behavioral sciences.* Hillsdale, NJ: Lawrence Erlbaum.
Coleman, J. S. (1988). Social capital in the creation of human capital. *American Journal of Sociology, 94,* S95–S120.
Cosgrove, J. (2000). *Breakdown: Facts about stress in teaching.* New York: Routledge Falmer.
Dionne, E. J. Jr. (2000, March 31). Michael Harrington's "America Can" reflects an optimism about America's social possibilities that needs to be rekindled. *Washington Post.*
Gupta, S. (2019, April 30). 19 Indian students kill themselves after controversial exam results. CNN. Retrieved from https://www.cnn.com/2019/04/30/health/india-exam-results-suicide/index.html
Harrington, M. (1962). *The other America: Poverty in the United States.* Baltimore: Penguin.
Harwell, M. R., & LeBeau, B. (2010). Student eligibility for a free lunch as an SES measure in education research. *Educational Researcher, 39*(2), 120–31.
Kelly, E. (2010). Equal opportunity, unequal capability. In H. Brighouse & I. Robeyns (Eds.), *Measuring justice: Capabilities and primary goods* (pp. 61–80). Cambridge: Cambridge University Press.
Krashen, S. (2011). Protecting students against the effects of poverty: libraries. *New England Reading Association Journal, 46*(2), 17–21.
Maslow, A. (1954). *Motivation and personality.* New York: Harper.
National Commission on Excellence in Education. (1983). *A nation at risk: The imperative for educational reform.* Washington, DC: US Department of Education.
National Conference of State Legislatures. (2019). Education legislation: Bill tracking. Retrieved from http://www.ncsl.org/research/education/education-bill-tracking-database.aspx
Nichols, S. & Berliner, D. C. (2005). *The inevitable corruption of indicators and educators through high-stakes testing.* Tempe, AZ: Education Policy Research Unit, College of Education, Arizona State University. Retrieved from http://www.greatlakescenter.org/pdf/EPSL-0503-101-EPRU.pdf

O'Dell, R. (2019, April 3). How we uncovered 10,000 times lawmakers introduced copycat model bills—and why it matters. *USA Today*.

Organisation for Economic Co-operation and Development. (2018). OECD family database: CO2.2: Child poverty. Retrieved from https://www.oecd.org/els/CO_2_2_Child_Poverty.pdf

Pekow, C. (2006, May 25). Federal offices disagree on monitoring under NCLB. *Grants for K–12 Hotline, 18*(10), 7.

Pogrow, S. (2018). *Authentic quantitative analysis for education leadership decision-making and EdD dissertations*, edition 2.2. Ypsilanti, MI: ICPEL Publications.

Sapolsky, R. (1994). *Why zebras don't get ulcers*. New York: Freeman.

Scherrer, J. (2014). The role of the intellectual in eliminating poverty: A response to Tierney. *Educational Researcher, 43*, 201–207.

Shim, M. K., Flener, R. D., & Shim, E. (2000, April). *The effects of family structures on academic achievement*. Paper presented at the Annual Meeting of the American Educational Research Association, New Orleans, LA.

Singh, A. (2017, October 31.). The scourge of South Korea: Stress and suicide in Korean society. *Berkeley Political Review*. Retrieved from https://bpr.berkeley.edu/2017/10/31/the-scourge-of-south-korea-stress-and-suicide-in-korean-society/

Sirin, S. R. (2005). Socioeconomic status and academic achievement: A meta-analytic review of research. *Review of Educational Research, 75*(3), 417–53.

Spencer, H. (1891). *Education: Intellectual, moral and physical*. New York: Appleton. (Originally published in 1861.)

Tanner, D., & Tanner, L. (2007). *Curriculum development: Theory into practice*. Upper Saddle River, NJ: Pearson.

Tienken, C. H. (2011). High school exit exams and mismeasurement. *Educational Forum, 4*(75), 298–314.

Tienken, C. H. (2017). *Defying standardization: Creating curriculum for an uncertain future*. Lanham, MD: Rowman and Littlefield.

Tienken, C. H. (2020). *Cracking the code of education reform: Creative compliance and ethical leadership*. Thousand Oaks, CA: Corwin Press.

Tienken, C. H., Colella, A. J., Angelillo, C., Fox, M., McCahill, K., & Wolfe, A. (2017). Predicting middle school state standardized test results using family and community demographic data. *Research on Middle Level Education, 40*(1), 1–13.

US Department of Commerce, Bureau of the Census. (2018). Current Population Survey, 2018 Annual Social and Economic Supplement. Retrieved from https://www.childrensdefense.org/wp-content/uploads/2018/09/Child-Poverty-in-America-2017-National-Fact-Sheet.pdf

Venkatramanan S., Armata I. E., Strupp, B. J., & Finkelstein, J. L. (2016). Vitamin B-12 and Cognition in Children. *Advances in Nutrition, 7*(5), 879–88. Retrieved from https://doi.org/10.3945/an.115.012021

World Bank. (2011). Social capital. Retrieved from http://go.worldbank.org/K4LUMW43B0

Yan, A. (2018, May 9). Child suicide covered up in China, says think tank as it calls on authorities to publish figures. *South China Morning Post*. Retrieved from https://www.scmp.com/news/china/society/article/2145372/child-suicide-covered-china-says-think-tank-it-calls-authorities

Chapter Six

High Stakes, Low Quality

The modern school reform movement aimed at solidifying a profit-driven dual system of education in the United States will continue to use standardized testing as the driving force to foment crises. The neoliberal case for the need to establish a dual system is fabricated. The fabrication is accomplished primarily by claims that student achievement, as measured by standardized test results, continues to stagnate.

The National Defense Education Act of 1958, *A Nation at Risk*, and America2000 and the Race to the Top federal competitive grant program all cited lagging student achievement as justification for neoliberal education reform proposals such as charter schools and vouchers for private school tuition. Dual system supporters routinely wheel out results from state, national, and international tests to prove their case that the public schools are failing.

Since the inception of No Child Left Behind in 2002, it has become easier to use standardized test results as a weapon of mass public school destruction. Federal education legislation created multiple pathways for dual system reformers to find flaws with public education and manufacture failure on a yearly basis. School quality and student achievement are increasingly evaluated through businesslike quarterly profit margin lenses, with standardized test results acting as the currency of judgment.

MANY PATHS TO FAILURE

NCLB and Every Student Succeeds Act regulations required schools and school districts to report separate test achievement data for at least fourteen subgroups: (1) economically disadvantaged, (2) White, (3) Black, (4) Native American, (5) Hispanic, (6) Asian, (7) multiethnic, (8) special education, (9)

English language learners, (10) migrants, (11) all students, (12) all students except special education, (13) male, and (14) female.

Results must be reported for reading/language arts and mathematics in grades 3–8 and once in high school, seven grade levels in total. Multiply the seven grade levels by the fourteen subgroups and that results in 98 reporting categories. Then an entry must be made for mandated science testing once before middle school, once during middle school, and once in high school, which translates to fourteen subgroups tested in three grade levels for 42 additional categories. Combine the 98 initial categories to the 42 additional categories and schools and districts have at least 140 indicators that schools need to pass to receive a clean bill of health.

Multiple Measures

Bureaucrats in many states use the results from the state-mandated standardized tests to make multiple decisions. Nine common decisions made based on a state mandated standardized test are: (1) the effectiveness of the school principal, (2) the effectiveness of the assistant principal(s), (3) the effectiveness of the some content area teachers, (4) student college readiness, (5) student career readiness, (6) a student's strengths and weaknesses in the tested area as reported on standardized test student report, (7) whether a school is "failing" and (8) whether a school district is "failing," and in some states, (9) whether a student can be promoted to the next grade or graduate high school.

Some school leaders voluntarily choose to use those same test results to (1) make judgments about the quality of the school district's subject area programs, like mathematics or language arts; (2) decide course placements for students; (3) identify students for gifted and talented programs; or (4) determine whether students must attend mandatory remedial courses. That equals thirteen determinations made totally or in part from one test score.

Failure to meet the arbitrary achievement expectations set by state bureaucrats on any one of the measures can bring the label of "failing" to the school, educators, and/or students. Like the albatross hung around the Ancient Mariner's (Taylor, 1857) neck, the failing label brings with it consequences such as increased state sanctions or even the closure of the school or district or takeover by a private education management company.

Potential Problems

Dewey (1929) warned that quantitative results do not tell the entire story about students' academic potential, socio-civic dispositions, or avocational interests and passions.

Exact quantitative determinations are far from meeting the demands of such situations, for they presuppose repetitions and exact uniformities. Exaggeration of their importance tends to cramp judgment, to substitute uniform rules for free play of thought, and to emphasize the mechanical factors that also exist in schools . . . they do not give any help in larger questions of reconstruction of curriculum and methods. (pp. 65–66)

Using multiple interpretations of one test score to make decisions raises issues of validity. The interpretations made about students and educators from standardized test results might not be accurate unless the test results have been validated for each type of interpretation made. People should not make decisions that can alter a student's educational trajectory or negatively impact an entire school or district based on the results from standardized tests alone. As of 2020, none of the test results obtained from the tests currently used around the country to satisfy ESSA are valid for all the ways those results are used.

Test Score Validity

Test-score validity is the leading actor and takes center stage in the debate about the use of results from standardized tests to make important decisions about school systems, educators, and students. Thompson (2002) defined validity as the "degree to which scores from a measurement measure the intended construct" (p. 5). Thompson's definition refers to a specific type of validity: construct validity.

McMillan (2004) defined a construct as an "unobservable trait or characteristic such as intelligence, reading comprehension, mathematics ability, honesty, self-concept, attitude, reasoning ability, learning style, and anxiety" (p. 63). Educators cannot measure those types of characteristics or traits directly, so they use proxies like tests of mathematics computation, tests of literal comprehension, student attitude questionnaires, perception scales, or other measures.

Construct Validity Examples

Not all constructs are created equal, and there can be multiple layers of construct validity concerns. A primary concern is when a high-stakes assessment defines the construct either too broadly or too narrowly. Take, for example, a hypothetical collection of standardized tests to measure the construct of Algebra I achievement. Three commercial standardized tests of Algebra I can define the construct of Algebra I in three different ways, measuring achievement differently and producing different results.

One test could present students with forty traditional algebra problems that require students to select the correct answer from a list of four or five possible answers. The students do not have to show their work. Students receive credit only if they select the correct answer from the choices provided. Demonstration of an understanding of the underlying algebra is not necessarily required on a multiple-choice format test. This example construct of Algebra I achievement rests solely on finding the correct answer, by hook or by crook.

The second test could present students with forty traditional Algebra problems that require them to select a correct answer and also show and explain their work, step-by-step. Full credit is given if the student selects the correct answer and provides the correct step-by-step procedures. This construct includes some expectation that one must at least demonstrate an understanding of the procedural aspects of Algebra I.

The third test presents forty algebraic word problems. Students must show their work and select the correct answer from a list of four or five choices. This construct includes an expectation that students can read, comprehend, and distill algebraic problems in word problem form, then represent the words symbolically in algebraic equations, show their understanding of the procedures in writing, and complete the procedures correctly.

Each test has a different construct of what Algebra I achievement means. The third test has much more of an emphasis on reading comprehension. The emphasis on reading comprehension could actually obscure a students' Algebra I achievement if that student is not a strong reader. The results from that student's test might reflect the student's reading ability more than the Algebra I achievement.

A second construct validity issue arises when the construct of the test does not match the construct of the state's content standards. In the hypothetical example of three Algebra I tests, construct validity of the test results could be impaired if the construct of the state's Algebra I content standards is not congruent with the construct of Algebra I on the test. There could be a construct mismatch if the state content standards do not stress Algebra I from the point of view of word problems and explanations of procedures. Student achievement in Algebra might appear to be low, when in fact the low achievement is an artifact of a mismatch in construct validity manifested in the test format.

A final layer of mismatch can occur between the textbook or primary instructional resource used by the school, the state content standards, and the mandated standardized test. Schmidt and colleagues (2001) and Polikoff (2015) found that most of the mathematics textbooks in use before and after the arrival of the Common Core State Standards in 2010 were not aligned to state standards. Schmidt and colleagues (2001) reviewed 185 math texts at all grade levels and found none of the texts matched state standards 100 percent. Polikoff's (2015) findings suggest that only 28 percent to 40 percent of the content in grade 4 mathematics textbooks matched the CCSS in terms of topics and emphasis.

Content Emphasis

Another problem occurs when the content emphasized on a test does not match the content emphasized in the state mandated standards and/or the texts being used or in the classrooms. For example, if the state's topical emphasis in its content standards for Algebra I vary significantly from the topical emphasis on the test of Algebra I, then a misrepresentation of achievement could manifest itself in the test results. The test results could be low, yet the students' understanding of Algebra I according to the content standards could be high. Different tests could emphasize content differently. The test might not be measuring what students are expected to learn. (See table 6.1.)

For instance, one test might have forty-two questions, with 55 percent of those questions focused on solving linear equations, 25 percent focused on visualizing linear functions, and only 5 percent of the questions focused on exploring real numbers, with the remaining concepts covered equally by the rest of the questions, including word problems. A second test might have thirty-eight questions, with 25 percent of the content focused on solving linear equations, 35 percent focused on visualizing linear functions, and 20 percent focused on real numbers, with the remaining concepts covered equally. The third test could have forty questions, with 25 percent of the questions focused on visualizing linear functions, 25 percent on solving linear questions, 25 percent on solving inequalities, 5 percent on real numbers, and the rest of the concepts covered evenly with the remaining 20 percent of questions.

The three tests emphasize the content of Algebra I differently. The same student could receive a different score on each of those tests and be judged to have three different levels of Algebra I acumen because the content covered and the emphases on the content vary greatly. Test 1 emphasizes solving

Table 6.1. Content Emphasis of Three Hypothetical Algebra I Tests

	Solving Equations	Visualizing Functions	Real Numbers	"The Rest"
Test 1 42 Questions	55%	25%	5%	15%
Test 2 38 Questions	25%	35%	20%	20%
Test 3 40 Questions	25%	25%	5%	40%

linear equations more than any other Algebra I concept. A student who has greater content readiness in solving linear equations might score higher on the first test compared to the other two tests. The student could potentially be rated proficient in Algebra I based on the results of the first test and rated deficient in Algebra I based on the results of the third test, yet all three tests are, in theory, tests of Algebra I.

Decisions

The Joint Committee on Standards for Educational Evaluation (1994) stated that validity "concerns the soundness or trustworthiness of the inferences that are made from the results of the information gathering process" (p. 145). The authors of the *Standards for Educational and Psychological Testing* (American Education Research Association, American Psychological Association, & National Council on Measurement in Education, 2014) defined test score validity as "the degree to which the evidence and theory support the interpretations of test scores for the proposed uses of tests" (p. 11). The test results must accurately represent the construct or characteristic being evaluated in the context in which the construct is used.

In a school context, educators should strive to ensure that the test results they use to make decisions about students are derived from tests specifically designed to measure the characteristic or construct they are attempting to measure, that the resulting score is an accurate representation of that characteristic within the context of the measurement, and that the interpretations made from the results of the test accurately reflect the construct being measured.

High-Stakes Boondoggles

There is no secret about the ineffectiveness of high-stakes testing as a school quality improvement tool. Much research has arrived since the NCLB era. The research coalesces around consistent themes: Standardized tests are blunt instruments that do not accurately measure how much a student knows, a student's academic potential, the quality of teaching or leadership in school, or the overall human potential of students.

Standardized tests do not help to move the needle in terms of educational improvement. Orlich (2003) found no positive impact on yearly student achievement as a consequence of the Washington Assessment of Student Learning (WASL). However, over a four-year period a small effect, an insignificant gain, does emerge. The effect size statistic is based on a normal distribution of scores. The larger the effect size, the greater the student gains. In Washington, the gains were negligible in a year-to-year comparison.

The results of Orlich's study paralleled the findings of Amrein and Berliner (2002a), who analyzed the consequences in eighteen states with high-stakes tests. They reported that in seventeen of the eighteen states, student learning remained at the same level as it was before the policy of high-stakes testing was instituted. Amrein and Berliner concluded that high-stakes tests might actually worsen academic performance and exacerbate dropout rates. The affective dimensions of high-stakes tests should be of great concern to policymakers and educators alike. In a separate study of twenty-eight states with high-stakes tests, Amrein and Berliner (2002b) concluded that these tests do little to improve student achievement.

Haney (2002) observed a "randomness" of school scores on the Massachusetts high-stakes test. That is, scores went up and down yearly, almost in a random manner. Braun (2004) cautioned that with all the variations in selecting and analyzing national test data, all conclusions about high-stakes tests and their impact on student achievement might be tentative at best. Wilson (1999) concluded that construct validity is insufficient for assuming large-scale educational assessment internal validity. High-stakes tests may not be testing what they are intended to test.

Review of High School Exit Exams as an Example of a Bankrupt Reform Strategy

One influence of decades of increased federal and state pressure to pursue assessment-driven education policies has been the use of high school exit exams. Broadly defined, a high school exit exam is any statewide standardized test given to all high school students in a specified high school grade or at the end of specified courses, such as Algebra II or Biology, in which the results become the basis for a judgment about whether students graduate from high school with a standard diploma, do not graduate, or receive a lesser diploma. More than half the states in the nation used high school exit exams in 2008. Since then, the number has dropped to about a dozen, but the exit exam idea has made its way into the lower grades, where some states use them for grade promotion out of elementary school.

State education bureaucrats began to use high school exit exams as a policy lever to affect change in the public school system in Virginia. The state education agency (SEA) and state board of education created a "minimum competency" test required for high school graduation (Sanger, 1978). In 1979 the New York SEA instituted a similar basic competency testing scheme for students in the ninth grade.

By 2001, prior to President George W. Bush signing the No Child Left Behind Act, eighteen SEAs required public school students to pass a standardized statewide exit exam for graduation (Education Commission of the States, 2008). As of 2012, more than 50 percent of the SEAs required youth to pass a standardized statewide test in at least language arts and mathematics to receive a standard high school diploma.

An overarching problem with state-mandated high school exit exams is that the results from all statewide tests of academic skills and knowledge at all grade levels have technical flaws that should restrict bureaucrats and school administrators from using the results as the only deciding factor in making life-changing decisions about individual students, such as whether a student graduates high school (American Education Research Association, American Psychological Association, & National Council on Measurement in Education, 1999; Joint Committee on Testing Practices, 2014). The limitations of the reported test results for individual students do not support the potential negative social and educational consequences raised by their use as a high school graduation requirement (Tienken, 2011).

Three common unintended consequences of using only high school exit exam results as a decision point include students being retained in grade, increases in the chance that economically disadvantaged students will not complete high school (Borg, Plumlee, & Stranaham, 2007), and placement in low-level courses which also increases the chances of not completing high school. Other consequences include not receiving a standard high school diploma or being denied graduation all together (Booher-Jennings, 2005; Burch, 2005).

All of the potential consequences listed cost taxpayers more money in the long term because of the depressed earnings of those students who do not attain a high school diploma. Levin (2009) found that reduced employment earnings result in lower local, state, and federal tax receipts, and lower earners also correlate with higher public medical costs, greater rates of incarceration, and greater use of the welfare system.

Another troublesome problem with results from all state tests, especially those used as exit exam gatekeepers, is conditional standard error of measurement (CSEM) and its effect on individual test score interpretation. The reported results for individual pupils might not be the true score.

Measurement Error

The CSEM is an approximation or estimate of the amount of error one must consider when interpreting a test score at a proficiency cut point (Harville, 1991). One can think of it as the margin of error reported in political polls (e.g., + or − 3 points). The individual student-level results from all the state standardized tests have a margin of error. The CSEM helps to describe how large that margin of error is and how much the reported test results might differ from a student's theoretical true score (Tienken & Rodriguez, 2010).

For example, if a student receives a reported scale score of 742, and there are + or − 8 scale score points of CSEM at the proficiency cut point, the minimum score a student must achieve to be considered proficient, then the possible true score could reside within the range of 734 to 750. Furthermore, if that state's proficiency cut score is 750, like it is in many states that used the PARCC test, then the student is categorized as not proficient or failing if the SEA does not account for CSEM in its calculations for individual students, even though the student scored within the CSEM band. This is especially troubling when bureaucrats and school administrators use a single test score determines if a student can graduate high school (Tienken, 2020).

If bureaucrats within SEAs and legislators do not provide policy safeguards for the CSEM, then some percentage of students might be wrongly denied a standard high school diploma when in fact they passed the exit exam. For example, based on information from the 2015 state test technical manual, about ninety-five hundred New Jersey high school students scored within the error range of the spring administration of their mathematics exit exam's CSEM at the proficiency cut score.

That means up to ninety-five hundred students were potentially categorized as not proficient and forced to take remedial coursework, retake the test, and/or participate in an alternative high school assessment process. These students lost out on valuable electives or other potentially rewarding school experiences. Similarly, almost fifty-four thousand students in California scored within the CSEM on their English language arts (ELA) exit exam.

This type of categorization error of students happens in every state on every high-stakes test, not just those given in high school. The reported student-level scores are not the true scores, yet education bureaucrats and school administrators make determinations about graduation eligibility as if scores were free of error (Tienken, 2011).

The Partnership for Assessment of Readiness for College and Careers (PARCC) suite of tests were no better at eliminating test score error. The average size of the errors on their high assessments were 7–13 scale score points. The error alone caused thousands of high school students in New Jersey to be initially denied high school graduation.

STANDARDS FOR EDUCATION TESTING

A joint committee represented by members of the American Educational Research Association (AERA), American Psychological Association (APA), and National Council on Measurement in Education (NCME) released the seventh edition of the *Standards for Educational and Psychological Testing* in 2014. The edition contains twelve categories of standards and provides specific guidance on topics that include appropriate test design, development, validity, and use of standardized tests and results (AERA, APA, & NCME, 2014).

Standard 1.0 provides general guidance regarding validity of results for uses related to various types of standardized testing contexts such as employment, education program placement, college entrance, and diagnostics. The standard states, "Clear articulation of each intended test score interpretation for a specified use should be set forth, and appropriate validity evidence in support of each intended interpretation should be provided" (AERA, APA, & NCME, 2014, p. 23).

Evidence Please

Standard 1.0 states that there needs to be evidence that the test was designed for the specific purpose for which its results are used and that the results are an accurate and consistent indicator of student performance relative to the purpose of the exam. The authors extend their warning about using test results for multiple interpretations in multiple contexts: "No test permits interpretations that are valid for all purposes or in all situations. Each recommended interpretation for a given use requires validation" (AERA, APA, & NCME, 2014, p. 23). Standard 1.1 further recommends, "A rationale should be presented for each intended interpretation of test scores for a given use, together with a summary of the evidence and theory bearing on the intended interpretation" (AERA, APA, & NCME, 2014, p. 23).

The authors of the standards present specific cautions about using results from standardized tests for multiple purposes. Standard 12.2 states, "In educational settings, when a test is designed or used to serve multiple purposes, evidence of validity, reliability/precision, and fairness should be provided for each intended use" (AERA, APA, & NCME, 2014, p. 195). A test designed to measure the effectiveness of a school principal may not be valid for measuring the effectiveness of a classroom teacher or college and career readiness of a student because of the differences in those constructs. The authors state clearly that one test cannot be a valid measure of multiple complex behaviors: "No one test will serve all purposes equally well" (AERA, APA, & NCME, 2014, p. 195).

More National Study Results

Tienken (2011) conducted a nonexperimental, descriptive, cross-sectional study to investigate the precision of the test results received from high school exit exams and to investigate the possible consequence of using those results for high-stakes decisions about students. Table 6.2 lists the name of each state, the most recently reported or approximate CSEM at the proficiency cut point for the ELA and mathematics portions of the high school exit exam, the number of opportunities to take and pass the exam, the method used to address the presence of CSEM, whether the state used a hard-and-fast cut score (i.e., did not allow for a range of scores at the proficiency cut point), and the number of students potentially affected by CSEM.

The range of CSEM at the proficiency cut point for ELA and/or mathematics tests given between 2004 and 2008 was 3.24 on the Idaho mathematics exit exam to 39 scale score points on the Texas mathematics exit exam. Hence, the true math scores for Texas students can be + or − 39 points from the reported test score. The actual size of the error is less of a concern because each state uses a hard-and-fast cut score. Therefore, even one scale score point of CSEM can cause misinterpretation and miscategorization of student performance.

SEAs do not formally publish the number of students potentially affected by CSEM. Tienken (2011) calculated or estimated the numbers from available SEA data. Although the calculations of students potentially affected by CSEM are tentative, they represent the best estimate possible given the lack of data provided by SEAs on this subject. The fact remains that students continue to be miscategorized today because SEAs have done nothing to account for CSEM. Students are subjected to inappropriate education decisions that carry high stakes for them and their families based on either an inability or an unwillingness of SEAs to address this issue.

Not all SEAs adhere to the recommendations regarding CSEM advocated in the *Standards for Educational and Psychological Testing* (AERA, APA, & NCME, 1999). For example, Standard 2.2 reads, "The standard error of measurement, both overall and conditional . . . , should be reported . . . in units of each derived score" (p. 31).

When SEA personnel choose not to report the CSEM (Standard 2.2), it creates a snowball effect of *Standards* violations. "When test score information is released to parents . . . , those responsible for the testing programs should provide appropriate interpretations. The interpretations should describe in simple language . . . the precision of the scores and common misinterpretations of tests scores" (AERA, APA, & NCME, 1999, Standard 5.10, p. 65). "When relevant for test interpretation, test documents ordinarily should include item level information, cut-scores . . . the standard errors of measurement" (AERA, APA, & NCME, 1999, Standard 6.5, p. 69).

School administrators, students, and parents in states where SEAs do not report CSEM or do not publish technical manuals in the public domain have no mechanism to judge the precision of individual student test results. Thus, stakeholders are limited in attempts to appeal the results or lobby for changes to the system (Tienken & Rodriguez, 2010). How can school administrators initiate policy remedies or safeguards for problems that they do not know exist? Where is the institutional accountability and where are procedural safety valves for children?

Is CSEM a real concern for students? Yes, according to the leadership of APA, AERA, NCME, and Joint Committee on Testing Practices (JCTP) and

Table 6.2. State CSEM in Scale-Score Points for the Language Arts and Mathematics Sections of High School Exit Exams (*n* = 23) and Number of Testing Opportunities

State/Year	LA CSEM	Mathematics CSEM	Testing Opportunities
Alabama	Did not respond	Did not respond	Not available
Alaska 2007	19	19	3
Arizona 2007	13	8	3
California 2007	11	9	8
Florida 2005	15	13	3
Georgia 2007	6	6	3
Idaho 2007	3.15	3.24	3
Indiana 2006	Did not respond	Did not respond	3
Louisiana 2006	3.54	3.98	3
Massachusetts 2007	Not reported	Not reported	3
Minnesota 2007	14	12	3
Missouri 2007	Approx. 8	Approx. 9	> 1
Nevada 2007	26	33	> 3
New Jersey 2006	Not reported	Not reported	3
New Mexico 2006	10	7	2
New York 2006	Not reported	Not reported	2
North Carolina	Not available	Not available	3
Ohio 2006	Approx. 8.59	Approx. 10.02	5
South Carolina 2004	5.6	5.5	3
Tennessee 2007	Not available	Not available	3
Texas 2007	Not available	Not available	3
Virginia 2004	24	17	Not available
Washington 2007	8.99	8.44	3

Adapted from Tienken, C. H. (2011). High school exit exams and mismeasurement. *Educational Forum, 4*(75), 298–314.

individuals in the field of educational testing like Messick (1996) and Koretz (2017), because even a small amount of CSEM can have severe consequences for students when SEA personnel do not account for it and instead simply require students to achieve a set cut score to demonstrate proficiency (Koretz, 2017), as do states in this study.

CSEM is a major issue that is not being addressed. We can be sure that perhaps hundreds of thousands of youth might have been potentially affected negatively in the NCLB era by what I perceive as inaction at the state and national levels to develop policy remedies aligned with standards and recommendations for appropriate testing practices.

Money, Money, Money

As introduced in a previous chapter, money matters when it comes to achievement on standardized tests. That's because standardized test results are susceptible to influences from the negative factors discussed in earlier chapters. The CSEM issue is even more potentially dangerous for students living in poverty. A review of test score data collected by the Center for Education Progress revealed that students labeled as economically disadvantaged, as a group, always score lower on all statewide and national exams, including all types of exit exams, than their non–economically disadvantaged peers.

The average effect size difference is greater than 0.50 in all cases in all states. Table 6.3 includes examples of effect size differences from several states' high school exams between students labeled as economically disadvantaged or eligible for free or reduced lunch and more advantaged students. The range of effect size in table 6.3 is 0.59 to 1.05, meaning if the average score of the non–economically disadvantaged group was at the 50th percentile, the group labeled as economically disadvantaged would score between the 30th and 14th percentiles, given the range of effect sizes. The effect size differences remain relatively consistent for statewide tests given in grades 3–11 (Tienken, 2011).

The Color of Poverty

In general, the relationship between poverty and test scores exists nationally on all state tests currently administered. According to an analysis of state test results data found on the Center on Education Policy website, at no grade level on any state test does the group of students labeled economically disadvantaged exhibit a higher mean score than the group of students labeled as non-economically disadvantaged.

Remember that one aim of the dual system of education is to provide benefits, through a better quality education, to the "haves" and relegate the "have-nots" to a more mechanistic, lower quality education. In the United States the association between quality education and less quality plays out in color; the color of children's skin because color associates with wealth in the United States.

Table 6.3. Example Mean Scale Scores and Effect Size Differences on Statewide High School Exams in Mathematics (M) and Reading/Language Arts (LA) for Students Labeled Economically Disadvantaged and Non-Disadvantaged

State	Economically Disadvantaged	Non-disadvantaged	Effect Size
CA (LA)	365.91	389.78	0.69
(M)	370.68	391.55	0.57
CT (LA)	211.40	254.50	1.05
(M)	218.20	264.30	1.02
DE (LA)	501.82	525.17	0.67
(M)	518.66	542.52	0.77
IL (LA)	148.39	159.69	0.81
(M)	147.62	160.60	0.94
PA (LA)	1220	1410	0.75
(M)	1210	1390	0.74
TX (LA)	2217	2296	0.60
(M)	2115	2217	0.59

Source: Tienken, C. H. (2010, fall). Social inequity and high school test scores: More strong correlations. *AASA Journal of Scholarship and Practice, 7*(3), 3–5.

The percentage of Black students living at or below the poverty line was approximately 22 percent, almost one in four, in 2018 and 19 percent of Hispanic students lived at or below the poverty line for a family of four. By comparison, only 9 percent of White students lived at or below the poverty line in 2018 (Kaiser Family Foundation, 2018). Black workers are paid only about 82 cents for every dollar paid to White workers, and Black unemployment approached twice as much as the rate for Whites in 2018 (Jones, Schmitt, & Wilson, 2018).

Median family wealth also favors White families, at a ratio of 10:1 compared to the median family wealth of Black families. The median family wealth for White families in 2018 was approximately $171,000, compared to $17,400 for Black families (Jones, Schmitt, & Wilson, 2018). Family wealth helps to provide more education support and resources and also pays for collateral learning opportunities like vacations and travel, extracurricular activities, summer camps, and other social capital resources. Family wealth results in lower college debt and the ability to pay for better colleges, and also transfers to children through inheritance.

Predictable Results

Results from studies conducted since 1999 in Michigan, Iowa, Connecticut, and Virginia have demonstrated consistently that family human capital and the social capital of the community in which a child lives and matures influence the child's achievement when measured by standardized test results (Darnell, 2015; Maylone, 2002; Sackey, 2014; Wilkins, 1999). Studies continue to demonstrate that standardized test results are influenced and can be predicted by family human capital and community social capital.

Caldwell (2017) predicted the percentage of students who would score proficient or above on the state tests of grade 4 mathematics and ELA in Massachusetts. The results suggest that language arts scores could be predicted for 73 percent of the school districts in the sample using just two variables: the percentage of families in a town with annual income less than $35,000 and the percentage of people in the community with a bachelor's degree. Likewise, the predictions for mathematics were accurate for 74 percent of the school districts using only two variables: percentage of households with income over $200,000 a year and the percentage of people in a community with bachelor's degrees.

Tienken and Lynch (2017) conducted a three-year longitudinal study that predicted test results in grades 6–8 for the New Jersey state-mandated standardized tests in mathematics and ELA for 70 percent and 78 percent of the schools in the samples, respectively. The samples ranged from 292 to 311 public schools that serviced grades 6–8 in New Jersey. The results suggested that in most cases three variables were able to predict the percentage of students in grades 6, 7, and 8 in each school who would score proficient or above on the New Jersey standardized tests: (1) percentage of families in a community with income over $200,000 a year, (2) percentage of people in a community in poverty, and (3) percentage of people in a community with bachelor's degrees. Tienken and colleagues conducted similar studies in grades 3,4,5, and 11 in New Jersey, Connecticut, and Iowa, finding similar results (Angelillo & Tienken, 2015; Maroun & Tienken, 2018; O'Leary, 2016; Tienken & Lynch, 2017; Tienken & Wolfe, 2014; Tienken & Turnamian, and Tramaglini, 2013).

Conclusions about State-Mandated Exams

Many countries around the world engage in standardized testing to sort students into academic and vocational tracks. Such countries overtly manage their social class structures and human capital. Sorting students in Europe via standardized testing is a leftover cultural practice from the days of the aristocracies and restrictive class systems. The meritocracy-based practice of sorting students is generally accepted culturally in other parts of the world, such as in some Asian countries, but it is not necessarily part of the democratic culture and ideals in the United States.

Those who hold equity-based views of education reject sorting systems, whether those systems are overt or covert. The public school system in the

United States is the only social institution that allows democratic values to be passed on to the next generation, and it is the only institution with the ability to socialize all Americans, citizens and immigrants alike, to the democratic ideals of the country (Commission on the Reorganization of Secondary Education, 1918). Sorting children into predetermined life trajectories or using tools and policies that result in de facto sorting is undemocratic and violates the right of individuals to pursue their own path.

The larger policy question remains: Given what is known about the limitations of standardized tests and the negative social and educational consequences to youth associated with their widespread use, do the ends (e.g., the mythical standardizing of the high school diploma) justify the means of using high-stakes tests with known technical flaws that effect score interpretation? Children do not have a seat at the decision-making table. Policy must speak for them. Adults make policy.

True Confessions from a High-Stakes Test Scorer

One brave soul, John Koudela III (2005), provided some very revealing insights into the scoring procedures used in the standard test industry. He submitted a report to Marda Kirkwood of Citizens United for Responsible Education (CURE), the essence of which is reported here with his permission.

At the time, Koudela held a BS degree and had been employed in the electronics manufacturing industry until he, like millions across America, was laid off from his job because of the cost-cutting functions of companies during the recession that started in 2001. He applied to a NCS Pearson Performance Scoring Center in 2003, while still continuing to seek work in his own field, and was hired to correct state high-stakes tests.

Allegedly, Pearson hired approximately 350 college-degreed individuals as a temporary employee pool to grade state high-stakes tests at $11.40 per hour. The work was full-time, five days a week, without benefits or days off. After two days of training, the fun began. Koudela observed that scorers discovered some test answers that were questionable, but that fact could not be discussed. Test scorers were told to accept only those answers approved by the Range Finding Committee regardless of their own college-educated knowledge base.

However, scoring criteria did change as scorers came up with more student test answers that were found to be acceptable but were not in the original rubrics. Those new answers were approved by supervisors on the spot, as was apparently allowed, although scorers were told that they were not to worry about rescoring previous tests that might also contain those correct answers.

One day's "correct" answers for a given question would be suddenly changed, and answers that had been wrong were suddenly correct! Whatever rubrics or criteria for grading were changed, it was of no concern to scorers; they were instructed to simply meet the work quota as accurately as they could with the approved answers. Scorers were constantly reminded about how many tests they needed to finish each day and how many days were left to score the remaining tests.

Each day, scorers were pushed by supervisors to read more tests. There were very few scorers who had both a high number of reads and high reliability percentages. More than thirty-eight different criteria were ultimately listed for just one open-ended science question alone. At the end of scoring a test, scorers were ordered to destroy all the notes they collected to assist them in scoring test answers.

Koudela closed his report stating, "Conformance was the main issue, not students' ability to logically arrive at their answers or rely on their own experience! This was true of all test scoring of all test answers." Test scorers were reminded daily to remember that "the chair is orange, if the 'committee' says so."

Not an Isolated Case

Providing more data and additional credibility to Koudela's report is the August 27, 2000, headline by reporter Jolayne Houtz of the *Seattle Times*: "Temps spend just minutes to score state test; A WASL math problem may take 20 seconds and essay, 2-1/2 minutes." The reporter visited the Iowa City NCS test-scoring facility. (NCS was purchased by Pearson PLC of the United Kingdom for $2.5 billion in 2000.)

Houtz reported that the scorers work at "assembly-line pace" and read as many as 180 writing essays a day with an average of two and a half minutes per essay. Houtz noted that nine of ten WASL exams were graded by a single reader and even if a second reader scored the exam, the first reader's score counted. In the year 2000, NCS expected to hand-score 82 million student responses. She quoted one NCS scorer as saying that when the pressure built to meet deadlines, supervisors announced: "Don't pay as much attention to accuracy." Houtz was never asked to withdraw her reported statements.

Take That!

Pearson replaced its human scoring system with an artificial intelligence system and started scoring more of its PARCC and other state mandated tests partially or entirely through the use of computer algorithms starting with the 2015–2016 testing season. Limitations of artificial intelligence scoring quickly made themselves known. New Jersey serves as a case study for the possible negative effects of artificial scoring. The state had a precipitous increase in the number of students who scored a 0 on the writing portion of the PARCC test in 2018, the year Pearson switched to 100 percent artificial intelligence scoring.

Some district leaders in New Jersey petitioned the New Jersey Department of Education to investigate the situation. At first, the department ignored the requests. Finally, after the issue reached a fever pitch, the department set up a meeting between a representative group of school superintendents and representatives from the Department of Education and Pearson. Pearson sent its team of lawyers to the meeting, and as of 2020, no comprehensive explanation that answered the superintendents' questions was given for the strange drop in scores.

Pearson and the New Jersey Department refused to release any details about the computer algorithm (scoring rubric) used by the artificial intelligence program. Not releasing details about the underlying scoring algorithm is problematic because it is the algorithm that becomes the actual scoring criteria, not the state writing standards. It is impossible to know if there is a mismatch between what the artificial intelligence program expects for writing proficiency and the state standards without seeing the algorithm.

POINTS TO REMEMBER

A social contract has long been made where organized societies and governments initiate interrelationships that support their citizenry. This social contract has been made to support public education by virtue of the Tenth Amendment to the US Constitution and the respective state constitutions. This unwritten contract endorses a positive support base for all school-aged youth. The No Child Left Behind Act, the Every Student Succeeds Act, Common Core State Standards, and other corporate education programs subversively negated this contract by removing the word "social" and substituting the word "corporate."

The corporate contract means that the schools are no longer social institutions with the primary mission of serving and educating youth. Current policy endorses a corporate-profit model instead. Millions of youth will fall into the social junkyard because they did not perform mechanistically like a programmed machine on one high-stakes test. Corporate-Ed USA has no need for losers. Only winners are rewarded by Corporate-Ed USA.

A LOOK AHEAD

Chapter 7 explores the Common Core State Standards initiative and provides evidence to suggest that both the project and the series of standardized curricula it spawned were misguided. Perhaps the most astonishing thing about the CCSS project is that there is no empirical evidence to support it. The chapter argues forcefully that standardization and homogenization of children is not only morally bankrupt, but empirically vapid as well.

NOTE

I thank the *Clearing House* journal for permission to use excerpts in this chapter from Orlich's "The No Child Left Behind Act: An Illogical Accountability Model" *78*(1), September/October 2004, 6–11. I also thank Dr. David C. Berliner for his insights leading to the section on the social contract.

REFERENCES

American Educational Research Association, American Psychological Association, & National Council on Measurement in Education. (1999). *Standards for educational and psychological testing*. Washington, DC: American Educational Research Association.

American Educational Research Association, American Psychological Association, & National Council on Measurement in Education. (2014). *Standards for educational and psychological testing*, 7th ed. Washington, DC: AERA.

Amrein, A. L., & Berliner, D. C. (2002a). High-stakes testing, uncertainty and student learning. *Educational Policy Analysis Archives*, *10*(18), 1–56. Review at https://epaa.asu.edu/ojs/article/viewFile/297/423

Amrein, A. L., & Berliner, D. C. (2002b). *An analysis of some unintended and negative consequences of high-stakes testing*. Tempe: Education Policy Research Unit, Education Policy Studies Laboratory, Arizona State University.

Angelillo, C., & Tienken, C. H. (2015). *Predicting grade 8 standardized test results using family census data: A statewide study*. Paper presented at the annual conference of the National Council of Professors of Educational Administration, August 6, 2015, Washington, DC.

Booher-Jennings, J. (2005). Below the bubble: "Educational triage" and the Texas accountability system. *American Educational Research Journal*, *42*(2), 231–68.

Borg, M., Plumlee, P., & Stranahan, H. (2007). Plenty of children left behind: High-stakes testing and graduation rates in Duval County, Florida. Educational Policy, *2*, 695–716.

Braun, H. (2004). Reconsidering the impact of high-stakes testing. *Education Policy Analysis Archives 12*(1). Review at http://epaa.asu.edu/ojs/article/view/157

Burch, P. (2005). The new educational privatization: Educational contracting and high-stakes accountability. *Teachers College Record*. Retrieved from http://www.tcrecord.org/content.asp?contentid=12259

Caldwell, D. G. (2017). *The influence of socioeconomic, parental and district factors on the 2013 MCAS Grade 4 language arts and mathematics scores*. Seton Hall University Dissertations and Theses (ETDs). Paper 2251.

Commission on the Reorganization of Secondary Education. (1918). *Cardinal principles of secondary education*. Bulletin No. 35. Washington, DC: US Bureau of Education.

Darnell, B. (2015). *The value of Iowa school district demographic data in explaining school district ITBS/ITED 3rd and 11th grade language arts and mathematics scores*. Seton Hall University Dissertations and Theses (ETDs). Paper 2075.

Dewey, J. (1929). *The sources of a science of education*. New York: Liveright.

Education Commission of the States. (2008). *State notes: Exit exams*. Denver, CO: Author. Retrieved from http://mb2.ecs.org/reports/Report.aspx?id=1357

Haney, W. (2002, May 6). Lake Woebeguaranteed: Misuse of test scores in Massachusetts, Part I. *Education Policy Analysis Archives, 10*(24). Review at http://epaa.asu.edu/ojs/article/view/303

Harville, L. M. (1991). Standard error of measurement. *Educational Measurement: Issues and Practices, 10*(2): 33–41.

Houtz, J. (2000, August 27). Temps spend just minutes to score state test: A WASL math problem may take 20 seconds; an essay, 2-1/2, minutes. *Seattle Times*.

Jones, J., Schmitt, J., & Wilson, V. (2018, February 26). 50 years after the Kerner Commission: African Americans are better off in many ways but are still disadvantaged by racial inequality. *Economic Policy Institute*. Retrieved from https://www.epi.org/publication/50-years-after-the-kerner-commission/

Kaiser Family Foundation. (2018). Poverty rates by race/ethnicity. Author. Retrieved from https://www.kff.org/other/state-indicator/poverty-rate-by-raceethnicity/

Koudela, J. III. (2005, February). *On scoring of OPT/WASL educational assessments*. Report submitted to Marda Kirkwood, Citizens United for Responsible Education, Burien, WA. (Reported with permission.)

Koretz, D. (2017). *The testing charade: Pretending to make schools better*. Chicago: University of Chicago Press.

Levin, H. M. (2009). The economic payoff to investing in educational justice. *Educational Researcher, 38*(1), 5–20.

Maroun, J., & Tienken, C. H. (2018). *Predicting PARCC algebra and English language arts results from human and social capital variables*. Paper presented at the Annual Conference of the University Council for Educational Administration, November 15, 2018, Houston, TX.

Maylone, N. (2002). *The relationship of socioeconomic factors and district scores on the Michigan educational assessment program tests: An analysis*. Unpublished doctoral dissertation. Eastern Michigan University, Ypsilanti, MI.

McMillan, J. H. (2004). *Classroom assessment: Principles and practice for effective instruction*. New York: Pearson.

Messick, S. (1996). Validity of performance assessments. In G. W. Phillips (Ed.), *Technical issues in large-scale performance assessment* (pp. 1–18). Washington, DC: National Center for Educational Statistics.

New Jersey Department of Education. (2015). Technical Report: New Jersey High School Proficiency Assessment. Spring 2015. Measurement Incorporated. Trenton, NJ. Retrieved from https://www.state.nj.us/education/assessment/hs/hspa/info/15TechReport.pdf

O'Leary, K. A. (2016). *The predictive accuracy of family and community demographic factors on the 2011, 2012, and 2013, grade 6 Connecticut Mastery Test*. Seton Hall University Dissertations and Theses (ETDs). Paper 2208.

Orlich, D. C. (2003). An examination of the longitudinal effect of the Washington Assessment of Student Learning (WASL) on student achievement. *Education Policy Analysis Archives, 11*(18). Review at http://epaa.asu.edu/ojs/issues/view/vol11

Partnership for Assessment of Readiness for College and Careers. (2019). Final technical report for the 2018 administration. Retrieved from https://files.eric.ed.gov/fulltext/ED599198.pdf

Polikoff, M. (2015). How well aligned are textbooks to the Common Core Standards in mathematics. *American Educational Research Journal, 52*(6), 1185–1211.

Sackey, A. N. L. Jr. (2014). *The influence of community demographics on student achievement on the Connecticut Mastery Test in mathematics and English language arts in grade 3 through 8*. (Unpublished doctoral dissertation). Seton Hall University, South Orange, NJ.

Sanger, D. (1978, April 3). Is "competency" good enough? *New York Times*.

Schmidt, W. H., McKnight, C. C., Houang, R. T., Wang, H. A., Wiley, D. E., Cogan, L. S., & Wolfe, R. G. (2001). *Why schools matter: A cross-national comparison of curriculum and learning*. San Francisco: Jossey-Bass.

Taylor, S. C. (1857). *Rime of the ancient mariner*. New York: Appleton.

Thompson, B. (2002). *Score reliability: Contemporary thinking on reliability issues*. New York: Sage.

Tienken, C. H. (2011). Structured inequity: The intersection of socioeconomic status and the standard error of measurement of state mandated high school test results. In B. J. Alford, G. Derreault, L. Zellner, and J. W. Ballenger (eds.), *Blazing new trails: Preparing leaders to improve and access and equity in today's schools.* Lancaster, PA: Desteeh Publications. Retrieved from https://files.eric.ed.gov/fulltext/ED523595.pdf

Tienken, C. H., & Lynch, C. (2017). *What standardized test results really tell us.* Paper presented at the Kappa Delta Pi International Honor Society Annual Conference, October 28, 2017, Pittsburgh, PA.

Tienken. C. H., & Rodriguez, O. (2010). The error of state mandated high school exams. *Academic Exchange Quarterly, 14*(2), 50–55.

Tienken, C. H., Turnamian, P., & Tramaglini, T.W. (2013). *Predicting the percentage of grade 3 students scoring proficient by using community wealth demographics.* Paper presented at the American Educational Research Association, April 28, 2013, San Francisco, CA.

Tienken, C. H., & Wolfe, A. (2014). *Three-year predictions of grade 5 state test results using community census data.* Paper presented at the National Council of Professors of Educational Administration Conference, August 6, 2014, Camarillo, CA.

Wilkins, J. L. M. (1999). Demographic opportunities and school achievement. *Journal of Research in Education, 9*(1), 12–19.

Wilson, R. J. (1999). Aspects of validity in large-scale programs of student assessment. *Alberta Journal of Educational Research, 45*(4), 333–43.

Chapter Seven

World-Class Standards That Are Too Big to Fail

The first installment of what became de facto national standards, the Common Core State Standards, represented a natural evolution of the ongoing attempts to homogenize and standardize public schooling. The ideas for mass standardization of education processes and output put forth were not much different from those presented by the Committee of Ten and Committee of Fifteen in 1893 and 1895, respectively, and Taylor's (1911) scientific management approach.

DEFACTO NATIONAL STANDARDS

Enter the Common Core State Standards Initiative

In March 2010, governors and education bureaucrats from forty-eight states, two US territories, and the District of Columbia endorsed the development and implementation of a common core of curriculum standards for mathematics and English language arts in grades K–12. Achieve, Inc., the Business Roundtable, the US Chamber of Commerce, the Gates Foundation, and a host of other business-oriented organizations supported the CCSS. The marketing of the CCSS included many of the typical catchphrases found in neoliberal education reform literature:

- Alignment with college and work expectations
- Internationally benchmarked to help students compete in the global marketplace

- Inclusion of rigorous content *and* application of knowledge through high-order skills
- Research-based development

Since 2010, approximately twenty-five states claimed to have either "revised" their content standards away from the CCSS or dumped the CCSS all together. The claims are fraudulent. Many states headed by Republican governors that originally adopted the CCSS began renaming them in 2014 and 2015 ahead of the 2016 presidential election because of intense political backlash against corporate standardization of education. Presidential hopefuls such as former New Jersey governor Chris Christie and Ohio governor John Kasich were racing to be the first to say they "dumped the Common Core" as they hit the campaign trail.

I conducted a review of the standards from states that "revised" or renamed the CCSS. The substance of the standards in those states did not change much at all. Some states changed the name from Common Core State Standards—for example, in New Jersey, to the New Jersey State Learning Standards—yet the content of the renamed standards was almost 100 percent identical to the CCSS. Other states maintained about 85 percent of the CCSS content. Most of the twenty-five states also maintained their CCSS-aligned standardized assessments. If states really made substantial changes or dumped the CCSS, then they should have made substantial changes to their student assessments. That did not happen.

Deeper Learning, Less Standards

One purported goal of the CCSS process was to produce a set of fewer, clearer, and higher-level thinking standards. Existing state standards were criticized as being a mile wide and an inch deep. When one actually dissects the CCSS standards into the specific learning objectives necessary to teach them, one sees that there are not fewer, clearer standards. There is actually more content for teachers to teach and more for students to acquire when you break the CCSS statements down into their teachable objectives. Another issue is that some of the standards are overly difficult and outside the range of normal cognitive development of the students, particularly at the K–3 levels.

Below is a breakdown of the grade 2 CCSS mathematics standard 2.OA.A.1 into its teachable objectives and their approximate cognitive developmental levels aligned to Piagetian (1950) theory based on later research by Shayer and Adey (1981). Shayer and Adey separated Piaget's concrete operations stage into early concrete and advanced concrete based on observable and important differences between student cognitive development within the concrete operations stage. They also separated formal operations into early formal and late formal. (See table 7.1.) The individual objectives of the example second grade CCSS math standard below align most closely with early concrete and advanced concrete stages. The standard itself actually has four distinct parts.

> Standard Statement (2.OA.A.1): *Represent and solve problems involving addition and subtraction. Use addition and subtraction within 100 to solve one- and two-step word problems involving situations of adding to, taking from, putting together, taking apart, and comparing, with unknowns in all positions, e.g., by using drawings and equations with a symbol for the unknown number to represent the problem.*
>
> Individual Objectives:
>
> Part 1:
>
> 1a. Use addition within 100 to solve one-step word problems involving situations of adding to with unknowns in all positions by using drawings, with a symbol for the unknown number to represent the problem. Cognitive level: *Early Concrete*
>
> 1b. Use addition within 100 to solve one-step word problems involving situations of taking from unknowns in all positions by using drawings, with a symbol for the unknown number to represent the problem. Cognitive level: *Early Concrete*
>
> 1c. Use addition within 100 to solve one-step word problems involving situations of putting together with unknowns in all positions by using drawings, with a symbol for the unknown number to represent the problem. Cognitive level: *Early Concrete*
>
> 1d. Use addition within 100 to solve one-step word problems involving situations of taking apart with unknowns in all positions by using drawings, with a symbol for the unknown number to represent the problem. Cognitive level: *Early Concrete*
>
> 1e. Use addition within 100 to solve one-step word problems involving situations of comparing with unknowns in all positions by using drawings, with a symbol for the unknown number to represent the problem. Cognitive level: *Early Concrete*
>
> Part 2:
>
> 2a. Use subtraction within 100 to solve one-step word problems involving situations of adding to with unknowns in all positions by using drawings, with a symbol for the unknown number to represent the problem. Cognitive level: *Early Concrete*
>
> 2b. Use subtraction within 100 to solve one-step word problems involving situations taking from unknowns in all positions by using drawings, with a symbol for the unknown number to represent the problem. Cognitive level: *Early Concrete*
>
> 2c. Use subtraction within 100 to solve one-step word problems involving situations putting together with unknowns in all positions by using drawings, with a symbol for the unknown number to represent the problem. Cognitive level: *Early Concrete*
>
> 2d. Use subtraction within 100 to solve one-step word problems involving situations of taking apart with unknowns in all positions by using drawings,

with a symbol for the unknown number to represent the problem. Cognitive level: *Early Concrete*

2e. Use subtraction within 100 to solve one-step word problems involving situations of comparing to with unknowns in all positions by using drawings, with a symbol for the unknown number to represent the problem. Cognitive level: *Early Concrete*

Part 3.

3a. Use addition within 100 to solve two-step word problems involving situations of adding to with unknowns in all positions by using drawings, with a symbol for the unknown number to represent the problem. Cognitive level: *Advanced Concrete*

3b. Use addition within 100 to solve two-step word problems involving situations of taking from unknowns in all positions by using drawings, with a symbol for the unknown number to represent the problem. Cognitive level: *Advanced Concrete*

3c. Use addition within 100 to solve two-step word problems involving situations of putting together with unknowns in all positions by using drawings, with a symbol for the unknown number to represent the problem. Cognitive level: *Advanced Concrete*

3d. Use addition within 100 to solve two-step word problems involving situations of taking apart with unknowns in all positions by using drawings, with a symbol for the unknown number to represent the problem. Cognitive level: *Advanced Concrete*

3e. Use addition within 100 to solve two-step word problems involving situations of comparing with unknowns in all positions by using drawings, with a symbol for the unknown number to represent the problem. Cognitive level: *Advanced Concrete*

Part 4:

4a. Use subtraction within 100 to solve two-step word problems involving situations of adding to with unknowns in all positions by using drawings, with a symbol for the unknown number to represent the problem. Cognitive level: *Advanced Concrete*

4b. Use subtraction within 100 to solve two-step word problems involving situations taking from unknowns in all positions by using drawings, with a symbol for the unknown number to represent the problem. Cognitive level: *Advanced Concrete*

4c. Use subtraction within 100 to solve two-step word problems involving situations putting together with unknowns in all positions by using drawings, with a symbol for the unknown number to represent the problem. Cognitive level: *Advanced Concrete*

4d. Use subtraction within 100 to solve two-step word problems involving situations of taking apart with unknowns in all positions by using drawings, with a symbol for the unknown number to represent the problem. Cognitive level: *Advanced Concrete*

4e. Use subtraction within 100 to solve two-step word problems involving situations of comparing to with unknowns in all positions by using drawings, with a symbol for the unknown number to represent the problem. Cognitive level: *Advanced Concrete*

This single second grade standard contained at least twenty individual objectives to teach, learn, and assess. That does not seem like more depth and less breadth.

Cognitive Conundrum

Half of the individual objectives from the grade 2 standard listed above require advanced concrete thinking to master. Students must be able to manipulate numbers and ideas in their heads when taking from, adding to, comparing, or taking apart unknowns in all positions of an algorithm to accomplish half of the objectives listed. In effect, major portions of the standard include the beginning of an algebraic equation in which a student must solve for a missing number. Some students in grade 2 still need to use manipulatives or have some other type of concrete experience first before engaging in more abstract work. They need to be able to "see it" in a form that is not symbolic, not a mathematical algorithm or equation.

Most students might be able to engage in more abstract work without the use of concrete supports, but they might not be able to demonstrate mastery. They can learn how to do the math, but just can't do it consistently enough to be considered to have mastered it. Problems occur when students are mandated to master content that is outside of the average developmental levels of their chronological ages. Students can be incorrectly labeled "not proficient" or "at-risk" or saddled with some other deficiency-oriented label. That label could simply be the result of a mismatch between the cognitive level of the standard and normal levels of cognitive development of children.

Table 7.2, adapted from Epstein (2002), presents the average percentage of general education students (non–cognitively disabled) in an average town, within an average ecological system, who are at each cognitive level of mastery by chronological age and associated grade level. The left side of the chart lists ages and grade levels and the cognitive levels are listed across the top. The table indicates that only about 10 percent of students in grade 2, at age eight, can be expected to have mastered advanced concrete operations. That *does not* mean eight-year-olds cannot learn content at abstract levels or think at abstract levels. It simply means eight-year-olds should not be expected to master content at abstract levels. Expecting all eight-year-olds to demonstrate mastery with content at the advanced concrete operations level is similar to asking all eight-month-old babies to walk. Both expectations are developmentally inappropriate.

Table 7.2 indicates that 55 percent of the students at age eight are in early concrete operations in terms of their learning mastery. This fact should inform educators that they need to present the more abstract portions of the grade 2 standards in concrete formats first and allow students to use concrete methods to work with such content. The cognitive developmental levels of

Table 7.1. Selected Concepts with Piagetian Descriptors Illustrating Concrete to Formal Development of a Child's Interaction with the World

Topic	Early Concrete	Late Concrete	Early Formal	Late Formal
Investigative Style	Unaided style does not produce models	Can serially order and classify objects	Is confused, needs interpretive model	Generates and checks possible explanations
Relationships	Can order a series but cannot make summarization	Readily uses the notion of reversibility	Can begin to use two independent variables	Reflects on reciprocal relationship between variables
Use of Models	Simple comparisons, one to one	Simple models: e.g. gearbox, skeleton	Deductive comparisons and models are taken as being true	Searches for explanatory model, uses proportional thinking
Categorizations	Objects are classified by one criterion: e.g., color, size	Partially orders and classifies hierarchically	Generalizes to impose meaning over wide range of phenomena	Abstract ideas generated, search for underlying associations
Proportionality	Needs whole sets to double or halve	Makes inferences from constant ratios and with whole numbers only	Makes inferences on ratio variables — Density=Mass/Volume	Knows direct and inverse relationship ratios
Mathematical Operations	Number is distinguished from size or shape	Works single operations but needs closure	Generalizes by concrete examples and accepts lack of closure	Conceives of a variable properly
Probabilistic Thinking	No notions of probability	Given equal number of objects knows there is 50/50 chance of one being drawn	Given set of objects can express chances in simple fractions	

Source: Shayer, M., & Adey, P. (1981). *Towards a science of science teaching: Cognitive development and curriculum demand.* London: Heinemann. Abstracted from table 8.1, pp. 72–78.

Table 7.2. Percentage of Students at Piagetian Cognitive Levels

Age	Grade	Intuition	Entry Concrete (a)	Advanced Concrete (b)	Entry Formal (a)	Middle Formal (b)
5.5	P	78	22			
6	K	68	27	5		
7	1	35	55	10		
8	2	25	55	20		
9	3	15	55	30		
10	4	12	52	35	1	
11	5	6	49	40	5	
12	6–7	5	32	51	12	
13	7–8	2	34	44	14	6
14	8–9	1	32	43	15	9
15	9–10	1	15	53	18	13
16	10–11	1	13	50	17	19
16–17	11–12	3	19	47	19	12
17–18	12	1	15	50	15	19
Adult	—	20	22	26	17	15

Table derived by Herman T. Epstein, personal communication, June 8, 1999. See also Epstein (2002). Level (a) in each category is composed of children who have just begun to manifest one or two of that level's reasoning schemes, while level (b) refers to children manifesting a half dozen or more reasoning schemes.

Smedslund, J. (1964). *Concrete reasoning: A study of intellectual development*. Lafayette, IN: Child Development Publications of the Society for Research in Child Development.

Arlin, P. K. (1975). Cognitive development in adulthood: A fifth phase. *Developmental Psychology*, 11: 602–6.

Wei, T. T. D., Lavatelli, C. B., and Jones, R. S. (1971). Piaget's concept of classification: A comparative study of socially disadvantaged and middle-class young children. *Child Development*, 42(3): 919–27.

Renner, J. W., Stafford, D. G., Lawson, A. E., McKinnon, J. W., Friot, F. E. and Kellogg, D. H. (1976). *Research, teaching and learning with the Piaget model*. Norman: University of Oklahoma Press.

Shayer, M., and Adey, P. (1981). *Towards a science of science teaching*. London: Heinemann.

students should also inform policymakers and education bureaucrats, as they set mastery targets and student achievement expectations on standardized tests.

Expecting 70, 80, 90, or 100 percent of students to master standards that are outside the normal developmental range of the majority of students is developmentally inappropriate. It is equally inappropriate to create high-stakes punishments for students and educators when students do not meet standards outside the average developmental levels. Creating accountability systems that mandate the mastery of developmentally inappropriate content is educational malpractice.

COMPLEXITY AND DIFFICULTY

The supporters of standardized curricula always claim their standards require greater emphasis on higher-level thinking than previous state standards. Dewey (1916) described two types of thinking that students can experience in school settings: higher-level and lower level. Dewey's conception of higher-level thinking includes the student engaging in original thinking with a purpose for eventually being able to use knowledge for taking action: action to solve a socially conscious problem. Socially conscious problem solving requires complex thinking: the interaction of academic content knowledge and active use of personal experience to generate original solutions to ill-defined problems, problems with more than one possible solution.

Although the conceptions of higher-level thinking in education are diverse, there appears to be a general theme in the research literature. Higher-level thinking includes purposeful, original thinking on the part of the student that can result in different outcomes or solutions. There is not a predetermined answer that the curriculum standard presupposes in most cases of higher-level thinking. Higher-level thinking is more divergent than lower-level thinking, which is aimed at remembering something, literally comprehending material, or following a prescribed process to arrive at a predetermined answer.

According to Webb (1997), thinking encompasses multiple dimensions, including the "level of cognitive complexity of information students should be expected to know, how well they should be able to transfer the knowledge to different contexts, how well they should be able to form generalizations, and how much prerequisite knowledge they must have in order to grasp ideas" (p. 15). Webb categorized thinking into four levels, known as Webb's Depth of Knowledge (DOK). The DOK levels define and categorize cognitive complexity of curriculum standards and tasks. The "DOK level of an item does not refer to how easy or difficult a test item is for students" (Wyse

& Viger, 2011, p. 188). The focus of DOK is on the cognitive complexity of required tasks or curriculum standards as opposed to difficulty.

DIFFERENCES BETWEEN DIFFICULTY AND COMPLEXITY

The differences between difficulty and complexity can be thought of as the difference between remembering a fact or imitating a procedure and developing an original solution, product, or process. Remembering facts and imitating procedures are less cognitively complex than developing an original solution, product, or process.

Difficulty is a static component of a learning objective or curriculum standard that refers to the amount of effort or work a student must expend to complete a task, and it frequently manifests itself in lower-level knowledge. Dewey (1916) described low-level knowledge when he wrote,

> Frequently it [knowledge] is treated as an end itself, and then the goal becomes to heap it up and display it when called for. This static, cold-storage idea of knowledge is inimical to educative development. It not only lets occasions for thinking go unused, but it swamps thinking . . . Pupils who have stored their "minds" with all kinds of material which they have never put to intellectual uses are sure to be hampered when they try to think . . . everything is on the same dead static level. (p. 114)

Asking students to solve a mathematics addition problem with two one-digit numbers is less difficult than solving an addition problem with four one-digit numbers. The complexity is at the "remember and imitate procedure" levels for both problems, but the second problem is theoretically more difficult because it requires more effort on the part of students to add more numbers. There is not original thinking involved in either addition problem. There are just more steps and more effort required. The complexity of thinking for both problems resides at the recall and imitation of procedure levels.

Solving multistep computation problems represents static thinking: recalling information from cold storage to arrive at predetermined answers. The multistep addition problems do not require complex thinking regardless of the amount of effort it takes a student to solve them. Difficulty only reinforces imitation and regurgitation of information and processes.

The Complexity of the CCSS and Its Spawn

Fitzhugh, Tienken, and Burns (2019) compared the revised 2017 New Jersey mathematics standards in grades 4–8 to the pre-CCSS version of New Jersey math standards. They found the pre-CCSS version of the mathematics standards included more higher-level thinking than the new version. Almost 30 percent of the pre-CCSS math standards in grades 4 and 5 in New Jersey required higher-order thinking compared to 1 percent of the CCSS-based 2017 standards. Similarly, 40 percent of the pre-CCSS middle school math standards required higher-level thinking compared to 28 percent of the 2017 standards.

Jarmon (2018) conducted a study that compared the pre-CCSS Massachusetts English language arts standards in grades 9–12 to the CCSS. Jarmon found the pre-CCSS standards included more higher-level thinking than the CCSS, 62 percent to 45 percent. Sforza, Tienken, and Kim (2016) compared the pre-CCSS New Jersey ELA and mathematics standards in grades 9–12 to the CCSS. We found the pre-CCSS ELA standards contained more higher-order thinking than the CCSS, 38 percent to 28 percent. The pre-CCSS New Jersey mathematics standards in grades 9–12 also required more higher-order thinking than the CCSS, 38 percent to 28 percent. Burns (2017) found that 40 percent of the pre-CCSS middle school math standards required higher-order thinking compared to just 28 percent of the CCSS.

Tienken, Sforza, and Burns (2017) compared the cognitive complexity of the pre-CCSS California ELA standards in grades 9–12 to the CCSS and found more higher-order thinking in the pre-CCSS versions. Almost 70 percent of the 1997 California ELA standards required some form of higher-order thinking, whereas only 28 percent of the CCSS required such thinking.

Translating the CCSS

The writers of the CCSS stated they "made unprecedented use of evidence" in deciding what to include—or not include—in the standards. In *no* case was there any field or pilot testing of any standard in a classroom. What the writers call evidence and research simply comes down to the opinions of individuals or organizations. Below are my pithy rebuttals of some of the CCSS claims.

Evidence Based

The vendors claimed they developed the CCSS based on the best available evidence. *Rebuttal:* Absolutely *no* experimental or control groups were used to evaluate the quality or efficacy of the standards! Empirical methods were not used to determine the efficacy of these standards. There is no independently verified empirical evidence supporting this initiative (Tienken, 2011). This point is most critical, because once again we see a batch of brief enthusiasms and ideological advocacy labeled as research! Thus, any revised content standards derived from the CCSS are likely not to be evidence based.

Internationally Benchmarked

The vendors claim that these standards are mirrors of standards of high-performing countries and states so that all students are prepared to succeed in a global economy and society. *Rebuttal:* The CCSS creators copied some language from some of the best test-taking nations, but we have no evidence that the ideas copied have any positive influence on student learning in the United States.

Appropriate for Special Populations

The standards are written with inclusionary language, or so the vendors tell us. *Rebuttal:* The creators of the CCSS assume the standards are accessible to different learners, but because the CCSS were never field tested prior to launch, the vendors do not have data to support the assertion.

Assessment

The authors of the CCSS claim that they did not develop an assessment system yet they supported the idea of a national system of standardized testing. *Rebuttal:* The creators of the CCSS did state that these standards will ultimately be the basis for an assessment system that will be a "national" assessment to monitor implementation. That is exactly what happened with tests such as Partnership for Assessment of Readiness for College and Careers and Smarter Balanced Assessment Consortium (SBAC). Although those consortia collapsed, their CCSS-aligned test item banks live on in revised state tests. Although almost all states dumped the PARCC, students in almost twenty states continue to be exposed to PARCC questions on revised state tests.

Twenty-First-Century Skills

The CCSS focuses on two areas—ELA and mathematics. The vendors claim that the standards incorporated twenty-first-century skills where possible. *Rebuttal:* The creators of the CCSS relegate twenty-first-century skills to a narrow conception of mathematics and English language arts. There is no guidance in the standards on how to develop authentic twenty-first-century skills such as (1) strategizing, (2) entrepreneurship, (3) persistence, (4) empathy, (5) socially conscious problem solving, (6) cross-cultural collaboration and cooperation, (7) intellectual and social curiosity, (8) compassion, (9) risk taking, (10) challenging the status quo, (11) leadership, or (12) creativity.

The vendors of the CCSS focus on the acquisition of content knowledge and the use of skills such as memory, verbal, and auditory, all skills that the World Economic Forum (2018) cited as having declining demand in the global economy. Memory, verbal, and auditory skills are already being replaced by artificial intelligence. The World Economic Forum surveyed 313 businesses in twenty of the world's largest economies, representing 70 percent of the world's gross domestic product, to determine the ten most important skills in highest demand in 2022 to 2030 (p. 12).

1. Analytical thinking and innovation
2. Active learning and learning strategies
3. Creativity, originality, and initiative
4. Technology design and programming
5. Critical thinking and analysis
6. Complex problem solving
7. Leadership and social influence
8. Emotional intelligence
9. Problem solving and ideation
10. Systems analysis and evaluation

None of the skills on the list are included in the CCSS.

Some might argue that analytical thinking is part of the CCSS, and those people might point to the fact that the word "analysis" is found in many of the CCSS standards. Although the word "analysis" is found throughout the CCSS, the focus of analysis in the CCSS is on finding a predetermined answer—the correct answer. That is different than analyzing to make sense of complex situations in which one correct answer does not exist. The CCSS focus on the analysis of certainty, whereas the real world requires analysis of uncertainty.

State Led and Collaborative

Another claim made about the CCSS is that it was a state-led initiative and collaborative, with many different stakeholders taking part. Many stakeholders were involved, just not from public education. Karp (2013) explained the characteristics of the main participants of the final versions of the CCSS when he wrote, "The standards were drafted largely behind closed doors by academics and assessment experts, many with ties to testing companies" (p. 13). Cody (2013) reported other associations between the CCSS and the business world:

> A "confidential" process was under way, involving 27 people on two Work Groups, including a significant number from the testing industry. Here are the affiliations of those 27: ACT (6), the College Board (6), Achieve Inc. (8), Student Achievement Partners (2), America's Choice (2). Only three participants were outside of these five organizations. Only one classroom teacher was involved—on the committee to review the math standards. (p. 1)

Karp (2013) and Cody (2013) reported that there was not representation by early childhood or primary grades K–3 educators on any CCSS committees. The K–12 educators were brought in at the end of the process to rubber-stamp the completed standards. The corporate education bias against public education in the development of CCSS was reinforced by the amount of private money used to market the standards. For instance, the Gates Foundation reportedly spent more than $160 million to promote the CCSS from 2010–2015, with other, smaller foundations also spending funds to do the same (Simon & Shah, 2013; Tienken, 2017). Mullen (2016) identified other edu-businesses that contributed to the support of the CCSS, like the College Board, the Broad Foundation, America's Promise Alliance, and Pearson, to name a few.

Frankly Speaking

The CCSS were not an improvement over the plethora of existing state standards. The CCSS were simply another list of standardized objectives. Ohanian (1999) cautioned that standardization schemes are usually camouflaged as improvements to the system, but they end up deskilling and deprofessionalizing teachers through reliance on canned programs. Standardization marginalizes children by making them fit into a mechanistic, one-size-fits-all education program instead of helping each child achieve his or her unique potential. All the benefits of standardization go to the edu-corporations.

Most large publishers had new texts on the market soon after the CCSS were released. It seemed as if publishers like Pearson had the books on the shelves ready to go before the CCSS were even released. The CCSS were supposed to be drastically different than what existed, yet within weeks of their release new CCSS materials were available for purchase.

Some state boards of education, like New Jersey, actually mandated school district use of the CCSS less than a year after they were released. Almost six hundred school districts had to purchase brand-new texts with millions of dollars of taxpayer money. It did not matter if the school district personnel had just revised their curricula and purchased new texts two years earlier. All that was now obsolete. The CCSS were a subsidy for text and test publishers. The CCSS were all about the business of education.

Common Core Standards: Where's That Evidence?

The CCSS do little to promote global literacy through cultural collaboration and cooperation. They do not stress socially conscious problem solving or strategizing. They are inert, sterile, socially static standards focused on having students arrive at predetermined answers.

When I reviewed the body of evidence offered by the National Governors Association (NGA), I found that it was not large (Tienken, 2011). The evidence was built mostly on one report, *Benchmarking for Success* (National Governors Association, Council of Chief State School Officers, & Achieve, Inc., 2008). That report was created by the same groups that created the standards, hardly independent research. The *Benchmarking* report had more than 135 endnotes, some of which were repetitive references. Only four of the cited pieces of evidence in the report could be considered empirical studies related to the topics of national standards and student achievement. The remaining citations were newspaper stories, armchair magazine articles, op-ed pieces, book chapters, and notes from telephone interviews.

Many of the citations in *Benchmarking* were linked to a small group of standardization advocates and did not represent the larger body of empirical thought on the topic. One claim included in *Benchmarking* was that better content standards will cause higher performance on international tests of academic achievement, and higher performance will cause the economy of the United States to improve, which in turn will make everyone's lives better. Wow, can curriculum content standards also cure cancer and bring about world peace? The fraudulent claim in *Benchmarking* about the power of standards to increase economic output comes from another dubious report, *The Role of Cognitive Skills in Economic Development* (Hanushek & Woessmann, 2008).

Hanushek and Woessmann (2008) claimed that a one-standard-deviation gain (this is a huge gain) in Programme for International Student Assessment scores would produce a large and noticeable gain in a country's gross domestic product. But the authors included all seventy countries that took PISA in their analysis. They did not cluster-sample based on the size of the economy. The country of Chad would see benefits from a large improvement in education because a majority of its children do not finish middle school and its economy is very small. In large, developed economies like the United States, Germany, France, or Japan, the education levels are already very high, and the economies so advanced, that a score on an international test is irrelevant.

Hanushek and Woessmann (2008) initially passed off their findings as if they are relevant for every country. But halfway through the sixty-two-page report, they admit that their findings are irrelevant for the United States:

> The United States has never done well on these international assessments, yet its growth rate has been very high for a long period of time. . . . In other words, simply providing more or higher-quality schooling may yield little in the way of economic growth in the absence of other elements, such as the appropriate market, legal, and governmental institutions to support a functioning modern economy. Past experiences investing in less developed countries that lack these institutional features suggest that schooling is not necessarily itself a sufficient engine of growth. (p. 637)

The authors admit that education does not drive the economies of highly developed countries like the United States. Tax, monetary, fiscal, labor, and other related policies drive economic growth in countries with high levels of education, like the United States. The fact that the Hanushek and Woessmann (2008) report played such an important role in supporting the CCSS is yet another example that the CCSS emperor has no clothes.

CCSS Good for Testing Companies

Students have been subjected to negative consequences of state-mandated curriculum and assessment schemes in terms of curricular reductionism. Study after study reports the elimination of the arts and physical education and the overteaching of mathematics and language arts to the detriment of science, social studies, foreign language, and other noncore areas of the education program (Tienken & Zhao, 2013). Meanwhile, computer-based testing is flourishing.

The CCSS exacerbated the high stakes testing environment. School districts now routinely give their own set of computer-based standardized tests to monitor student acquisition of the CCSS-aligned state standards. In some cases students are taking computer-based tests once a marking period, once every six weeks, or once a month. Then they must take state-mandated tests, along with regular classroom tests that average about ten assessments per marking period. Students routinely take forty to sixty assessments a marking period! All the testing is prescribed in the name of standards-based reform.

Corrupting Force of Standards

The increase in testing was always part of the CCSS plan. The Council of Chief State School Officers (CCSSO, 2009) wrote, "States know that standards alone cannot propel the systems change we need. The common core state standards will enable participating states to . . . develop and implement an assessment system to measure student performance against the common core state standards" (p.2). Campbell's law (Campbell, 1976) predicted what eventually happened to the academic programs of many schools in terms of the hyper-quantitative accountability environment. The subjects aligned to the CCSS and tested as part of state accountability schemes became the most important subjects in terms of time and resources allotted. The opportunities students had to explore and delve into other subjects and educational activities, especially those seen as not academic enough, were bludgeoned by standardization and testing.

Within two to three years after the release of the CCSS, almost every state had new state assessment schemes. Students who did not meet the arbitrary levels of achievement on the standards-based tests were labeled "at-risk."

Many students were forced to do more work by attending remedial courses, depriving them further of the opportunity to participate in other educational activities.

Teachers in schools in which students did less well were punished. The punishments drove them to narrow their curriculum, teach less creatively, and turn themselves into test-preparation instructors. In effect they stripped themselves of their own professionalism and created a death spiral of mechanistic education, exactly what the dual system runs on.

House of Cards

Standardization is a Pollyanna approach to policy making. One cannot separate curriculum from culture, emotions, personal backgrounds, prior experiences, prior knowledge, and stages of cognitive and social development. Cognitive development theory (Piaget 1950), ecological systems theory (Bronfenbrenner & Evans, 2000), sociocultural theory (Vygotsky 1978), and even Maslow's (1943) hierarchy of needs, for that matter, all tell us that we cannot pretend curriculum operates in a vacuum, separate from other factors.

Seminal works emphasized the importance of curriculum as a proximal variable, developed and customized at the level of the student. The mountains of curricular knowledge created by Francis Parker, John Dewey, Horace Mann, Ralph Tyler, and Hilda Taba, to name just a few, support proximal curricula development. The landmark Eight-Year Study (Aikin, 1942) demonstrated that less standardized curricula, locally developed and based on demonstrated research and theories of learning, produced superior results compared to distally produced curricula. Results from other well-known earlier studies (e.g., Wrightstone, Rechetnick, McCall, & Loftus, 1939; Jersild, Thorndike, Goldman, Wrightstone, & Loftus, 1941) demonstrated that there is not one best curricular path for students and standardized curricula is not necessary to achieve superior results.

Wang, Haertel, and Walberg (1993) demonstrated that curriculum has the greatest influence on student achievement when it is a proximal variable in the education process. They found that the closer to the student the curriculum is designed, deliberated, and created, the greater influence it has on learning. When curriculum is treated as a distal variable—created distant from the student—its influence is weakened. National policy mandates have the weakest influence of all on student learning because they are distal to the actual learning process (Wang, Haertel, & Walberg, 1993).

DeTuro (2015) and Luciano (2015) conducted quantitative studies of the influence of curriculum customization on student achievement in mathematics and language arts in grades 3 and 5 in more than one hundred schools located in New Jersey's thirty poorest school districts. The researchers found similar results to those of Wang, Haertel, and Walberg (1993): The more proximal the curriculum development in a school, the better the students performed on the state's standardized tests. Local involvement and input from educators and students matter in terms of the influence of curriculum on learning.

Life, Liberty, and the Pursuit of Standardization

The notion that a human being can be standardized rests upon theories of behaviorism and efficiency. Both theories have served education poorly, but they retain their attractiveness with policymakers and some educators. As Callahan (1962) exposed, education leaders in the early 1900s eagerly supported Frederick Taylor's scientific management (1911) and tried to make education more efficient like business. No one questioned whether business was more efficient or more effective for children. Superintendents acted like business wannabees and jumped on the efficiency train (Callahan, 1962). Unfortunately, it was the students who got taken for a ride.

The same thing happened with CCSS. More than 150 organizations supported the CCSS and thousands of school administrators were tripping over each other to find ways to implement the standards rather than questioning the entire endeavor. Few educators took the time to evaluate the quality of the standards. Many simply accepted the claims made by the developers and state education bureaucrats. They drank the school reform Kool-Aid.

Efficiency is not the same as effectiveness and effectiveness is not always efficient. Efficiency is concerned with maximizing profit at all costs. Taylor's ideas of efficiency and scientific management were created in the steel mills and focused on shoveling coal. They were never tested or intended to be applied to student learning or teaching.

There is no evidence that the efficiency movement of the late 1800s and early 1900s improved education, in fact evidence exists that the opposite was true. Consider that the public high school graduation rate in 1918, well into the efficiency movement, was about 4 percent and remained that way until the height of the progressive education movement in the late 1930s and early 1940s.

TAKING ACTION

Democracy and local control are not standardized, not efficient, and not easily managed; their benefits are not easily quantifiable. A democratic education system is not for the faint of heart. It requires constant tending and vigilance. It is not paint by numbers. Education can be a society's greatest democratic gift or a government's greatest undemocratic weapon. Educators must work for effective local control.

Consider the example of China's revolution that began the Mao era in 1949. One of the first things the new Communist government did was change the school curricula. No local control or provincial input. The centralized government decided for the people what was best based on government's need to control the people. Now the Chinese government is desperately trying to un-standardize education (Zhao, 2014). The Soviets did the same thing when they invaded countries during the 1950s through the 1980s as part of a program known as Russification. History has demonstrated time and time again that a key part of controlling a country's citizenry is through central control of the school curriculum.

Although some supporters of national standards no doubt mean well, we should all remember the words of Thomas Paine: "The greatest tyrannies are always perpetrated in the name of the noblest causes." I believe we can do better in the United States than develop and implement policies for our children driven by disinformation, frauds, and anti-intellectualism. The diversity of the United States is one of its greatest strengths. The intellectual, creative, and cultural diversity of the US workforce allow it to be nimble and adapt quickly to changes in the marketplace.

A LOOK AHEAD

Chapter 8 examines the frauds, myths, and lies associated with charter schools: the neoliberal dual system's other weapon of mass public school destruction. A review of some pertinent research on the lack of effectiveness of charter schools and some notable scandals are presented.

REFERENCES

Aikin, W. M. (1942). *The story of the eight-year study*. New York: Harper.
Bronfenbrenner, U., & Evans. G. W. (2000). Developmental science in the 21st century: Emerging questions, theoretical models, research designs and empirical findings. *Social Development, 9*(1), 115–25.
Burns, C. R. (2017). *A comparison of complex thinking required by the middle school New Jersey Student Learning Standards and past New Jersey Curriculum Standards*. Seton Hall University Dissertations and Theses (ETDs). Paper 2308.
Callahan, R. E. (1962). *The cult of efficiency*. Chicago: University of Chicago Press.
Campbell, D. T. (1976, December). *Assessing the impact of planned social change*. Hanover, NH: Public Affairs Center, Dartmouth College.
Cody, A. (2013, November 16). Common Core Standards: 10 colossal errors. *Education Week Teacher*. Retrieved from http://blogs.edweek.org/teachers/living-in-dialogue/2013/11/common_core_standards_ten_colo.html
Council of Chief State School Officers. (2009). Standards and accountability. Retrieved from http://www.ccsso.org/What_We_Do/Standards_Assessment_and_Accountability.html
DeTuro, M. (2015). *The influence of curriculum customization on grade 3 student achievement in language arts and mathematics in New Jersey's 30 poorest school districts*. Seton Hall University Dissertations and Theses (ETDs). Paper 2063.

Dewey, J. (1916). *Democracy and education.* New York: Macmillan.
Epstein. H. T. (2002). Biopsychological Aspects of Memory and Education. *Advances in Psychology Research, 11,* 197–203.
Hanushek, E. A., & Woessmann, L. (2008). The role of cognitive skills in economic development. *Journal of Economic Literature, 46*(3), 607–68.
Fitzhugh, G., Tienken, C. H., & Burns, C. (2019). *The shifting sands of higher order thinking policy in state curriculum content standards: Rhetoric versus reality.* Paper presented at the Annual Conference of the University Council for Educational Administration, November 23, 2019, New Orleans, LA.
Jarmon, M. (2018). *Content complexity in high school English: An analysis of Common Core State Standards and past Massachusetts curriculum.* Seton Hall University Dissertations and Theses (ETDs). Paper 2574.
Jersild, A. T., Thorndike, R. L., Goldman, B., Wrightstone, J. W., & Loftus, J.J. (1941). A further comparison of pupils in "activity" and "nonactivity" schools. *Journal of Experimental Education, 9*(4), 303–309
Karp, S. (2013). The problems with the Common Core. *Rethinking Schools, 28*(2), 10–17.
Luciano, J. (2014). *The influence of curriculum quality on student achievement on the New Jersey Assessment of Skills and Knowledge (NJ ASK) language arts and mathematics for fifth-grade students in the lowest socioeconomic school districts.* Seton Hall University Dissertations and Theses (ETDs). Paper 2017.
Maslow, A. H. (1943). A theory of human motivation. *Psychological Review, 50*(4), 370–96.
Mullen, C. A. (2016). Corporate networks and their grip on the public section and education policy. In C. Tienken & C. Mullen (Eds.), *Education policy perils: Tackling the tough issues.* (pp. 27–62). Philadelphia: Taylor Francis Routledge.
National Governors Association, Council of Chief State School Officers, & Achieve, Inc. (2008). *Benchmarking for success: Ensuring US students receive a world-class education.* Washington, DC: National Governors Association.
Ohanian, S. (1999). *One size fits few: The folly of educational standards.* Portsmouth, NH: Heinemann.
Piaget, J. (1950). *The psychology of intelligence.* London: Routledge & Kegan Paul.
Sforza, D., Tienken, C. H., & Kim, E. (2016). A comparison of higher-order thinking between the Common Core State Standards and the 2009 New Jersey Content Standards in high school. *AASA Journal of Scholarship and Practice, 12*(4), 4–30.
Shayer, M., & Adey, P. (1981). *Towards a science of science teaching.* London: Heinemann.
Simon, S., & Shah, N. (2013, September 18). The common core money war. *Politico.* Retrieved from https://www.politico.com/Story/2013/09/education-common-core-standards-schools-096964
Taylor, F. W. (1911). *Principles of scientific management.* New York: Harper and Brothers
Tienken, C. H. (2011, winter). Common Core State Standards: An example of data-less decision-making. *AASA Journal of Scholarship and Practice, 7*(4), 3–18.
Tienken, C. H. (2017). *Defying standardization: Creating curriculum for an uncertain future.* Lanham, MD: Rowman and Littlefield.
Tienken, C. H., Sforza, D., & Burns, C. (2017). *A comparison of the cognitive complexity of the Common Core State Standards in English language arts and the 1997 California Standards.* Paper presented at the Annual Conference of the University Council for Educational Administration, November 18, 2017, Denver, CO.
Tienken, C. H., & Zhao, Y. (2013). How common standards and standardized testing widen the opportunity gap. In P. Carter and K. Welner (Eds.), *Closing the opportunity gap: What America must do to give every student a chance.* (pp. 111–22). New York: Oxford University Press.
Vygotsky, L. (1978). *Mind in society: The development of higher psychological processes* ed. M. Cole, V. John-Steiner, S. Scribner, and E. Souberman. Cambridge, MA: Harvard University Press.
Wang, M. C., Haertel, G. D., & Walberg, H. J. (1993). Toward a knowledge base for school learning. *Review of Educational Research, 63*(3), 249–94.

Webb, N. L. (1997). *Criteria for alignment of expectations and assessments in mathematics and science education.* Research Monograph No. 6. Washington, DC: Council of Chief State School Officers.

Wyse, A. E., and Viger, S. G. (2011). How item writers understand depth of knowledge. *Educational Assessment, 16*(4), 185–206.

World Economic Forum. (2018). *The future of jobs report 2018.* Author. Geneva, Switzerland. Retrieved from http://www3.weforum.org/docs/WEF_Future_of_Jobs_2018.pdf

Wrightstone, J. W., Rechetnick, J., McCall, W.A., & Loftus, J. J. (1939). Measuring social performance factors in activity and control schools of New York City. *Teachers College Record, 40*(5): 423–32.

Zhao, Y. (2014). *Who's afraid of the big bad dragon.* New York: Jossey-Bass.

Chapter Eight

Charter Schools

Separate but Legal

Up to this point in the book I have provided an examination of some threshold events, legislation, and reform-related issues that acted as examples of ways the modern unitary system has come under attack. This chapter provides a look into a concrete example of the dual system in action: charter schools. The purpose of the chapter is to provide some evidence-based commentary about the rhetoric used to support charter school proliferation. Although the overall evidence is negative toward charters, this chapter is not meant to attack those who work in charters. In many cases people who work in charters are looking to make a positive difference in the lives of children. Unfortunately, as this chapter will explain, they are working in organizations that have—most likely unbeknownst to them—become increasingly predatory and discriminatory.

THE MOVEMENT

The charter school movement has grown from a small grassroots effort to improve or provide education options on a very small scale to some schools that faced overwhelming odds, becoming the big-box store version of education consumerism. Charter schools are often marketed as the panacea to all the ills that supposedly ail public schools. The charter school movement in many states has now been taken over by big business interests via commercial charter school chains. The movement is seen by many neoliberals as the chance to install the dual system and then move on from there.

The Center for Education Reform reported in 2009 that there were approximately five thousand charters schools serving almost 1.5 million students in the United States. The number of students more than doubled by 2018, with 3.2 million, and the number of schools increased to more than seven thousand (David & Hesla, 2018).

In the Beginning

The birth of the modern-day charter school movement is often credited to University of Massachusetts Amherst professor Ray Budde (Kolderie, 2005). Although Budde was the first to use the term "charter," Robert Kennedy proposed an idea that I believe to be the genesis of the charter school movement in a press release on May 31, 1968 (Guthman & Allen, 1993). Kennedy wrote:

> We must create experimental elementary and secondary schools not run by traditional administrative methods—competitive schools—both as a means for encouraging innovation and as a yardstick for measuring the effectiveness of our schools. (p. 396)

US secretaries of education, legislators, education bureaucrats, and other charter proponents use similar rhetoric today to forward the charter movement. I am not claiming that Kennedy was calling for charter schools specifically, but it does appear at least that the movement co-opted the language he used in this press release to make the case for charters.

The idea picked up steam in 1988 when Albert Shanker, president of the American Federation of Teachers, supported the idea to establish schools that were not constrained by the typical state and local bureaucracy and able to operate semiautonomously, both financially and legally. Perhaps Shanker recognized that overregulation and bureaucratization of the public schools by the federal and state governments were constraining innovation and stifling the educational imagination.

However, Shanker (1994) later stepped away from his enthusiastic support of charters when he stated that any common ground that existed between charters and public schools could be wiped out by a large-scale charter movement. I wonder what Shanker would think now about the confluence of pro-charter, anti–public school alliances on Wall Street and the bludgeoning of public school regulations fostered by No Child Left Behind, Race to the Top, and the Every Student Succeeds Act.

The presidential administrations of Ronald Reagan and George H. W. Bush helped to strengthen support for the idea of charter schools. Reagan supported vouchers and school choice. He attached the conservative revolution to school choice and provided political strength to supporters of the charter school concept. The Bush administration, with support from then

Assistant Secretary of Education Diane Ravitch, pushed the choice agenda and rhetoric further.

Minnesota and California were the first states to adopt charter school legislation, in 1991 and 1992, respectively. By the start of school in 2009, forty one states had adopted charter school laws and more were planning to do so in order to be eligible for a portion of the federal $4.3 billion RTTT program created by the Obama administration. Many states had previously placed caps on the number of charters that could exist, but RTTT guidelines mandated that all caps be lifted.

Charter schools are legally defined as public schools that are free from some of the financial and regulatory restrictions placed on the unitary public school system. In some respects, they operate outside of the public school system, yet they are marketed as public schools.

So far the rhetoric that supports charter schools sounds pretty innocuous and somewhat helpful on the surface. What a great idea—free schools from overregulation to spur innovation and serve student needs, give parents and students a choice and help those who struggle. But things are not what they seem. What is the connection between charter schools and the marginalization of the unitary system in favor of the expansion of the dual system? What is really going on?

The Smoking Gun

The charter cartel tipped its hand about its predatory plans in 2008 when Andy Smarick wrote the following set of instructions for taking over public education:

> First, commit to drastically increasing the charter market share in a few select communities until it is the dominant system and the district is reduced to a secondary provider. The target should be 75 percent. Second, choose the target communities wisely. Each should begin with a solid charter base (at least 5 percent market share), a policy environment that will enable growth (fair funding, non-district authorizers, and no legislated caps), and a favorable political environment (friendly elected officials and editorial boards, a positive experience with charters to date, and unorganized opposition). Third, secure proven operators to open new schools. To the greatest extent possible, growth should be driven by replicating successful local charters and recruiting high-performing operators from other areas. Fourth, engage key allies like *Teach for America*, *New Leaders for New Schools*, and national and local foundations to ensure the effort has the human and financial capital needed. Last, commit to rigorously assessing charter performance in each community and working with authorizers to close the charters that fail to significantly improve student achievement.
>
> As chartering increases its market share in a city, the district will come under growing financial pressure. The district, despite educating fewer and fewer

students, will still require a large administrative staff to process payroll and benefits, administer federal programs, and oversee special education. With a lopsided adult-to-student ratio, the district's per-pupil costs will skyrocket. . . . That is, eventually the financial crisis will become a political crisis. . . . The district could voluntarily begin the shift to an authorizer, developing a new relationship with its schools and reworking its administrative structure to meet the new conditions. Or, believing the organization is unable to make this change, the district could gradually transfer its schools to an established authorizer.

Smarick recommends that charters cease cooperation and collaboration with traditional public schools and simply look to replace them. That is exactly what happened in New Orleans after Hurricane Katrina, and in Camden, New Jersey. Corporate schooling interests infected the Louisiana and New Jersey departments of education at the highest levels and began to dismantle the public systems, shifting millions in public money to private coffers, and the dual system was established. Charter schools are now predatory organizations.

A VISION FOR ACADEMIC EXCELLENCE: WHAT DOES THE RESEARCH SUGGEST?

Supporters of charter schools often cite improved academic performance as a major advantage over traditional public schools. The Center for Education Reform (2009) published an interesting piece of pseudo-research titled *The Accountability Report: Charter Schools*. It is chock full of methodologically flawed results and conclusions that attempt to make charter schools sound like the magic pill for all that ails student achievement.

Many charter school special interest groups report and publish similar pseudo-research. Independent research released since 2005 based on results from national and regional studies show that charter schools offer no significant advantages related to student achievement when controlling for the socioeconomic backgrounds of the students attending the charter schools and their academic achievement prior to entering the charter school.

McEwan (2009) conducted an independent analysis of the report *Everybody Wins: How Charter Schools Benefit All New York City Public School Students* (Winters, 2009), published by the special interest group Center for Civic Innovation at the Manhattan Institute. The analysis revealed no statistically significant gains ($p < .05$) for students as a result of competition from charter school.

The original report claimed an advantage of 1 percentage point in English language arts test scores for students who left the traditional public school for the charter and an effect size of 0.02 and a non–statistically significant gain of 1 percent on the mathematics test scores. An effect size of 0.02 is microscopic and not worth the money. In contrast, consider experimental studies on the effects of class size reduction on student achievement in mathematics and language arts consistently find effects of 0.25 to 0.60, moderate to large effects (Finn & Achilles, 1990).

Several other methodologically strong studies revealed that the claims made by charter school proponents that charters improve the education for our neediest students are unsubstantiated (Mishel & Roy, 2005; Skinner, 2009; van Lier, 2009). In most cases, the student populations of many charter schools are not comparable to the schools in the surrounding community (Weber & Rubin, 2019). Charters generally have fewer students who are economically disadvantaged and admit fewer students with special education or English language learning needs. In a sense, charters practice selective enrollment.

More Shoddy Research from the Charter Crew

Hoxby (2004) published two highly publicized reports on charter achievement that I consider pseudo-research. At the very least, independent analyses have determined those reports to be methodologically flawed. The report that received the most attention, *A Straightforward Comparison of Charter Schools and Public Schools in the United States*, was shown to be anything but straightforward (Mishel & Roy, 2005).

Hoxby put forth the following claims based on her analysis of grade 4 reading and mathematics achievement scores from 99 percent of charter schools:

- Charter school students were 3.8 percent more likely to be proficient in reading.
- Achievement in reading is even stronger, with 4.9 percent more likely to be proficient, when the racial composition of the charter was similar to that of the local public school.
- Charter school students were 1.6 percent more likely to be proficient in math, and that rises to 2.8 percent when "controlling" for student composition in the types of schools.
- "Initial indications are that the average student attending a charter school has higher achievement than he or she otherwise would" (p. 3).

Unfortunately, when Mishel and Roy (2005) looked behind the curtain they found some serious statistical sleight-of hand being conducted in terms of the methods Hoxby used to "compare" the student composition at the charter schools to their local traditional public schools. There were significant demographic differences between the students in the charter schools and those in the "similar" local public schools. This was a classic case of apples versus oranges. As a university professor who mentor doctoral students, this issue is something I cover early on in the mentoring process.

Making claims that sound like apples to apples when they are really apples to oranges is a Research 101 no-no. Mishel and Roy (2005) found that the charter school sample used by Hoxby had significantly fewer economically disadvantaged students, 49 percent versus 60 percent for public school. The charter sample had significantly fewer Hispanic students, one of the lowest-scoring racial/ethnic groups of students on the National Assessment of Education Progress assessments, 18 percent versus 30 percent. Hoxby's samples had more White students, the second highest-scoring racial group behind Asians on NAEP assessments, 43 percent versus 36 percent.

The charter schools in Hoxby's study were anything but similar to the traditional public schools she used as the comparison group. Mishel and Roy (2005) went beyond just identifying the errors—they conducted the type of analysis that should have been conducted the first time. Their results are somewhat different than Hoxby's. Below are just a few of the findings from Mishel and Roy's reanalysis:

- When controlling for the racial composition of the student samples, the math advantage for charters disappears, and only charters in California retain a small statistically significant advantage in reading.
- When controlling for race and economic status, the positive effects for math and reading evaporate.
- In the states where the charter school students were actually similar to those in traditional public schools (Michigan, North Carolina, Ohio, and Texas), the effect of charters on student achievement is negative, but not always statistically significant.
- No attempts to account for selection bias—students who attend charters, or their parents, *choose* to do so. Selection bias is a major threat to the validity of the findings in this case.

Hoxby, Murarka, and Kang (2009) produced a report for the New York City Charter Schools Evaluation Project, *How New York City's Charter Schools Affect Achievement*. The authors made the following claim, among others: New York City charter schools that students attend for kindergarten through grade 8 closed the rich/poor achievement gap by 66 percent in ELA and 86 percent in math compared to traditional public schools. The authors' claim is stunning given that charters in New York City were able to seemingly erase the achievement gap in math and cut it by two-thirds in ELA, when most other charters around the country produce achievement gains that are generally identical to or lower than those of the traditional public schools.

As with the other Hoxby report presented in this chapter, this one suffered from some basic methodological flaws along with some more complex issues. Reardon (2009) conducted an independent evaluation of this report and found that the above claims, and others made in the report, did not stand up to scrutiny. Reardon found in his reanalysis that the students who attend New York City charters are "disproportionately non-Hispanic, black, or poor relative to students in all New York City's schools" (p. 5). Once again, we have apples versus oranges. As for the second claim that the achievement on the Regents Exams and the graduate rates are significantly affected, that depends on how one defines statistically significant.

In social science research, it is generally accepted that statistical significance is $p < .05$, or that there is a 95 percent percent chance that he results obtained did not occur randomly or by chance. Hoxby and colleagues, claim statistical significance at $p < .15$—not even close. Any reputable peer-reviewed research journal would reject such a claim.

Another well publicized report from the Center for Research on Education Outcomes (CREDO, 2009) reviewed the academic performance of charter school students in sixteen states. The report analyzed results from 2,403 charter schools. The main findings related to student achievement were as follows:

- Thirty-seven percent of charter schools had achievement that was statistically significantly lower achievement than if their students attended the local traditional public school.
- Seventeen percent of charter schools had achievement that was statistically significantly higher than if their students attended the local traditional public school.
- Forty-six percent of charter schools had achievement that was not statistically significantly different from their local traditional public school.
- The learning gains for Black and Hispanic students were statistically significantly lower than their similar peers in the traditional public schools.

The pooled average achievement for charter schools at the grade 4 level compared to the grade 4 achievement posted on the NAEP in reading and math was -0.01 and -0.03, respectively. The report stated, "Charter school students on average see a decrease in their academic growth in reading of .01 standard deviations compared to their traditional school peers. In math, their learning lags by .03 standard deviations on average. While the magnitude of these effects is small, they are both statistically significant" (p. 12).

A CREDO (2014) report on the academic achievement of charters in California provides an example of how charter school underachievement is camouflaged in hard-to-understand language and descriptions to make it sound as if they are superior to public schools. The report makes the following claim: "California charter schools make larger learning gains in reading and learn less in mathematics. These results show overall improvement in charter school learning in both subjects" (p. 4).

The problem is that the claim is based on questionable assumptions and methods. The authors predicted learning gains for charter school students based on the assumption that the students had stayed in public schools and that their achievement would remain unchanged. This is problematic because predictions like that assume that the education quality in the public schools remains stagnant over time. It does not. Another issue is that the authors never show the actual scores of charter students compared to public school students.

Pogrow (2018) warned of statistical shenanigans by authors who use a lot of statistical language and ambiguous claims but never show the actual scores. How do we know if the actual scores of students in charters were better? The authors report on growth, not ultimate achievement. Students can demonstrate large growth but still be underachieving. For example, a group of students might demonstrate 20 percent growth in math over one year but still know less mathematics than students who demonstrate 2 percent growth.

Another issue with the CREDO (2014) report is that the authors never proved that the two groups of students, charter versus public school, were even comparable. A final problem is that the effect size changes that charters make, as a group, are very small, only a maximum of 0.15. That size change is not even worth spending money on. In fact, it is a waste of money. In my opinion, charters in California are a waste of money. Even with the questionable methodology slanted toward showing charter academic gains, the report states that only about a third of all charters in California outperform public schools!

SEPARATE, UNEQUAL, YET LEGAL

Charter proponents trumpet choice as the hallmark of a democratic public education system. They put "parents' right to choose" at the forefront of their argument for expanding the charter market and put the parent in the role of consumer. On its face, it sounds very logical. Anything less than free choice would be un-American, right?

The argument made by charter proponents for free choice usually goes something like this: *Education is the civil rights issue of our lifetime. Students should not be made to attend schools that are persistently unsafe and that do not deliver a quality education. Parents should have the right to choose a school that is right for their child.* Sounds very democratic and consumer-chic, yes?

Sometimes choice can be undemocratic, especially when the choices result in segregation and/or discrimination against students by race/ethnicity, English language learner (ELL) status, socioeconomic status, or learning disabilities. By allowing people to engage in unrestrained choice, there is potential in a weakly regulated system like the current charter system for certain parents to choose certain schools based on factors that create greater segregation. This is exactly what is happening. But remember that the majority of parents *choose* to remain in their local public school.

Bergman and McFarlin (2018) conducted a nationwide study in which the researchers sent e-mails, posing as fictitious parents, to 6,452 charter schools and traditional public schools in twenty-ninth states and Washington, DC. The researchers specifically sent e-mails to traditional public schools within the enrollment zones of the charter schools to ensure they were selecting enrollment zones in which traditional public schools were in competition with charter schools. The authors asked each school about their application process and whether any student was eligible to attend the school.

Each e-mail contained a randomly assigned characteristic of the child. The characteristics included (a) the need for special education services, (b) behavioral issues, (c) low and/or high academic achievement, (d) race, (e) gender, and (e) household makeup in terms of single-parent status. The research found that charter schools were less likely to respond to e-mails in which the researchers described students with disabilities. In addition, "no-excuses" charter schools—schools that have zero tolerance policies for misbehavior that results in expulsion—were most likely not to respond to e-mails in which students were described as having special needs.

New Jersey provides a case study of how charters insulate and segregate themselves from students that have learning needs or do not fit the mold of high achieving. New Jersey's increase in charter schools goes hand in hand with the state's being sued as having the one of the most segregated school systems in the country. The situation of racial/ethnic segregation is so severe in New Jersey that a group of plaintiffs filed a lawsuit in the Superior Court of New Jersey on May 17, 2018, *Latino Action Network v. the State of New Jersey*. The plaintiffs allege the state of New Jersey is complicit in the segregated system. The plaintiffs seek a ruling by the courts to alleviate the issue. The lawsuit cited charter schools as a contributing factor in school segregation:

> New Jersey's charter schools exhibit a degree of intense racial and socioeconomic segregation comparable to or even worse than that of the most intensely segregated urban public schools. Indeed, 73% of the state's 88 charter schools have less than 10% White students and 81.5% of charter school students attend schools characterized by extreme levels of segregation, mostly because almost all the students are Black and Latino. (p. 10)

As of this writing, the case was expected to go to court in 2020 or early 2021 and could have monumental ramifications for education in New Jersey and charter school regulation.

New Jersey continues to be a representative example of how charter schools reshape district demographics in their favor. Charter school student populations are rarely similar to those of the districts from which they take students. Weber and Rubin (2018) documented that on average, charter schools in New Jersey enroll about half as many students with disabilities than their corresponding districts, 9.7 percent compared to 15.6 percent. The enrollment of students with high-cost disabilities such as autism or intense medical disabilities is also much lower in charters. Charters purposefully seek to enroll students with less expensive disabilities for monetary gain.

> Charter schools receive additional funds for every special education student they enroll, regardless of disability, with the exception of speech/language disabilities. This creates a potential problem for hosting public school districts: the classified students they send to charter schools are likely to have less expensive disabilities than the classified students who remain in the district. However, districts must send the same amount of additional funding to charter schools for each classified student. This can result in districts educating a higher percentage of students who have more expensive disabilities while having less funding to meet those students' needs. (p. 15)

There is a stark difference in the percentages of ELL students educated in the public schools compared to the charter schools. The average percentage of ELL students in charter schools is 2.8 percent, compared to 11.4 percent in the corresponding districts; an 8.6 percent difference. Charter schools like the one in Red Bank Boro and Plainfield City appear to be the most egregious in New Jersey in their not enrolling ELL students. The Red Bank Charter School enrolls 31.1 percent fewer ELL students than the Red Bank public schools, 35.1 percent and 4 percent, respectively. Almost 34 percent of the students in Plainfield public school district qualify for ELL services, whereas only 4 percent of the students in the charter schools receive ELL services.

Many charter schools in New Jersey enroll fewer students who are economically disadvantaged. Red Bank Charter School is the winner in this category. Only 37 percent of its students were considered economically disadvantaged, whereas almost 82 percent of students in the Red Bank public schools were economically disadvantaged—a difference of almost 45 percent! Hoboken City is the runner-up, with its charter schools enrolling less than 10 percent of students categorized as economically disadvantaged compared to 47 percent of district students (Weber & Sass-Rubin, 2018).

Siphoning Students and Cash

Not only are charter schools segregating populations, they are siphoning off money from families that *choose* to stay in public schools. The public schools lose much-needed funding because children who go to the charter school take a majority of their per-pupil funding with them. This system of funding following the student effectively creates a public dual system based on the all-American right of free choice. But what does the research suggest?

Results from reviews of charters consistently show that the students in charter schools either come from homes that are more economically stable; have higher prior achievement levels; do not require special education, ELL, or intense medical services; and exhibit patterns of white flight or minority flight from the public school to the charter schools. One example of charters enrolling fewer poor students, fewer students in need of ELL services, and fewer students with disabilities comes from Philadelphia.

The Education Law Center of Pennsylvania (2019) found that only 54 percent of students in Philadelphia charter schools were economically disadvantaged, whereas the district of Philadelphia average was 70 percent. There were fewer students with severe disabilities and about one-third fewer students who needed ELL services enrolled in Philly charters. About one-third of Philadelphia public school students—seventy thousand children—attend charter schools.

Of course, not all charters segregate in every situation, but as a group, their student populations are more segregated than the surrounding public schools. There are charters that are more inclusive and less segregated, and that offer better programs than their surrounding schools, but that is not the overall characteristic of the population of charter schools. Over 70 percent of Black students in charter schools were in schools that were 90–100 percent Black, lacking almost any racial diversity, whereas only 34 percent of Black students in the public schools were in schools that were 90–100 percent Black (Frankenberg, 2011).

Unrestrained Choice

I think it is important to remember that at various times in our country's history, people have "chosen" to keep slaves, not allow women to vote, create separate and unequal facilities for non-White citizens, institute voting laws to make it difficult for certain citizens to vote, restrict who can get married, ban bilingual education, and fire people who are not heterosexual. These types of discriminatory and nondemocratic choices weaken our country.

Unrestrained choice leads to the trampling of democratic rights and subjugation of the "greater good of society" to individual prejudice and hate.

Choice for choice's sake is irresponsible, reckless, and in some cases, undemocratic. Passing laws and policies that have been shown to weaken the democratic fabric of the country by facilitating people's choice to segregate is immoral, and those who knowingly create and support such laws and policies are engaging in social and moral malpractice.

Students in public schools attend more racially diverse schools, on average, than their peers in charter schools. If your goal is to facilitate the segregation of students, and thus eventually society, by race, ethnicity, achievement, special needs and ELL status, and economics, all based on the "free choice" of parents supported by law, then charters are good.

If your goal is a unitary system in which people of all races; ethnicities; and economic, language, special needs, and cognitive backgrounds learn, collaborate, and deliberate together, side-by-side, in the rich pool of diversity, then charters are not so good. I argue for the more democratic and diverse system.

Selection Bias

Some charter schools practice selective admissions. Yes, the practice is illegal, and in most states charter schools must hold lotteries to admit students—and they do. The issue is what happens after lottery. I had private discussions with the current and former charter directors and teachers of multiple charter schools in multiple states as part of my research for this chapter. We spoke about their admissions practices and their practices of "returning students to their home schools" in an attempt to determine why charter school populations differ so much from their local public schools in terms of the percentage of students with special needs and ELLs. The charter heads represented schools that spanned the K–12 spectrum.

The scenario for admissions generally goes something like this: (1) All students who win the lottery must fill out a detailed student intake form. The form requires parents to disclose any special needs the child might have and in some cases free/reduced lunch status. (2) Parents and students must submit to an "intake interview" with the leadership of the charter school to be oriented to the "expectations" of the school. (3) In some schools, students must produce a writing sample. (4) Students who have special needs, behavior issues, are ELLs or other factors that might influence achievement negatively are gently counseled about the possible mismatch between their needs and the school's mission.

In some cases, parents are told that their student might not fit the school or that the school does not offer the level of service needed. They might also be made to feel uncomfortable or not quite the type of clientele served by the school, similar to when an African American couple go house shopping in some communities, they may be shown homes in one section of town rather than another, or dissuaded from purchasing a home in a traditional White, middle-class neighborhood. Yes, that still happens.

Charters often have high rates of attrition for students who do not score well on standardized tests. Those students are "returned to their home schools," never to return to the charter. The scenario for returning students follows the same pattern of "counseling" used in admissions.

Selective admissions and attrition practices only exacerbate an already troubling situation of segregation. Subtly counseling parents or creating an uninviting environment during an intake interview, especially for parents of students with special needs, ELLs, or those who struggle academically, is illegal and immoral, but difficult to prove. Of course, not all charter schools participate in selective admissions or attrition counseling. But it happens more often than people might realize.

Not Quite a Separation of Church and State

A quiet trend is taking place within the charter movement: Blurring the lines between church and state. There are currently charter schools that focus on Turkish language and culture or Hebrew language and culture, and some charters are housed in Christian church buildings. Charter schools devoted to other languages and cultures also exist, all publicly funded. This creates a context in which covert or subtle religious instruction or indoctrination can take place.

Justice and Macleod (2017) chronicled the trend of how charters are blurring religious lines in an article in the *Atlantic*:

> Sometimes, religious schools simply close at the end of the school year and reopen in the fall as public charter schools, hiring many of the same teachers and taking on most of the same students. . . . A Greek Orthodox community opens a charter school in Brooklyn with a Greek language and culture theme, with a predominantly Greek staff and clientele; a Florida Jewish school reopens as a Hebrew-theme academy that focuses on Jewish history and culture and teaches the Hebrew language, explicitly serving "Jewish communal purposes." A different kind of conversion, more typical of Roman Catholic parochial schools, reconstitutes a religious school that serves no particular cultural group or even religious one, but hews instead to a mission of Christian service and (usually) light evangelism. In Washington, D.C., Roman Catholic schools serving primarily African American children have recently begun converting to charters.

Now there exists a situation in which religion can be brought into the public classroom through the study of culture and language. It is very hard to separate Hebrew language and culture from Judaism or Turkish language and culture from aspects of Islam. In terms of housing charter schools founded by

Christian church pastors in church-owned buildings, I'll let the reader ponder that one.

The Turkish language and cultural schools have raised some concerns in the United States. Many of the more than one hundred Turkish language and culture schools that service more than thirty-five thousand students have financial and philosophical connections to Fethullah Gülen. Gulen, a Turkish nationalist, now living in exile in Pennsylvania is well known for proposing that Islam should take greater precedence in Turkish society.

Groups affiliated with or inspired by Gülen operate schools in twenty-five states. Although most Gülen-inspired schools distance themselves from the exiled nationalist, the money flows from those committed to his teachings into organizations that support the charter schools. Some of these Turkish language and culture schools have been cited for crossing the line between church and state. For example, in Minnesota, the Tarek ibn Ziyad Academy authorized by Islamic Relief USA was cited by state education officials for having teachers take part in Friday prayers voluntarily.

Questions also surround the Hebrew language and culture charter schools that have opened in New York City and Florida. In the case of New York, Ravitch (2009) described a situation surrounding the opening of the Hebrew Language Academy Charter School in Brooklyn, funded in part by Michael Steinhardt. Steinhardt is known as a philanthropist who has donated millions of dollars to promote Jewish culture and identity. Ravitch wrote:

> His generosity is unquestionable. In this case, however, he is asking taxpayers to support an institution that has obvious religious overtones. In a city with a great variety of Jewish schools and other agencies that encourage Jewish identity, it makes no sense to create a public school with the same purpose. . . . The proposal to the Regents asserts that the school will not engage in any devotional activities. Even so, the Hebrew language is so closely aligned with the Jewish religion that it is baffling that the Regents are willing to treat the proposed charter school as a nonsectarian institution.

The Hebrew Language Academy charter school is another example of a school that raises some questions in terms of blurring the lines between church and state. On its website one can see students waving Israeli flags, Israeli flags hanging throughout classrooms, and teachers' classes with Hebrew names such as Hertzeliya, an Israeli city named after Theodor Herzl, the founder of modern Zionism. Another class is named Eilat, another city that is also known for being part of the book of Exodus.

As Ravitch stated, it is very difficult to separate Hebrew language and culture from religion. The Hebrew culture is rich with history, and much of that history revolves around religion.

Justice and Macleod (2017) reference Dewey's (1916) warning that allowing the public to segregate itself into tribes or ganglike groups can result in destructive ends, ends that are dangerous to a diverse democracy and discriminatory:

> Whether or not charter schools are former sectarian schools with a makeover, the lack of public accountability for charter-school providers encourages fraud. The financial cases are many and disturbing, and reports of intellectually bogus curricula are common too, particularly as Christian fundamentalists make war on history and science. RES, the Texas-based charter-school organization, is a powerful example of the perils of charter-school curriculum, and the fallacy that "the marketplace" will police itself. RES charter-school curriculum materials include a biology text that presents creationism and evolution as equally valid theories, with the latter presented as being widely questioned and full of inconsistencies and contrary evidence (which is nonsense). Other examples of a desperately right-wing agenda include teaching that the feminist movement "created an entirely new class of females who lacked male financial support and who had to turn to the state as a surrogate husband"; that Democrat John Kerry's war medals for bravery were "suspect at best"; and that the decline in Christian values caused World War I.

My purpose is not to single out religions or cultures. My purpose is to provide examples of how allowing specific culturally and religiously oriented charters to receive public tax dollars can facilitate the blurring of the line between church and state and result in miseducation, anti-intellectualism, and discrimination. Publicly funding and encouraging things like pre-Enlightenment thinking and discrimination moves the United States further away from the original unifying visions of people like Thomas Jefferson, Horace Mann, W. E. B. Du Bois and John Dewey.

THE UNDERLYING PHILOSOPHY OF CHARTER SCHOOLS

The original charter school movement driven by local needs has since been replaced by a new movement, Charter 2.0: money and religion. Charter 2.0 is personified by the ideas to marketize the system and marginalize local public schools and local control of local tax dollars in order to install a tiered system of for-profit and publicly funded schools. Many charter school chains are not accountable to the public. They operate financially outside of public input.

Most charters do not have a democratically elected board of community members. The community has no say what happens to public tax money. Charters are a concrete example of how neoliberal policies fleece the taxpayer by transferring public services and money to private coffers that trample democratic principles and actively promote discrimination.

Postmodern Consumerism

Postmodern consumerism is one component of neoliberal ideas and it is a hallmark of charter school expansion. In postmodern consumerism, the felt needs and desires of the individual trump the social needs of the greater population. Personal choice rules and there is no shortage of must-have products marketed to create those felt needs (Corrigan, 1998). Success is measured by consumption and the accumulation of material goods at any cost. Consuming becomes the way people self-identify in postmodern consumerism (Jessup, 2001).

Truth becomes marginalized within the growing space of the market. Product marketing replaces empirical fact in an effort to drive consumption and increase it. The convergence of neoliberalism and postmodern consumerism creates a fertile field for big business to become more financially involved in the movement. It's a perfect fit for speculation, market manipulation, and new market creation. Therefore, it is no wonder there has been a surge in the amount of money business is investing in the movement.

BIG BUSINESS ENTERS THE BUILDING

It only makes sense that a movement with roots in neoliberal postmodern consumerism would sooner or later be influenced, if not in some ways hijacked, by big business. For-profit education management organizations (EMOs) like Connections Academy, K12, EdisonLearning, National Heritage Academies, Imagine Schools, Charter Schools USA, and White Hat Management are some of the largest for-profit corporations managing charter schools. As of 2008 there were fifty EMOs operating in twenty-eight states, with more than 250,000 students enrolled. (Molnar, Miron & Urschel, 2008).

Remember, these are for-profit operations. Their objective is to make money. This raises the possibility that decisions will be made first on the effect on profits, not children. The information to support this claim is not hard to find. Simply search the internet for things like "White Hat Management and scandal" (e.g., http://charterschoolscandals.blogspot.com/2010/05/white-hat-management.html) or "EdisonLearning school management and scandal" (e.g., http://www.pasasf.org/edison/pdfs/042105.pdf) or any of the large for-profit EMOs and the term "scandal." White Hat is a model scandal in terms of what will happen across the country as charter schools proliferate the landscape—well worth reading.

But there is another major player besides EMOs: big banks. Yes, they are back, fresh off their victory from the 2008 worldwide economic catastrophe that the taxpayers will own for many years to come. Big banks are deeply rooted in the charter school start-up business, and business is booming. It seems as if there is money to be made financing charter schools, and big banks are hurtling themselves into the market with tens and hundreds of millions of dollars at a time.

Big banks are actively campaigning and buying off legislators to help feed the charter frenzy. Gabriel and Medina (2010) wrote an exposé in the *New York Times* that provides a representative example of the current landscape:

> Wall Street has always put its money where its interests and beliefs lie. But it is far less common that so many financial heavyweights would adopt a social cause like charter schools and advance it with a laser-like focus in the political realm. Hedge fund executives are thus emerging as perhaps the first significant political counterweight to the powerful teachers unions, which strongly oppose expanding charter schools in their current form. They have been contributing generously to lawmakers in hopes of creating a friendlier climate for charter schools. More immediately, they have raised a multimillion-dollar war chest to lobby this month for a bill to raise the maximum number of charter schools statewide to 460 from 200. The money has paid for television and radio advertisements, phone banks and some 40 neighborhood canvassers in New York City and Buffalo—all urging voters to put pressure on their lawmakers.

Gabriel and Medina describe in their article the current environment, fed by a little-known law signed in 1999 by Bill Clinton and passed by the Republican Congress, that allows banks to cash in on up to 39 percent tax credits for financing the creation of "new markets." Charter schools qualify as a new market. Gonzalez (2010) reported on this phenomena through the microcosm of Albany, New York.

> Wealthy investors and major banks have been making windfall profits by using a little-known federal tax break to finance new charter-school construction. The program, the New Markets Tax Credit, is so lucrative that a lender who uses it can almost double his money in seven years.
> Under the New Markets program, a bank or private equity firm that lends money to a nonprofit to build a charter school can receive a 39% federal tax credit over seven years. The credit can even be piggybacked on other tax breaks for historic preservation or job creation. By combining the various credits with the interest from the loan itself, a lender can almost double his investment over the seven-year period. No wonder JPMorgan Chase announced this week it was creating a new $325 million pool to invest in charter schools and take advantage of the New Markets Tax Credit. Albany is Exhibit A in the web of potential conflicts that keep popping up in the charter school movement. . . . If wealthy investors and banks can double their money simply by building charter schools, taxpayers deserve to know exactly who arranged those deals, who will benefit and what they will ultimately cost each school.

In an economic environment where most of those big banks are paying you less than 0.5 percent interest on your savings accounts, doubling my money in just seven years sounds like a good deal to me. Unfortunately, you and I are not eligible for that deal. We are stuck with the 0.5 percent, and we get to fund the interest and principal payments those charter schools must make to the big banks; guaranteed money. So that's how the new dual system works.

POINTS TO REMEMBER

Creating a multitiered, balkanized education system will not solve the problems we face as a society. It seems that charter schools fall flat in terms of achieving their stated goals of superior achievement. Charter schools can't overcome broken housing policy that favors the nonpoor (Schwartz, 2010), broken health policy that allows indigent pregnant women to be denied consistent healthcare, and fiscal policies that keep low wage earners in low-wage jobs with no way to pay their children's way out of poverty. Charters only exacerbate those issues and undermine democracy

A LOOK AHEAD

In chapter 9 I provide some ideas for education reform that strive to promote equity, democracy, and education quality. As can be expected, the chapter does not provide a standardized recipe. It provides some guiding ideas that others can use to create customized reform proposals. I do not see any evidence that distal bureaucrats should be creating specific regulations and mandating specific education practices at the local level beyond those that protect everyone's legal rights to equity and equality. Local control of curriculum, instruction, and assessment should be just that: local control.

REFERENCES

Bergman, P., and McFarlin, I. Jr. (2018). *Education for all? A nationwide audit study of school choice*. NBER Working Papers 25396. Cambridge, MA: National Bureau of Economic Research.

Center for Research on Education Outcomes (CREDO). (2014). *Charter school performance in California*. Author. Palo Alto, CA. Retrieved from https://credo.standford.edu/sties/g/files/sbiybj6481/f/ca_report_final.pdf

Center for Research on Education Outcomes (CREDO). (2009). *Multiple choice: Charter school performance in 16 states*. Retrieved from http://credo.stanford.edu/reports/MULTIPLE_CHOICE_CREDO.pdf

Corrigan, P. (1998). *The sociology of consumption*. London: Sage.

David, R., & Hesla, K. (2018). *Estimated public charter school enrollment: 2017–2018*. Washington, DC: National Alliance for Public Charter Schools. Retrieved from https://www.publiccharters.org/sites/default/files/documents/2018-03/FI-NAL%20Estimated%20Public%20Chater%20School%20Enrollment%2C%202017-18.pdf

Finn, J. D., & Achilles, C. M. (1990). Answers and questions about class size: A statewide experiment. *American Educational Research Journal, 27*, 557–77.

Education Law Center–Pennsylvania. (2019). *Safeguarding educational equity: Protecting Philadelphia students' civil rights through charter oversight.* Author. Philadelphia, PA.

Frankenberg, E. (2011). Educational charter schools: A civil rights mirage? *Kappa Delta Pi Record, 47*(3), 100–105.

Gabriel, T., & Medina, J. (2010, May 9). Charter schools' new cheerleaders: Financiers. *New York Times.* Retrieved from http://www.nytimes.com/2010/05/10/nyregion/10charter.html

Gonzalez, J. (2010, May 7). Albany charter cash cow: Big banks making a bundle on new construction as schools bear the cost. *New York Daily News.* http://www.nydailynews.com/ny_local/education/2010/05/07/2010-05-07_albany_charter_cash_cow_big_banks_making_a_bundle_on_new_construction_as_schools.html

Guthman, E. O., & Allen, R. C. (1993). *RFK: Collected Speeches.* New York: Penguin.

Hoxby, C. M. (2004, September). *A straightforward comparison of charter schools and regular public schools in the United States.* Cambridge, MA: National Bureau of Economic Research.

Hoxby, C. M., Murarka, S., & Kang, J. (2009, September). *How New York City's charter schools affect achievement.* Second report in series. Cambridge, MA: New York City Charter Schools Evaluation Project. Retrieved from http://www.nber.org/~schools/charterschoolseval/

Jessup, M. (2001). Truth: The first casualty of postmodern consumerism. *Christian Scholar's Review, 30*(3), 289–304.

Justice, B., & Macleod, C. (2017, February 9). Does religion have a place in public schools? *Atlantic.* Retrieved from https://www.theatlantic.com/education/archive/2017/02/does-religion-have-a-place-in-public-schools/516189/

Kolderie, T. (2005). Ray Budde and the origins of the charter concept. Education Evolving. Retrieved from http://www.educationevolving.org/pdf/Ray_Budde.pdf

Latino Action Network v. State of New Jersey. (2018). Retrieved from https://docs.wixstatic.com/ugd/9214ff_cb8a627911e5464d8b912446ec8dc914.pdf

McEwan, P. J. (2009). Review of *Everyone Wins: How Charter Schools Benefit All New York City Public School Students.* Boulder, CO. Retrieved from https://nepc.colorado.edu/thinktank/review-everyone-wins

Mishel, L., & Roy, J. (2005). *Re-examining Hoxby's findings of charter school benefits.* Washington, DC: Economic Policy Institute.

Molnar, A., Miron, G., & Urschel, J. (2008). *Profiles of for-profit educational management organizations: Tenth annual report.* Boulder, CO: Education in the Public Interest Center. Retrieved from http://nepc.colorado.edu/publication/profiles-profit-education-management-organizations-2007-2008

Pogrow, S. (2018). *Authentic quantitative analysis for education leadership decision-making and EdD dissertations*, edition 2.2. Ypsilanti, MI: ICPEL Publications.

Ravitch, D. (2009, January 18). New schools flunk the unity test. *New York Daily News.* Retrieved from http://www.nydailynews.com/opinions/2009/01/18/2009-01-18_new_school_flunks_unity_test_hebrewlangu.html

Reardon, S.F. (2009). Review of *How New York City's Charter Schools Affect Achievement.* Boulder, CO: National Education Policy Center. Retrieved from http://epicpolicy.org/thinktank/review-How-New-York-City-Charter

Shanker, A. (1994). *Where we stand: The Chicago reform.* Washington DC: American Federation of Teachers.

Skinner, K. J. (2009). *Charter school success or selective out-migration of low achievers.* Boston: Massachusetts Teachers Association.

Smarick, A. (2008, winter). Wave of the future: Why charters should replace failing urban schools. *Education Next, 8*(1). Retrieved from http://educationnext.org/wave-of-the-future/

Schwartz, H. (2010). *Housing policy is school policy: Economic integrative housing promotes academic success in Montgomery County, Maryland.* New York: Century Foundation.

Van Lier, P. (2011, May 17). Testimony of Piet van Lier, Senior Researcher, before the Senate Finance Committee. Policy Matters Ohio. Retrieved from http://www.policymattersohio.org/wp-content/uploads/2011/10/PvanLierHB153Testimony2011_0517.pdf

Weber, M., & Sass-Rubin, J. (2018). *New Jersey charter schools: A data-driven view—2018: Update, Part I.* http://doi.org/10.7282/T39Z983M

Chapter Nine

A Way Forward

Because education in the United States has a long history as being a local endeavor, local control is a key factor in the revitalization of the unitary system. The impact and effectiveness of many education interventions are influenced by the contexts in which they are used. Student characteristics, teacher skill and ability, school resources, and other local factors all work to facilitate or inhibit education interventions used with students. Educators must have the freedom to customize interventions at the local level.

It is up to those with the courage, ethical fortitude, and will to save the public schools to develop locally innovative means to connect children to evidence-based practices that will tap into local talents while also propelling students to make global connections. Think of it as local globalism—look globally and act locally.

LOCAL CONTROL

It is important to return public education to the public through increased local control for the sake of democracy, creativity, and innovation. Neoliberal policies aimed at installing a dual system have reduced local control and creativity and innovation of important school functions such as curriculum content, teaching methods, teacher evaluation, assessment, and high school graduation requirements.

Not all communities are created equal, and the ecological system in which a group of students live can change dramatically, even within the span of a few square miles. Zhao (2010) described one approach to return public education to the public as "mass localism." Zhao explained that local control is the key to creativity because each locale can address its needs through customized solutions that draw on evidence-based practices and ideas.

Each locale can express its interests and values while exposing its children to the larger world through technology-enabled collaboration. The ideas of mass localism flow from the progressivist philosophy and an acknowledgement of the learner as an active constructor of meaning who has prior knowledge and needs to connect that prior knowledge to new learning in developmentally appropriate and authentic situations. Local control does not have to mean a parochial or hyper-local approach to topics. It simply means that the local level can decide more of the content and the methods of implementation and evaluation.

Losing Democracy

Martin Gilens of Princeton University and Benjamin Page of Northwestern University published a study in which they concluded that the United States had been transformed from a marjoritarian electoral democracy and replaced with a government whose policies reflect the wishes of a small minority of economic elites, known as economic-elite domination. Forms of government characterized by economic-elite domination are also known as plutocracies, or government by the wealthy. Gilens and Page (2014) explained that "in the United States, our findings indicate, the majority does not rule—at least not in the causal sense of actually determining policy outcomes. When a majority of citizens disagrees with economic elites or with organized interests, they generally lose" (p. 576).

Public intellectual Noam Chomsky characterized the devolution of democracy in the United States this way in a 2018 interview: "What's wrong with today's democracy is its decline, with the attendant attack on prospects for a decent life as the political system falls even more than usual under the control of concentrated private power and hence becomes less responsive to human needs" (Polychroniou, 2018). The rise of elitist governments, even within countries that claim to be democracies, such as Brazil, India, the United States, Turkey, Hungary, Poland, and Russia, should come as a clarion call to educators across the globe to educate a new generation of citizens to the tenets of a socially just government, representative of the interests and needs of the common good.

The Idea of Democracy

Democracy is simply an idea, and as such, it is open to evolution in positive and negative ways. Realizing the promise of a democratic and socially just education to reinvigorate interest in a representative democracy should be at the forefront of education reform. If the next generation of citizens is not initiated into the tenets of a socially just democracy, then how will the generation after that ever come to realize it?

DEMOCRACY AND EDUCATION

John Dewey (1916) defined democracy in chapter 7 of his landmark text *Democracy and Education*:

> A democracy is more than a form of government; it is primarily a mode of associated living, or conjoint communicated experience. (p. 248)

Dewey viewed interactions in the form of civic engagement among people as a key feature of democratic living. Citizens in a democratic society should be concerned about each other's well-being, not just their own. Democracy does not function well if people act as islands unto themselves. He noted that "democracy is not an alternative to other principles of associated life. It is the idea of community life itself" (1927, 148).

Dewey (1916) explained the power of associated living in the democratic and educative processes: "One cannot share in interactions with others without learning, without getting a broader point of view and perceiving things of which one would otherwise be ignorant" (p. 354). Dewey rejected the notion of individualism and narrow, elite interests. He suggested that democracy is not only a type of government but a way of living together and concerning oneself with the greater good.

Dewey (1916) explained the importance of considering the viewpoints and concerns of others in a democratic society as a way to advance socially conscious progress in a country:

> The extension in space of the number of individuals who participate in an interest so that each has to refer his own action to that of others, and to consider the action of others to give point and direction to his own, is equivalent to the breaking down of those barriers of class, race, and national territory which kept people from perceiving the full import of their activity. (p. 249)

Dewey sides with individual responsibility in the service of social justice in society and awareness of the ways in which one's actions affect others. He clearly calls for education to support socially just democratic life so that all people can achieve their potential in ways that improve life for all.

EDUCATING DEMOCRATICALLY

Dewey (1916) discussed the importance of equality in education to strengthen a democratic society. He put forth education as the vehicle for people to teach the next generation of citizens how to study the problems of democracy and take responsible actions to improve democracy and improve life in a democratic society:

> A society which makes a provision for participation in its good of all its members on equal terms and which secures flexible readjustment of its institutions through interaction of the different forms of associated life is democratic. Such a society must have a type of education which gives individuals a personal interest in social relationships and control, and habits of mind which secure social changes without introducing disorder. (p. 283)

Dewey (1916) viewed socio-civic education as one important function of education. He drew upon a foundation of the three functions of education initially put forth by Lester Ward (1883). Dewey used the ideas developed by Ward to build his conception of the purposes of public school. Public school in the United States historically had specific purposes centered around the fulfillment of three complimentary functions: (1) economic: students experience a general set knowledge and skills they can use as platform go on to specialized education for a vocation, (2) socio-civic: knowledge and skills that help students gain experiences in being a responsible and participating citizens in a democracy and the global community, and (3) avocational: experiences to help students develop their personal interests, passions, and hobbies (Tanner & Tanner, 2007).

One historic role of public education has been socio-civic in nature: the incubator of democracy. Public education has a history of uniting diverse peoples through exposure to a liberal education and democratic principles while also providing outlets for people to specialize in diverse academic, career-oriented areas (Commission on the Reorganization of Secondary Education, 1918). It is the unifying and specializing characteristics of a public school system that make it unique from other forms of school. Public school in the United States has historically provided a unique mixture of common, yet diverse thinking and opportunities for people to follow their interests and passions while still learning the democratic traditions of the country in order to carry on and improve society for all (Aikin, 1942).

Dewey explained the socio-civic role of public education in nurturing a democracy in *The Sources of a Science of Education* (1929):

> For the creation of a democratic society we need an educational system where the process of moral intellectual development is in practice as well as in theory a cooperative transaction of inquiry engaged in by free, independent human beings who treat ideas and the heritage of the past as means and methods for the further enrichment of life, quantitatively and qualitatively, who use the good attained for the discovery and establishment of something better. (p. 84)

Dewey continued to be mindful of the tension between the roles of education in the development of the individual and the development of the society in the context of a country with a culture based in part on "rugged individualism" such as the United States. He was concerned with the confusion of individual development with individualism and the impact that a focus on individualism could have on the policy making within a democracy. Research seems to support Dewey's concerns with individual development morphing into individualism (Bazzi, Fiszbein, & Gebresilasse, 2018).

Individualism Rules the Individual

The United States provides an important example of how an aspect of a country's culture can affect the evolution of democracy in that county. The United States has a cultural tradition of embracing "rugged individualism". The results published in 2018 suggests some residents within areas of the United States that were part of the western frontier experience between 1790 and 1890 still possess a frontier mentality.

People in the former frontier zones are more likely to embrace rugged individualism as a worldview and less likely to support government policies that provide for a more equitable distribution of income. They are more likely to support limited government and limited regulatory safeguards for the society, and they are more likely to favor cuts to domestic social programs (Bazzi, Fiszbein, & Gebresilasse, 2018). The affinity toward a worldview based on rugged individualism continues to play out in policy making as residents of the United States continue to see policies enacted that hollow out government and attack social programs that address the larger needs of society.

The Rise of Individualism

One problem with rugged individualism is the underlying mindset of "leave me alone and let me do whatever I want." Giles, McCutchen, and Zechiel (1942) reiterated Dewey's concerns about the threat of individualism to a democracy and explained how it can impede personal, cultural, and societal growth:

> In a democracy, however, the assumption is made that significant personalities can be developed only through the mutual sharing of interests and purposes. The development of the individual as a goal is not to be confused with individualistic action as a method for its achievement. Unrestrained individualism is inconsistent with democratic values since it will not guarantee others the realization of their potentialities. . . . [A] sharing of responsibilities are essential for the development of personalities to their maximum. (p. 10)

The development of one individual should not impinge upon or impede the growth of another individual in a socially just democracy. One aspect of education for individual development within a democracy is learning that there are responsibilities that individuals must assume in a democracy to ensure that the rights and liberties of all people are respected: "Individuals must learn that there are responsibilities, as well as advantages, in the sharing of concerns involved in group living" (Giles, McCutchen, & Zechiel, 1942, p. 10).

One challenge for today's educators in realizing Dewey's vision of democratic education is the rise of authoritarian education via reforms that standardize what students learn, how they learn it, and how they demonstrate their learning. How can students learn to actively participate in a democracy, critique ideas, and think creatively and innovatively if they are essentially educated in a system that is standardized and decidedly autocratic?

UNSTANDARDIZED EDUCATION

Standardized education products such as one-size-fits-all curriculum content standards, high-stakes standardized tests, and commercially prepared teacher evaluation systems share two externally imposed aims: conformity of performance and monitoring conformity. Dewey (1916) explained some fundamental flaws with externally imposed standardized aims in *Democracy and Education*:

> The vice of externally imposed ends has deep roots. Teachers receive them from superior authorities; these authorities accept them from what is current in the community. The teacher imposes them upon children. As a first consequence, the intelligence of the teacher is not free; it is confined to receiving the aims laid down from above. Too rarely is the individual teacher so free from the dictation of authoritative supervisor, textbook on methods, prescribed course of study, etc., that he can let his mind come to close quarters with the pupil's mind and the subject matter. (p. 311)

Standardization of student output and teaching methods is an antidemocratic conception of education. Dewey's conception of education, and hence curriculum, as the "reorganization of experiences which adds to the meaning of experience and which increases ability to direct the course of subsequent experiences" (p. 220) portrays education as something in which the student is as involved as the teacher: a partnership of growth, if you will. The outcomes of such an education are decidedly unstandardized and not always predetermined.

Education must allow students to learn and use their learning in ways that empower them in a reciprocal process in which education affects the student and the student affects education. There is inherent flexibility in Dewey's definition of education because each student is seen as an active constructor of meaning who brings skills and prior experiences to the learning situation. Dewey acknowledges that students will experience and influence the curriculum in a unique way and take away individual interpretations and understandings—some of which are not planned for by the teacher. Greater local control of education goals provides the opportunities for educators to customize curriculum and instruction to the students in front of them, not the students that a group of distal bureaucrats think should exist.

Dewey (1916) warned that an education that required all students to know and be able to do the same things in the same way on the same day in the same format was ineffective and dangerous to democracy. That is a mechanistic education. The economic elite have the means to exclude their children from mechanistic education through their wealth and tax subsidies, such as vouchers and private school tax credits, to buy relevant, nonmechanistic education in the private market. Dewey explained the consequences to the nonelite class and to democracy itself of a two-tiered system of education:

> Otherwise the influences which educate some into masters, educate others into slaves. . . . A separation into a privileged and a subject-class prevents social endosmosis. (p. 241)

The policy degradation of public education into mechanistic training through standardization while simultaneously providing public dollars to private options more frequently accessed by the wealthy create a two-tiered system of education.

Dewey (1916) identified negative consequences of a two-tiered system to the elite as well:

> The evils thereby affecting the superior class are less material and less perceptible, but equally real. Their culture tends to be sterile, to be turned back to feed on itself; their art becomes a showy display and artificial; their wealth luxurious; their knowledge overspecialized; their manners fastidious rather than human. (p. 241)

The ultimate results of a two-tiered system of education is one of social subjugation of one class over another and the degradation of the democratic fabric of society:

> The more activity is restricted to a few definite lines, as it is when there are rigid class lines preventing adequate interplay of experiences, the more action tends to become routine on the part of the class at a disadvantage, and capricious, aimless, and explosive on the part of the class having the materially fortunate position. (p. 242)

What's That Knowledge Worth?

No one can predict with accuracy the exact content knowledge that will be of most worth ten, twenty, or fifty years in the future. However, there are unstandardized skills that transcend time and subject matter that logically seem useful in an ever-changing global community. An uncertain future requires students to gain not only content knowledge, but also experience in developing and using unstandardized skills to study and solve the problems of a democratic society such as collaboration, leadership, empathy, developing social networks, adaptability, creativity, persistence, cultural literacy, self-esteem, courage, and compassion (Tienken, 2017).

Advances in artificial intelligence and assistive technology make standardized curricula that are focused on knowledge acquisition and storage obsolete as soon as they are released. The content and skills can already be acquired or demonstrated by computer technology. The Common Core State Standards and their derivatives in the United States provide a good example of curricular content that was obsolete upon its release (Tienken, 2011).

The rise of artificial intelligence does not mean that students no longer need to learn content, but the overwhelming emphasis of education policy across many countries deals with knowledge acquisition and storage. The content seems to be solely in service of itself—that is, the entire purpose of most state standards is the mastery of the standards. Dewey (1916) rejected the selection of content knowledge for solely utilitarian purposes. He wrote, "Democracy cannot flourish where the chief influences in selecting subject matter of instruction are utilitarian ends narrowly conceived for the masses, and for the higher education of the few, the traditions of a specialized cultivated class" (p. 553).

The Problem Method

Democratic education in the Deweyian tradition of the problem method calls for students to acquire, create, and use content through interdisciplinary study of socially conscious issues, to (a) identify problems, (b) propose solutions, (c) identify the strengths and the problems associated with the solutions, (d) test hypotheses or solutions, and (e) reflect upon and revise those solutions in light of their impact on the greater good. By its nature, Dewey's problem method facilitates the development, use, and refinement of unstandardized skills because education becomes experiential instead of an exercise in acquiring facts. The problem method facilitates the unleashing, facilitation, and development of skills and dispositions in ways that are unique to each student.

DEMOCRATIZING OPPORTUNITIES TO UNSTANDARDIZE

Democratic education is not teaching students about democracy by just reading about it or listening to a lecture. Learning about democracy is best conducted through living democratically and helping to solve the problems that face a democracy. One method for democratic education includes the way students experience education. Dewey's conception was that students will make personal connections to the content and derive customized meaning from some content and assimilate some of that content into their lives for use going forward to improve themselves, their culture, and their country. Other content will have little to no meaning to them.

Socially conscious problem-based learning activities are an effective way to operationalize the aspirations of democratic education. Problem-based learning can be effective regardless whether the curricula and programs currently in place in a school are standardized. Educators and students can work together to recreate entire units of studies or individual learning activities around problems.

Superior Structure

Regardless of how one conceives of problem-based learning, whether it be as a complete unit of study or a short-term activity, problem-based learning is a superior structure from which to organize curricula to facilitate the "reorganization of experiences which adds to the meaning of experience and which increases ability to direct the course of subsequent experiences" (Dewey, 1916, p. 220). But the type of problem matters. Dewey recommended socially conscious problems.

A problem for study must be "an outgrowth of existing conditions. It must be based upon a consideration of what is already going on; upon the resources and difficulties of the situation" (Dewey, 1916, p. 298). The ways students come to experience, interact with, and influence knowledge, skills, and dispositions, and the voice they have in the processes, influence their personalized experienced curriculum and ultimately what they take, use, and create outside of the classroom (Tienken, 2017).

Lived Democracy

Democracy must be lived. As such, democratic education must be experiential in nature and related to the human condition, otherwise education itself becomes utterly utilitarian and socially vapid: "Democratic society is peculiarly dependent for its maintenance upon the use in forming a course of study of criteria which are broadly human" (Dewey, 1916, p. 552). The further the course of study moves toward socially conscious consideration of content and skills, the further democratic education moves from the student and into the historical archives.

Developmentally Appropriate and Relevant Curriculum

Locally developed standards should play a role in local control (Tienken, 2017). I do not advocate that a set of locally developed rigid standards should replace the current set of national and state-imposed standards. I am floating the idea that standards, when developed at a cognitively, socially, and morally appropriate level and used as guidance, not mandates, could help to structure a comprehensive creative local curriculum.

Consider the following kindergarten mastery mathematics standard from the CCSS in light of the cognitive development chart. (See table 9.1.)

- *Compose and decompose numbers from 11 to 19 into ten ones and some further ones, e.g., by using objects or drawings, and record each composition or decomposition by a drawing or equation (such as 18 = 10 + 8); understand that these numbers are composed of ten ones and one, two, three, four, five, six, seven, eight, or nine ones.*

Although there is room for debate, this standard seems to reside somewhere between early concrete and advanced concrete development, depending on how it will be assessed—multiple choice, close-ended short response, or open-ended—and whether students can use concrete objects or must use abstract symbols.

What is not a question is whether the standard is expected to be mastered by 100 percent of kindergarten students as part of the CCSS initiative. It is expected to be mastered because the CCSS and state standards derived from the CCSS are mastery standards. To receive full credit the student would probably have to move from pictures to symbolic representation and show through a set of symbols how to construct the various numbers, as shown in the example. Therefore, to receive full credit, the student would be operating more in advanced concrete than early concrete.

The problem arises because most children are not operating at the early or advanced concrete levels developmentally. That does not mean schools should not expose their kindergarten students to that level of work. In fact, they should. However, it is developmentally dangerous and professionally reckless to require all students to master standards that lie outside of normal human cognitive development when less than half of the national kindergarten population operates consistently and at a mastery level in the concrete stage of development.

Using table 9.1 as an example, only a small percentage of students without cognitive disabilities in kindergarten should be expected to master the standard quoted above. That does not mean that schools should not *teach* that challenging standard or those students cannot *learn* challenging material.

School should teach it and students can learn it. They just might not be able to demonstrate mastery in kindergarten.

Vygotsky (1978) demonstrated that students can access and work with challenging content with the guidance of a teacher, through guided practice, but that content needs to be within the zone of proximal development of the student. Even with the help of a teacher, it is still foolish to believe that all students can *master* all these concepts if they are not developmentally ready. Yes, they can learn many of the standards, and they should be exposed to them, but they should not be made to master those standards that reside outside their normal developmental range.

Curriculum activities for each standard and/or objective can be differentiated—tiered—to include two or three levels of cognitive complexity. The activities used to teach students and to assess their understanding can include two or three cognitive tiers. Teachers who differentiate their instruction by "readiness" already know about this. It is an idea that has been around for more than one hundred years, first proposed formally in the *Cardinal Principles of Secondary Education* (Commission on Reorganization of Secondary Education, 1918).

Tiered differentiation simply adjusts the levels of complexity at which students encounter, interact with, and demonstrate the understanding of content and skills. For example, providing students with more or less structure, examples, modeling, and/or scaffolding can change the level of complexity at which a student experiences content. The level of direct teacher support to a student is another example of how to change complexity.

Curriculum Quality

Local entities should be held responsible for developing challenging curriculum and assessments that capitalize on local strengths, address local needs, and prepare students for a globalized world, but they must be based on what we know about cognitive development. The curriculum should reflect the broad goals that the general public, school board members, and state legislators identified as being important.

Those broad goals include (a) basic academic skills and knowledge, (b) critical thinking, (c) appreciation for arts and literature, (d) preparation for skilled employment, (e) social skills and a general work ethic, (f) citizenship, and (g) physical and emotional health (Rothstein, Jacobsen, & Wilder, 2008, p. 43). Can educators still use standards as a guide and adopt standards at the local level? Of course they can.

State standards can act as a skeleton upon which to build a more complete curriculum, but they need to be reduced in number, as most standards can be accomplished via artificial intelligence and assistive technologies. I see the need for no more than 50 percent of the CCSS at most. However, some

Table 9.1. Cognitive Development Chart

Age	Grade	Intuition	Entry Concrete (a)	Advanced Concrete (b)	Entry Formal (a)	Middle Formal (b)	Ref.
5.5	P	78	22				J
6	K	68	27	5			A
7	1	35	55	10			A, W
8	2	25	55	20			A
9	3	15	55	30			A
10	4	12	52	35	1		S
11	5	6	49	40	5		S
12	6–7	5	32	51	12		S
13	7–8	2	34	44	14	6	S
14	8–9	1	32	43	15	9	S
15	9–10	1	15	53	18	13	S
16	10–11	1	13	50	17	19	S
16–17	11–12	3	19	47	19	12	R
17–18	12	1	15	50	15	19	R
Adult	—	20	22	26	17	15	R

Level (a) in each category is composed of children who have just begun to manifest one or two of that level's reasoning schemes, while level (b) refers to children manifesting a half dozen or more reasoning schemes.

Table derived by Herman T. Epstein, Personal communication, June 8, 1999. See also Epstein 2002.

J: Smedslund, J. (1964). *Concrete Reasoning: A Study of Intellectual Development*. Lafayette, IN: Child Development Publications of the Society for Research in Child Development.

A: Arlin, P. Personal communication with H. t. Epstein.

W: Wei, T. D., et al. (1971). Piaget's Concept of Classification: A Comparative Study of Socially Disadvantaged and Middle-Class Young Children. *Child Development* (42): 919–27.

R: Renner, J. W., Stafford, D. G., Lawson, A. E., McKinnon, J. W., Friot, F. E. and Kellogg, D. H. (1976). *Research, Teaching and Learning With the Piaget Model*. Norman: University of Oklahoma Press.

S: Shayer, M. and Adey, P. (1981). *Towards a Science of Science Teaching*. London: Heinemann.

districts might choose some of the CCSS along with some standards from national organizations as well as locally developed goals and objectives. The choice of content standards depends on the district's goals, the students' needs, and the community's vision for education. It does not have to be an either/or decision, but the decision does need to be cognitively appropriate and the requirements for mastery via formal state assessments must match the cognitive developmental level of the students.

The selection and creation of content is not enough. Content not connected to the experiences, lives, and needs of the students subjected to that content becomes irrelevant and counterproductive. Not only do more children learn less when content is not relevant to their lives, irrelevant content breads discontent among the most dispossessed and fragile of children: the poor living on the margins of society in our urban centers.

Those dispossessed by the larger society are only going to take so much in terms of having irrelevant content heaped upon them before they drop out or react in other ways. The *Report of the National Advisory Commission on Civil Disorders* (1968; also known as the Kerner Commission), created as a result of the many riots in US cities during the 1960s, found that a lack of meaningful, relevant, responsive curriculum was an issue contributing to poverty and unrest in the cities. Content without a conscience and a connection to the student is just another recipe for failure.

The problem-based, socially conscious curriculum was demonstrated to be superior to traditional forms and needs to be returned to the classroom through local development. It should come as no surprise that our best medical and nursing schools use problem-based curricula. If it is good enough for some of our most important professionals who care for children, why is not good enough for our children? Curriculum organization must blend the subject matter disciplines with student experiences related to democratic concerns.

RICE

Problem- and project-based curricula are effective because they can tap into four key points that facilitate student learning: relevancy, interest, choice, and engagement—RICE. Relevant curricula have meaning to students right now, not at some distant point in the future that the student cannot relate to or understand. Relevant curricula include skills and content that can students can use immediately in their lives. Interesting curricula package static content into issues of importance to students at their developmental levels. Interesting content is organized around socially conscious topics and themes either chosen by or chosen with input from students. The topics facilitate real-world use of the content and skills the students learn.

Choice provides students opportunities for input and options for things such as how they do schoolwork, the content and skills they learn, the ways in which they learn, and the output they create (Tienken, 2017). Engagement is fostered by curricula that go beyond compliance. Engaging curricula involve students in important work—work that has purpose beyond school. It does not focus on standardized testing because standardized testing has little relevance outside of education reform policy.

Standards are not evil. Irrelevant, disconnected, rigidly mandated, and cognitively inappropriate standards that all students must master are educationally bankrupt. Standards that bog students down with acquisition of static content are a waste of time and resources. General standards that are developmentally appropriate and address the RICE concepts can be informative for local decision makers, free teachers to be more creative and innovative, and ultimately facilitate learning for all students They can act as a starting point or a framework from which innovative practices can emanate.

Assessment

One stated purpose of education accountability is to inform the public about the efficacy of the publicly funded system of schools. Each state must implement a school accountability system as part of the Every School Succeeds Act. States must implement a system to identify the lowest-performing schools as in need of comprehensive support or targeted assistance. The ESSA accountability mandate also requires a mandatory public "report card" in which schools within the state are graded and/or ranked and/or labeled in some way. Most states use standardized test results as the deciding factor for school ratings.

Standardized test results do not capture accurately what or how well students learn, especially when students are subjected to large doses of test preparation. Test preparation is a form of gaming the system and it invalidates the results as indicators of learning (Koretz, 2008). Standardized test results do not explain how well teachers teach or how well principals lead. In short, results from standardized tests are poor measures of academic achievement. Standardized test results—including the SAT and ACT tests—can be predicted with a good deal of accuracy based on demographic factors found in US Census data (Tienken, Colella, Angelillo, Fox, McCahill, & Wolfe, 2017). Also, none of the state-mandated standardized test results have been validated as accurate measures of quality teaching or leadership or overall school quality. Perhaps the most insidious issues with using standardized test results as education accountability criteria is that the act of testing itself does not nothing to improve learning or teaching.

Accountability 3.0: Assessment to Inform Learning

In its most basic sense, education accountability at the state level is about answering the question of quality: How is the school doing? A comprehensive accountability program should address the three historic purposes of public schools in order to fully answer the quality question: (1) prepare students for a vocation or career, (2) prepare students for socio-civic life, and (3) avocational pursuits, or pursuing one's hobbies or interests (Dewey, 1916).

One way to move away from the current system of false and developmentally inappropriate accountability and toward comprehensive education accountability is to create a layered system that addresses the question of quality within the context of the historical purposes of education through multiple measures.

There exists historical precedent for deemphasizing standardized testing without losing the ability to provide accountability. After the thirty high schools and districts that were involved in the Eight-Year Study (Aikin, 1942) made the decision to cut the standardized testing cord, they were left to develop a more comprehensive system. They could not rely on the prophesized ease of making decisions from just one test per year. They actually had to take stock of their educational goals and objectives and develop a system to meet them: thirty unique systems for thirty unique populations with the common goal of developing quality programs to educate well-rounded citizens.

Quality programs require quality feedback. Below is a partial list of the summative assessments developed and used during the Eight-Year Study, their reliability estimates, and whether they were useful for individual student diagnosis or diagnosis of groups. More than 150 assessments, summative and formative, were eventually used with students during the study. (See table 9.2.)

The majority of the assessments used during the Eight-Year Study were not developed by assessment corporations or organizations. They were developed by a collaboration of teachers, school administrators, and university faculty in what are now known as professional learning communities. Although it is true that some "off-the-shelf" psychological tests were used to assess some aspects of social and emotional development, many of the assessments used were created by educators for students. This partial list of assessments provides evidence that we need not rely on the current system of myopic tests vended to us at much cost. It is possible for educators to develop high-quality assessments that produce fine-grained diagnostic results.

The reliability estimates are stronger than many of those found on the subsections of most state-mandated tests. Because the staff members from the Eight-Year Study were concerned with developing an education experi-

Table 9.2. High Reliability Assessments Developed for the Eight-Year Study

Assessment Table	Grades Assessed	Realiability* Estimate	Use with Individual (I) or Group (G)
Ability to Make Original Interpretations (of data)	7–8	.85	I or G
Application of Principles of Logical Reasoning	9–12	.94	I or G
Tests on Beliefs of Social Issues*	11–12	.85	I or G
Analysis of Controversial Writing (Propaganda)	10–12	.70–.82	I or G
Art Appreciation	12	.77	I or G
Personal and Social Adjustment	7–12	.75–.78	I or G

Source: Aikin, W. M. (1942). *The story of the eight-year study.* New York: Harper.

ence that attended to the social, emotional, and academic needs of all students, they recognized the need to develop feedback loops to inform instructional and leadership decision-making.

The District Layer

The first layer of the comprehensive accountability system resides at the school district level, the local level. School districts should be accountable for assembling a portfolio of district-wide indicators that provide information on how well students are developing academically, socio-civically, and avocationally. The district level is ideal for providing in-depth information about those three purposes because districts can draw upon the many types of teacher-made assessments to help paint a picture of student development. District personnel identify threshold skills and create a portfolio of standardized teacher instruments, quantitative and qualitative, including projects, and report those results to the public and state education agency.

Districts can use high-quality teacher-designed, criterion-referenced assessments that foster effective teaching methods. Examples include assessing reading levels through running records and readers workshop formats, writing prompts, literary analyses, and problem-based assessments that include socio-civic concepts and use of mathematics. Schools can also be judged on the types of avocational opportunities (clubs, hobbies, and organizations) they offer and how many students take advantage of those pursuits and/or have an avocational support outside of school.

Quality models and assessments already exist that district personnel can call upon for assistance support as they transition to this type of multidimensional accountability. The New York Performance Standards Consortium is a group of thirty-eight public, noncharter schools that has developed authentic and problem-based assessments in areas such as higher-order thinking, writing, mathematical problem solving, technology use, science research, appreciation and performance in the arts, service learning, and career skills. The schools use outside experts from universities and the community, along with the teachers to review student work and provide real-world feedback to students.

The Mission Skills Assessment (MSA) is one assessment districts can use as a way to gain information about socio-civic skills and unstandardized skills such as creativity, resilience, and teamwork. The assessment is formative in nature and seeks to provide ongoing feedback to school personnel and students about the development and use of important skills The College and Work Readiness Assessment Plus (CWRA+) is a standardized problem-based assessment that provides feedback on complex thinking skills like written communication, critique, mathematical reasoning, and evaluating information. Questions are designed around problem-based activities and reading passages. The MSA and CWRA+ are just two examples of assessments that are formative in nature and meant to inform instruction and learning on a wide range of unstandardized skills.

A clear framework for the district layer of accountability structure already exists. known as the School-based Teacher-led Assessment and Reporting System (STARS) program, it was first implemented in Nebraska under Commissioner of Education Dr. Doug Christensen during the 2000–2001 school year (Dappen and Isernhagen, 2005). The Partnership for 21st Century Skills (2005) called it the "nation's most innovative assessment system" (p. 13). The system operated successfully until the 2009 school year, when the political winds changed and a NCLB-friendly state legislature changed the system to an all-commercial standardized-test-based system, but the framework—including state policy documents, assessments, and protocols—still exists and state education leaders could easily reinvigorate the system without having to reinvent the accountability wheel.

The State Layer

The second layer could involve state department of education personnel in a three-part role organized under a newly organized Office of Accountability and Development: (1) assessor, (2) auditor, and (3) professional developer.

The state could administer low-stakes, nonintrusive, off-the-shelf standardized assessments of basic skills, such as arithmetic and reading comprehension. Such tests can be administered in thirty or forty-five minutes and are cheap to administer and score. The results would carry little weight in the overall accountability system because of the known issues that invalidate standardized test results as high-stakes decision-making tools, but they would satisfy the federal ESSA testing requirement for compliance purposes.

The more important roles for state education personnel are those of auditor and professional developer. State personnel provide job-embedded professional development on quality assessment design, problem-based activity development, and scoring protocols and processes. State personnel also provide an auditing system in which they audit a percentage of district-level accountability assessments to maintain quality control of the scoring processes and also identify professional development needs to help inform and enhance classroom instruction and assessment processes.

National Accreditation Layer

The final layer is the capstone of the multidimensional accountability system: accreditation from third-party accreditation organizations. There exist at least six national accreditation agencies that provide accreditation assessment processes to public schools. The processes include a broad set of criteria that require districts to demonstrate quality practices and procedures that relate directly and indirectly to the historic functions of education. For instance, the Middle States Association of Colleges and Schools (2014) process includes twelve components that cover all aspects of public schooling at the school level:

- School Mission
- Governance and Leadership
- School Improvement Planning
- Finances
- Facilities
- System Organization and Staff
- Health and Safety
- Information Resources
- Educational Program
- Assessment and Evidence of Student Learning
- Student Services
- Student Life and Student Activities

National accreditation involves a comprehensive, multiyear process of intense self-study by the school and district. It includes a rigorous external review capped by a multiday visitation by an independent team of accreditation auditors. The auditors prepare a detailed visitation report written by the team. Then, the district must send yearly updates to the accreditation agency that explain how the district is following through on its accreditation plan. There is a midterm reporting process after three years that includes a follow-up team visit if it is the district's or school's first time being accredited.

National accreditation is an important capstone because it is not part of the state or district political environment, and as such, the accreditation agencies are less apt to have political pressure contaminate their findings. The process goes beyond typical state education monitoring process that focuses mostly on standardized test results. Accreditation looks at how schools are functioning on a broad range of components that affect all areas of schooling.

An Example State System

A three-layered approach to accountability provides triangulated data points from which to inform all areas of the education process. It is a "three-legged stool" of accountability that brings a sense of balance in which one indicator cannot make or break the rating of a school district. The entire structure acts to inform the education and provides actionable formative data that school personnel can use for more informed school enhancement efforts.

Standardized tests that are developmentally appropriate can play a part in a comprehensive assessment system, but simply as one data point among many. Their results should not be given any greater consideration than the results from other locally developed assessments. Other assessments can provide feedback on things such as:

- Social sensitivity
- Ability to apply social facts and generalizations
- Democratic values
- Applying facts and generalizations to social problems
- Evaluation of social attitudes
- Beliefs on economic issues
- Student reading inventory
- Student reaction to reading
- Questionnaire on voluntary reading
- Critical mindedness in the reading of fiction
- Judging the effectiveness of written composition
- The novel questionnaire
- The drama questionnaire
- Evaluation of literature
- Student interest inventory
- Socially conscious problem solving

But these ideas are not lost in education's past. They were used successfully in recent times. STARS was in place in Nebraska since 2000, and until approximately 2004–2005 it relied on local assessments graded by teachers (Dappen & Isernhagen, 2005; Roschewski, Isernhagen, & Dappen, 2006).

When the STARS system was first developed, the Nebraska Department of Education required that districts either adopt the state-approved core standards or create their own set of standards that were at least of the same quality. Districts that opted for local standards were also allowed to develop a local set of assessments to demonstrate evidence of student learning (Dappen & Isernhagen, 2005).

The state's department of education acted as a support system with professional development in how to design various assessments, how to design and use rubrics, how to report assessment results, and how to interpret the results to inform instruction. The department of education also acted as part of the auditing process in terms of helping to ensure assessment quality. This locally developed curriculum and assessment system was in place for approximately seven years until a new superintendent of state instruction chose to follow a traditional approach to implementing NCLB. The STARS system stands as the modern-day example that localism can work on a large scale. (There are more than five hundred school districts in Nebraska.)

ADDRESS THE ROOT CAUSES OF UNDERACHIEVEMENT

The latest wave of reformers claim they are concerned with underachievement, especially for student of color and those who come from poverty. That is an interesting concern in light of the fact that poverty is the largest predictor of ultimate academic achievement on traditional standardized tests in this country. If education reformers truly want to increase achievement, they need to work to decrease poverty.

Children living in poverty are more likely than students who do not grow up in poverty to be plagued with chronic illnesses, psychological stress, preventable disabilities, low cognitive functioning and learning disabilities, dental problems, hearing and sight issues, and heart and digestive system disorders. Children living in poverty are more likely to need emotional and behavioral services compared to their non-poor peers. They underachieve compared to their non-poor peers, as a group, on every state mandated academic test of skills and knowledge (Tienken, 2011) and they are more likely to have health issues later in life due to the stressors during their childhood created by poverty.

Two international longitudinal studies revealed some long-term negative effects of living in poverty as a child. Winning, Glymour, McCormick, Gilsanz, and Kubzansky (2015) reported results from a 1958 birth cohort longitudinal study conducted in Britain. The results demonstrated that forty-five-year-old participants in the cohort who experienced psychological distress during their childhood had an increased risk of cardiovascular disease in adulthood, even when the psychological distress abated during adulthood.

A meta-analysis conducted by Pillas, Marmot, Naicker, Morrison, and Pikhart (2014) reviewed 201 studies conducted in thirty-two European countries of the lasting effects of poverty. The results suggested that factors from multiple levels of a child's ecological system can negatively affect health and development, and those effects can be long-term. The researchers cited things like the neighborhood in which students live, the people they and their family associate with, lower parental income, unemployment and job strain, and housing instability as factors that can cause long-term negative issues for children.

Fundamental Support

Children living in poverty lack fundamental supports that the children of more wealthy means access on a regular basis. For example, appropriate center-based childcare (Loch, et al., 2004) has a positive influence on cognitive development and academic achievement, as does universal healthcare. Children of poverty have less frequent access to quality childcare and healthcare. In contrast, the G20 nations that outscored the United States on the 2018 PISA math had universal healthcare for children, universal childcare, or a combination of both.

Schwartz (2010) demonstrated that appropriate housing policy affects student achievement more than the education interventions being proposed by the latest crop of *reformanistas*. Many children of poverty live in substandard housing in neighborhoods that are less than conducive to cognitive, social, and emotional growth. Some opponents of liberty and justice for all might retort that America can't afford to do the things necessary to alleviate the negative effects of poverty. Not true.

Gale and Kotlikoff (2004, pp. 1288–90) demonstrated how tax cuts to corporations and the wealthy benefit those who already have enough and further disadvantage those who need more. The authors estimated that if the George W. Bush–era tax cuts from 2003, later extended by Barack Obama, were not allowed to continue, there would have been net gain to government revenue, the amount equal to 2 percent of GDP. That gain alone would have been more than enough to provide meaningful support to poor children. But that did not happen, and instead, the wealthiest 2.5 percent of all Americans received another income benefit: a cash payment, if you will.

Society Can Do More

Gale and Kotlikoff (2004) concluded there would have been enough money to provide for indigent families: (a) an increase in the child allowance cash payment to bring families to or above the poverty line, (b) comprehensive prenatal and perinatal screenings, (c) universal health coverage for children up to the age of eighteen, (d) universal preschool, (e) center-based childcare so families can work, (f) equitable parent leave programs to care for newborns and sick children, and (g) services for emotionally and behaviorally disturbed children, among other productive measures. Add in even a portion of $130 billion a year the United States spent on wars in Iraq and Afghanistan, and there certainly seems enough money to solve the problems of poverty. What we lack is the moral conscience and courage to do something.

It seems undemocratic to deny a group of people full access to the democratic society due to the preexisting condition of poverty or an unanticipated fall into poverty. Of course, there are those who blame poverty on the poor and a lack of work ethic. Racist tropes will not end poverty. Jobs that pay living wages and provide family healthcare will help more than politics based on demonizing and blaming the victims of neoliberal policies. Therefore, it is in the interest of the greater good to support those who find themselves without a living wage by providing them with a living wage. They are consumers as well, and any money that makes its way toward ending poverty will ultimately find its way back into the system through the capitalist economic process, thus generating tax revenue and added wealth for everyone.

POINTS TO REMEMBER

Some groups in the United States have been trying to impose national standards on public schools since the 1980s. Look what we got: nineteenth-century standards copied almost directly from the Committees of Ten and Fifteen, circa 1893 and 1895. At this pace it will take another two hundred years to get standards turned around that begin to address current needs. Instead, we should unleash the power of innovation locally. People concerned with the degradation of public school must advocate for a return to greater local control.

Hold policymakers accountable for helping to create conditions and provide resources to support authentic, innovative student learning. There exists today no accountability for student learning in the current summative high-stakes system. The results tell us more about the community in which students live than the quality of the education they receive. Hold educators accountable for developing quality curricula, instruction, and assessment systems that provide for equality and equity and that allow for diversity in achievement. The goal should not be to have students arrive at a finite point.

One goal of education should be avocation in the sense of helping students develop themselves into lifelong learners.

The words of the democratic reformers like Horace Mann (1848), along with John Dewey, Francis Parker, and the other giants of the education field, sometimes fall on deaf ears, but there is no more urgent task than to safeguard liberty and justice for all. Some of my colleagues say it is useless to fight the current wave of dataless reforms like standardization and testing. They say such policies will continue to be useless until our policymakers adopt a more enlightened attitude toward evidence and science.

Let us not be silent. Draw upon the thoughts of Martin Luther King Jr. to support our voices of dissent about current policies: "In the end, we will remember not the words of our enemies, but the silence of our friends." Remember the words of Robert Kennedy, adapted from Bernard Shaw, to push us to consider policies that might seem "extreme" or Pollyanna in their proposals for a way forward: "Some men see things as they are, and ask why. I dream of things that never were, and ask why not."

REFERENCES

Aikin, W. M. (1942). *The story of the eight-year study*. New York: Harper.

Bazzi, S., Fiszbein, M., & Gebresilasse, M. (2018). *Frontier culture: The roots and persistence of "rugged individualism" in the United States*. NBER Working Papers 23997. Retrieved from https://www.nber.org/papers/w23997

Commission on the Reorganization of Secondary Education. (1918). *Cardinal Principles of Secondary Education*. Bulletin No. 35. Washington, DC: US Bureau of Education.

Dappen, L., and Isernhagen, J. C. (2005). Nebraska STARS: Assessment for learning. *Planning and Changing, 36* (3–4), 147–56.

Dewey, J. (1916). *Democracy and education*. New York: Macmillan.

Dewey, J. (1927). *The public and its problems*. Chicago: Gateway.

Dewey, J. (1952). Foreword. In Elise Ripley Clapp, *The Use of Resources in Education*. New York: Harper.

Gale, W., & Kotlikoff, L. (2004, June 7). Effects of recent fiscal policies on children. *Tax Notes*.

Giles, H. H., McCutchen, S. P., & Zechiel, A. N. (1942). *Exploring the curriculum: The work of the thirty schools from the viewpoint of curriculum consultants*. New York: Harper.

Gilens, M., & Page, B. I. (2014). Testing theories of American politics: Elites, interest groups, and average citizens. *Perspectives on Politics, 12*(3), 564–81.

Kerner Commission. (1968). *Report of the National Advisory Commission on Civil Disorders*. Washington, DC: US Government Printing Office.

Loch, S., Fuller, B., Kagan, S., & Carrol, B. (2004). Child care in poor communities: Early learning effects of type, quality, and stability. *Child Development, 75* (1), 47–65.

Mann, H. (1848). *Twelfth annual report of the board of education together with the twelfth annual report of the secretary of the board*. Boston: Dutton and Wentworth State Printers.

Pillas, D., Marmot, M., Naicker, K., Goldblatt, P., Morrison, J., & Pikhart, H. (2014). Social inequalities in early childhood health and development: A European-wide systematic review. *Pediatric Research, 76*(5), 418–24.

Polychroniou, C. J. (2018, July 25). The resurgence of political authoritarianism: An interview with Noam Chomsky. *Truthout*. Retrieved from https://truthout.org/articles/resurgence-of-political-authoritarianism-interview-with-noam-chomsky

Roschewski, P., Isernhagen, J. C., and Dappen, L. (2006). Nebraska STARS: Achieving results. *Phi Delta Kappan, 87*(6), 433–37.

Rothstein, R., Jacobsen, R., & Wilder, T. (2008). *Grading education: Getting accountability right.* Washington, DC, and New York: Economic Policy Institute and Teachers College Press.

Schwartz, H. (2010). *Housing policy is school policy: Economic integrative housing promotes academic success in Montgomery County, Maryland.* New York: Century Foundation.

Tanner, D., & Tanner, L. (2007). *Curriculum development: Theory into practice.* New York: Allyn & Bacon.

Tienken, C. H. (2011). Structured inequity: The intersection of socioeconomic status and the standard error of measurement of state mandated high school test results. In B. J. Alford, G. Perreault, L. Zellner, J. W. Ballenger (Eds.) *Blazing new trails: Preparing leaders to improve access and equity in today's schools.* Lancaster, PA: Destech Publications. Retrieved from https://files.eric.ed/gov/fulltext/ED523595.pdf

Tienken, C. H. (2017). *Defying standardization: Creating curriculum for an uncertain future.* Lanham, MD: Rowman and Littlefield.

Tienken, C. H., Colella, A. J., Angelillo, C., Fox, M., McCahill, K., & Wolfe, A. (2017). Predicting middle school state standardized test results using family and community demographic data. *Research on Middle Level Education, 40*(1), 1–13.

Vygotsky, L. (1978). *Mind in society: The development of higher psychological processes.* Cambridge, MA: Harvard University Press.

Winning, A., Glymour, M. M., McCormick, M. C., Gilsanz, P., & Kubzansky, L. D. (2015). Psychological distress across the life course and cardiometabolic risk: Findings from the 1958 British Birth Cohort Study. *Journal of the American College of Cardiology, 66*(14), 1577–86.

Zhao, Y. (2010, May 23). Mass localism: How might the Race to the Top money be better spent. Retrieved from http://zhaolearning.com/2010/05/23/mass-localism-how-might-the-race-to-the-top-money-be-better-spent/

Index

Achieve, Inc., 16
Achilles, C. M., ix–xi, 139
accountability, 169
ACT, 63
Adey, P., 130–131
Adler, M., 26, 29
Aikin, W., 18, 19, 130, 158
ALEC, American Legislative Exchange Council, 27–28
Allen, R. C., 136
Amata, I. E., 84
American Educational Research Association, American Psychological Association, & National Council on Measurement in Education, 101
Amrein, A. L., 99
Angelillo, C., 33, 168
Atkinson, A. B., 29

Babad, E. Y., 38
Badger, E., 33
Baker, D., 45
Bannister, R., 32
Barbuti, S. M., 53
Becker, G. S., 79
Bergman, P., 143
Berliner, D. C., 46, 51, 68, 87, 99
Biddle, B. J., 46, 51, 68, 87
business values, 67
Bloom, B., 85
Bon Jovi, J., 46

Booher-Jennings, J., 32, 100
Borg, M., 100
Bourdieu, P., 26
Bracey, G., 52–53, 55, 58
Bazzi, S., 158–159
Bredo, E., 66
Brindley, S., 26
Bronfenbrenner, U., 81, 130
Bryk, A., 65
Buber, M., 70–71
Bui, Q., 33
Building America, 21
Bullough, Jr., R. V., 19
Burch, P., 100
Burns, C. R., 123–124
Bush, G. W., 30, 31

Caldwell, D., 107
Callahan, R. E., 22, 68, 131
Campbell, D. T., 87, 129
Campbell, J. K., 9–10
Campbell's Law, 87
Cardinal Principles of Secondary Education, 12, 13, 14–15, 16, 17–18, 18–19
Carney, J., 28
Carrol, B., 175
Carr, N. K., 26
Carson, C. C., 54
Carter, J., 7, 8
Central Intelligence Agency, 89

charter schools, 6, 9, 25, 27–28, 29, 31, 55–56, 63, 67, 69, 78, 93, 135, 171
Chomsky, N., 68
Chubb, J. E., 69
Cody, A., 126
Cogan, L. S., 96
Cohen, J., 84
Colella, A., 33, 168
Coleman, J. S., 79, 80
collective punishment, 66
College Board, 53, 126
Commission on the Reorganization of Secondary Education, 13, 108, 158
Committee of Ten, 12–13, 16, 115
Committee of Fifteen, 12, 13, 115
Committee on Testing and Basic Skills, 61
Common Core, 16, 51, 96–97, 110, 115, 116, 127, 129, 162
complexity versus difficulty, 122–124
consumerism, 25, 30, 31, 32, 37–38, 150
Corrigan, P., 150
Cosgrove, J., 86
Council of Chief State School Officers, 128, 129
Center for Research on Education Outcomes (CREDO), 141–142
Cremin, L. J., 52
curriculum: activity based, 16–17; corporate, 70; macro-curriculum, 16; objectives, 127, 130; problem-based, 17; standardized, 122

Dappen, L., 171, 174
Darnell, B., 107
David, R.,, 136
democracy, 19, 20–21, 22–23, 38, 43, 58, 66, 68, 70, 74, 131, 148–149, 152, 155, 156–157, 158–159, 159–160, 161, 162, 163
Denney, J. T., 33
DeTuro, M., 130–131
developmentally appropriate, 77, 119, 156, 164, 168, 173
Dewey, J., 2, 9, 10–12, 16, 19, 25, 27, 37, 77, 94, 122, 123, 130, 148–149, 157–159, 159–161, 162–163, 169, 177
Dionne, Jr., E. J., 88
Doubilet, S., 33
Draper, N., 72

Duncan, A., 44, 45

Ecological systems theory, 81–82, 83, 84, 86, 89, 106, 119, 130, 155, 175
economic-elite domination, 156
Edson, C. H., 55–56
Education Commission of the States, 99
educational corruption, 87
The Education Law Center of Pennsylvania, 145
education management organizations (EMO), 150
Educational Policies Commission, 18; Education for All America's Youth, 18
effect size, 17, 84–85, 98, 105, 138–139, 142
egalitarianism, 5, 14, 15–16, 25, 29, 38, 58
Elmore, R. F., 73
Eight-Year Study, 18, 20–21
Eisenhower, D. D., 39, 44–45, 46–49, 50–51
Elementary Secondary Education Act, 34
English, F. W., 26
Epstein, H. T., 119
equity, 6, 12, 13, 15, 17, 20, 21, 29, 33, 37, 38, 53, 64, 68, 82, 107–108, 152, 176
Evans, G. W., 130
Every Student Succeeds Act (ESSA), 34–35, 37, 93, 95, 168, 172

Fair Test, 72–73
Felner, R. D., 84
Finkelman,, 7
Finkelstein, J. L., 84
Finn, J. D., 138–139
Fiszbein, M., 158–159
Fitzhugh, G., 123–124
Foster, J. B., 30
Fox, M., 33, 168
Frankenberg, E., 29–30, 145
Freire, P., 26, 31; banking model, 25–26
Friedman, N., 29
frontier mentality, 159
Fuller, B., 175

Gabriel, T., 151
Gale, W., 175
Gates, W., 9
Gebresilassev, M., 158–159

Index

Geiser, S., 45
Gilens, M.,, 156
Giles, H. H., 11, 159
Gilsanz, P., 174
Gleason, E. S., 46
Glymour, M. M., 174
Goldblatt, P., 175
Goldman, B., 17, 130
Golem effect, 38
Gonzalez, J., 151
Goodpaster, 46, 47–48
Gupta, S., 87
Guthman, E. O., 136

Haney, W., 99
Hanushek, E., 128, 129
Harrington, M., 88
Haertel, G. D., 130–131
Harville, L. M., 100
Harwell, M. R., 79
Heinrich, C. J., 62
Hermanson, K., 65
Hesla, K., 136
high school exit exams, 38, 84, 99, 102
Houang, R. T., 96
Houtz, J., 109
Hoxby, C. M., 139, 140, 141
Huelskamp, R. M., 54
human capital, 79–80, 81
Hungerford, T. L., 29
Hursh, D., 33–34

International Monetary Fund, 28, 52
Isernhagen, J. C., 171, 174

Jacobsen, R., 165
Jarmon, M., 124
Jerslid, A. T., 17, 130
Jefferson, Thomas, 6–7, 8, 11, 20, 25, 149
Jessup, M., 150
Jewett, T. O., 6
Jones, J., 106
Justice, B., 147

Kagan, S., 175
Kaiser Family Foundation, 106
Kakoyiannis, A., 29
Kang, J., 140
Karier, C. J., 33–34

Karma, R., 33
Karp, S., 126
Kelly, E., 81
Kennedy, R., 177
Kerner Commission, 167
Kim, E., 124
Kolderie, T., 136
Korbin, J. L., 53
Kotlikoff, L., 175
Koudela, III, J., 108–109
Kozol, J., 70–71
Koretz, D., 103–105, 168
Krashen, S., 85
Kridel, C., 19
Kubzansky,, 174

LaBeau, B., 79
Lancaster method, 8; monitorial instruction, 5, 8
Latino Action Network, 143
learned helplessness, 86
Lee, J., 62
Leigh, A., 29
Leith, C., 35
Levin, H. M., 100
Loch, S., 175
Loftus, 16, 130
Lubienski, C., 69
Lubienski, S., 69
Luciano, J., 130–131
Lynch, C., 107

Macleod, C., 147
Mann, Horace, 8, 12–13, 130, 149, 177
Mathis, W. J., 29–30
Mattern, K. D., 53
Madaus, G., 72
Marmot, M., 175
Maroun, J., 107
Maslow, A., 86, 130; hierarchy of needs, 86
Maylone, N., 107
McCall, 16
McCahill, K., 33, 168
McCormick, M. S., 174
McCutchen, S. P., 11, 159
McEwan, P. J., 138
McFarlin, Jr., I., 143
McLean, B., 28

McMillan, J. H., 95
McNeil, M., 35
McKnight, C. C., 96
McNown, R., 27–28
measurement error, 100; conditional standard error of measurement (CSEM), 100–101, 102–105
Medina, J., 151
meritocracy, 5, 29–30, 32, 37–38, 38–39, 50, 107
Messick, S., 103–105
Miller, J., 54
Miron, G., 29–30, 150
Mishel, L., 139–140
Moe, T. M., 69
Molnar, A., 69, 150
Morrison, J., 175
Mullen, C., 26, 127
Muraka, S., 140

Naicker, K., 175
National Assessment of Education Progress (NAEP), 52, 56, 57, 58, 63, 69, 140, 141
National Academies of Sciences, Engineering, and Medicine, 33
National Alliance for Public Charter Schools, 27
National Center for Education Statistics, 30
National Commission on Excellence in Education, 51, 55–56, 77
National Conference of State Legislatures, 78
National Governors Association, 128
Nation at Risk, 23, 37, 51, 54, 55–56, 77, 93
neoliberalism, 25, 26, 27, 37–38, 51, 61, 62, 74, 78, 83, 93, 115, 135, 149, 150, 155, 176
Nichols, S., 87
Nisar, H., 62
Nocera, J., 28
No Child Left Behind Act, 33–34, 37, 61–62, 73, 74, 88–89, 93, 98, 105, 171, 174

Obama, B. H., 30, 34, 44–45, 137, 175
O'Brien, J., 38

O'Dell, R., 78
Ohanian, S., 127
O'Leary, K., 107
Open Secrets, 27
opportunity gap, 89
Organisation for Economic Co-operation and Development (OECD), 83, 87
Orlich, D., 98

Padover, S. K., 7
Page, B. I., 156
Paige, R., 45
Pareto efficiency, 26
Parker, F., 9–10
Patterson, B. F., 53
Pekow, C., 88
Piaget, J., 116–117, 130
Pikhart, H., 175
Pillas, D., 175
Plumlee, P., 100
Pogrow, S., 84, 142
Polikoff, M., 96
Polychroniou, C. J., 156
poverty, 8, 26, 30, 33, 57, 63, 75, 78, 79–80, 81, 83–84, 85–86, 88, 89, 105, 107, 152, 167, 174–176
psychological stress, 87

Ravitch, D., 136–137, 148
Rayman, R., 8
Reardon S. F., 141
Rechetnick, J., 16
Reeves, T., 62
Rhodes, K., 72
R.I.C.E. (relevancy, interest, choice, engagement), 167
Riley, R., 45
Rodriquez, O., 103
Roemer, J., 29
Rogers, R. G., 33
Romano, L., 72
Roschewski, P., 174
Rothstein, R., 165
Rowe, W. G., 38
Roy, J., 139–140
Roy, M. J., 35
Roy, R. R., 27
Rubin, J., 29–30
rugged individualism, 159

Index

Ryan, C., 72

Sackey, A. N. L., 107
Sambora, R., 46
Samier, E. A., 26
Sandel, M., 25
Sandia Report, 54–55
Sanger, D., 99
Santelices, M. V., 45
Sass-Rubin, J., 144
SAT, 53, 54–55, 63–64, 72, 168
Sapolsky, R., 86
Scherrer, J., 79, 80, 81
Schmidt, W. H., 96
Schmitt, J., 106
school reform, 6, 10, 23, 31, 39, 43, 44, 45, 50, 51, 56, 65, 74, 77, 79, 85, 88, 93, 131
Schwartz, H., 152, 175
segregation, 30, 84, 143, 146, 147
Sforza, D., 124
Shanker, A., 136
Shayer, M., 116–117
Shaw, E. J., 53
Shaw, N., 127
Shim, E., 84
Shim, M. K., 84
Simon, S., 127
Simpson's Paradox, 57–58
Sinclair, S., 35
Singh, A., 87
Sirin, S. R., 29, 79
Skinner, K. J., 139
Slouka, M., 62
Smarick, A., 137–138
Stranahan, H., 100
Strupp, B. J., 84
social Darwinism, 32–33, 37–38, 55–56
socioeconomic status, 29, 30, 33, 54–55, 63, 69, 73, 79, 138, 143
Spencer, H., 77
Sputnik, 4, 43–46, 47–48, 50
standardized: curricula, 111, 122, 130, 162; tests, 26, 30, 32, 33–34, 37, 52–53, 55, 62–64, 71–73, 74, 77, 78, 79, 80, 81, 85, 86, 89, 93–94, 95, 96, 98, 99–100, 101–102, 105, 106, 107–108
Stanovich, K. E., 30
Statista, 52

Steger, M. B., 27
Stiglitz, J., 28–29
Strauss, V., 74
student achievement, 16–17, 18, 29, 52–53, 63, 64, 70, 73, 79, 86, 93, 96, 98–99, 119–122, 126, 128, 130, 137, 138–139, 140, 141, 175
suicide, 87

Tanner, D., 1, 7, 15, 21, 34, 80, 82, 158
Tanner, L., 1, 7, 15, 21, 34, 80, 82, 158
Taylor, F. W., 21, 94, 115; scientific management, 21, 115, 131; Gary Plan, 22
Taylor, S. C., 94; Rime of the Ancient Mariner, 94
Thompson, B., 95
Thompson, D., 9
Thorndike, E. L., 15–16
Thorndike, R. L., 17, 130
Tienken, C. H., 33, 38, 53, 69–70, 78, 79, 80, 85, 100, 101, 102, 103, 105, 107, 123–124, 127, 128, 129, 162, 163, 164, 168, 174
Title I, 88–89
Tornquist, E., 29–30
Tramaglini, T., 107
Turnamian, P., 107
Tyler, R., 20

United States Department of Commerce, 83
United States Department of Education, 51, 54, 56, 57, 62
United States Patent and Trademark Office, 52
unstandardized education, 160, 161–162, 171
Urschel, J. L., 29–30, 150

validity, 95; construct, 95
Van Lier, P., 139
Veblen,, 30
Venkatramanan, S., 84
Viger, S. G., 122
Vygotsky, L., 130, 165

Walberg, H. J., 130–131
Wallis, C., 62

Wang, H. A., 96
Wang, M. C., 130–131
Ward, L. F., 16, 19
Webb, N. L., 122
Weber, M., 29–30, 144
Welner, K. G., 89
Wilder, T., 165
Wiley, D. E., 96
Wilkins, J. L. M., 107
Williams, F. D., 6
Wilson, R. J., 99
Wilson, V., 106
Winning, A., 174

Woessmann, L., 128, 129
Wolfe, A., 33, 168
Wolfe, R. G., 96
Woodall, T. D., 54
Worldbank, 28, 80
World Economic Forum, 119
Wrightstone, J. W., 16, 17, 130
Wyse, A. E., 122

Yan, A., 87

Zhao, Y., 68, 129, 132, 155
Zechiel, A. N., 11, 159

About the Author

Christopher H. Tienken is an associate professor of education leadership, management, and policy. His research interests include curriculum and assessment policy at the state, national, and international levels. His recent books include *Cracking the Code of Education Reform: Creative Compliance and Ethical Leadership* by Corwin Press (2020) and *Defying Standardization: Creating Curriculum for an Uncertain Future* by Rowman & Littlefield (2017).

Made in the USA
Middletown, DE
15 January 2024